Housebirth®

Your Guide to Buying an Energy-Efficient, Healthy New Home that Pays You Back

Sara Lamia, MA, MCSP, CAPS, CGA

Home Building Coach, Inc.

Published by Home Building Coach, Inc.
3149 San Luis Street
Fort Collins, Colorado 80525 USA
(970) 402-2600 / (877) 444-4534
http://www.homebuildingcoach.com

Drawings created by Sarah Saunders
Cover design by F + P Graphic Design, Inc. Fort Collins, CO

Library of Congress Control Number: 2007923023

ISBN: 978-0-9723390-2-5

Congratulations on the planned arrival of your new home!

The birth of my children and the "birth" of my new home were two big, creative, adventurous experiences! The tools I learned to use during childbirth helped me to accomplish my goal: deliver a healthy, beautiful baby in the best way possible.

This workbook provides information, tools and strategies for you to use in order to have an efficient, enjoyable homebuilding experience that results in getting the home you really want.

We all know that quality in automobiles, and almost every product, commands a higher price, which we willingly pay. Your "high performance" new home may cost slightly more initially, because it is better made. The lower monthly energy bills, plus the likelihood of increased resale value will result in less overall cost to you, and provide a healthier, safer, more comfortable home that is more respectful of our planet.

Why Should I Use This Book?

If you've ever painted a room, you probably discovered that to do it right, you spent more time preparing (choosing colors, laying tarps and taping around windows and baseboards) than painting. But, after all that "work before the work" was done, you were pleasantly surprised at how smoothly and well the actual painting went!

So it is with building a home. If you educate yourself about how this process generally works, focus on choosing the right home plan for your lifestyle and budget, and finding the right builder to build it, you will have paved the way for a smooth journey.

How To Use This Workbook

Sections 1 through 5 present the entire building process in quick, easy-to-follow checklists. Section 6 offers more detailed information about many of the checklist items.

Don't let this "candy store" overwhelm you; it isn't designed to all be eaten by one home's budget. Your planning process must therefore include making many choices, and you'll want them to be the right choices for you.

Bring this compact-size workbook along as a reference and working tool as you shop. Writing important information directly on the specific worksheet will be a tremendous help when you need to refer back to it later. Some information is mentioned in several places because it needs to be considered when making each decision.

Have fun shopping! With the attitude that you will find the items and features that are just right for your new home, you are paving your road to success. Let's get started!

Look for these symbols throughout Section 6.

Environmentally-friendly

Saves money

My stories

Foreword to Homebuyers

It has been stated that a Huge Tidal Wave of Change is upon the Home Building Community. It is a change driven by rapidly escalating energy prices, the evolution of Building Science, Environmental/Sustainable concerns and educated homeowners and builders. This is resulting in an amazing demand for High Performance Homes (Extremely energy efficient, comfortable, healthy, strong and durable.) Good builders always benefit when consumers demand a quality product and when their clients know how to properly partner with them to define and identify what that means when having a home built. This is never truer than with High Performance Homes.

Consumers will find that this easy-to-use workbook will be helpful in finding the right builder, staying on budget, and avoiding conflicts, so their experience will be enjoyable from start to finish. Builders will appreciate working with consumers who are able to make informed decisions on time and be a helpful part of this creative building process.

I gladly supply this workbook to our clients as I find it an invaluable tool to assist them in working through the vast array of decisions that are necessary in building a High Performance Home. Our clients appreciate a method to organize the process into bite size pieces.

I trust you will enjoy this book and that your Home Building endeavor brings you many years of comfortable, healthy living with energy bills that will be the envy of your neighbors.

Donald Ferrier

CEO / President
Ferrier Custom Homes, LP
Fort Worth, Texas
2005, 2006, 2007 NAHB Energy value award-winning green builder

Who Will Benefit From This Workbook?

Homebuyers who want to:

- Select a model of home with the right floor plan and features (**production**)
- Choose a floor plan to modify slightly or significantly (**semi-custom**)
- Create a unique design and customize all features (**custom**)

About the Author

Sara Lamia is an educator and clogging instructor who moved to Colorado with her husband, son and daughter in 1996. After having her home built, she dove in to understanding the building process from the inside out.

She wrote How to Enjoy Building Your Dream Home in 2003 and has since produced a DVD entitled "Your 21st Century High Performance Home." She provides builder seminars and continuing education courses for REALTORS® nationwide. She is a contributing editor to *Green Builder Magazine* and hosts a local radio show in Fort Collins, Colorado.

My Building Story

Our REALTOR located exactly what we were looking for: a row of homesites that abutted an open space designated to become a city park. Since the land was owned by a group of builders, we visited each builder's models and chose what we guessed was the highest quality from among them.

We chose one of our builder's existing plans but wanted to make structural changes, requiring additional architectural drawing. And so the process began. I spent many hours studying and trying to make sense of the blueprints, so that I'd make the right decisions as deadlines approached. I was haunted by the fact that this was a very complex undertaking, involving an enormous amount of money. I didn't even know what questions to ask, much less where to find answers.

As construction progressed, I would learn about a particular product or feature and only then realize that I'd made the wrong decision. Oh, no! Was it too late to submit another change order? Sometimes no, but if at all possible, my builder accommodated the change. I didn't fully understand at the time how much of a problem I was creating for him with each late change.

My builder knew how to build a house, but he couldn't know what I needed my home to be. I tried to be a good client, but I just didn't know enough to participate correctly. The same thought kept recurring: I'm spending an enormous amount of money, without knowing what I'm doing or how to make the right choices.

I began a little notebook. I visited showrooms, gathering stock numbers for items I wanted as upgrades. I then contacted my builder's assistant to find out what the charge would be for each. This process filled my notebook. I wish I had a nickel for every time I searched through that little book for a particular piece of information that was *somewhere*. Dollar signs and scribbled phone numbers flew from every page. I still have that little book. What a mixed memory.

I thought it was a shame that the process had been so stressful and inefficient. Having a home built should be fun! I began to visit model homes, noticing wonderful features, designs that *didn't* work, and questionable building practices. Only when homebuyers gain an understanding of the importance of quality and good design in the building of their home will they absolutely want to spend some of their money on quality rather than on extras that could be added later.

This practical workbook can help to keep you organized. It will raise questions and help you to focus on your specific needs and wants. The information can help you to determine your budget and stay within it. You will be able to do your research much more easily, so that you can make the right decisions in a timely way. Enjoy the building of your home and get the restful sleep that you, the new homebuyer who drives this whole industry, deserves.

Sara Lamia

Table of Contents

Section 5
Contract, Construction, Communication..........................84

Section 6
Learn More About It...100

Table of Worksheets

Section 1
Planning: The Foundation of Success

Why Build?

- I want to build in a particular subdivision or on a particular homesite
- I have specific land/home requirements not currently available in resale
- I like everything to be new
- I love creating my own home
- I can build more cheaply than what I can find on the resale market
- I need to start with specific basics but can add on gradually
- This is a good investment

Financial Investment or Dream Home?

Financial investment

REALTORS® can tell you how to maintain and increase the value of your investment in your home: choose a less expensive home in the most expensive neighborhood, one that looks attractive from the street and has features that are classically and currently in demand. This always includes an impressive kitchen, the most luxurious master bathroom, and for baby boomers or those with live-in, elderly relatives, a one-story home or first-floor master suite.

Dream home

When you've made a list of priorities in descending order, those at the top of the list, those we'll call "core priorities" may dictate where and what to build. Do you want to be near a particular urban area but outside of city limits so that you can have some acreage? This area may not be the best financial decision but still be the right choice for you.

The decision

How long are you planning to live in this home? How important is it that your most valued wishes be realized in this home? Are you building to achieve the greatest possible profit when you sell, so that you will be able to buy that retirement haven? The answers to these questions will help you to plan the very best home for you.

What to Build?

Is land available that

- Is in
  - a planned community
  - a particular climate
  - the mountains
  - the country
  - an urban center
- Is near
  - water
  - a golf course
  - a particular school
  - public transportation
  - employment
  - shopping
  - wildlife
- Is zoned for horses
- Is on
  - hilly terrain
  - level ground
- Has
  - a beautiful view
  - open space/privacy in the back/side/front
  - acreage
  - a place to garden
  - tranquillity
  - an exciting environment
  - a safe environment

Home style

- One story/ranch style
  - one main living level
  - no stairs
  - can finish basement for
    - ‣ guest rooms
    - ‣ media room
    - ‣ entertainment area
- Multi-level
  - master bedroom on main level
  - additional bedrooms above or below
  - common areas on first-floor, all bedrooms upstairs
  - raised entrance for above-ground lower level
- Income property with all or part of the home to rent
- Home with professional office

Floor plan style

- Open – rooms flow into each other, many interior walls omitted
- Partially open – generally open but with doors to close off specific rooms
- Closed – most rooms with walls and doors for privacy, defined function and décor

The first worksheet, Choosing Priorities, will help you to bring the right home into clearer focus.

Identify "Core" Priorities and More

"Core priorities" is a concept I learned from a successful custom builder named John Brockett who had been a marriage counselor for 20 years! The answers below should be your "gut reactions" to what is most important to you. (More in-depth strategies begin on page 93.) After painting your new home with this broad brush, move on to a little helpful analysis.

When I think of my/our new home, I picture_____
    (Such as: everyone in the family room together, enjoying the solitude of my study, working at my workbench, gardening, spaciousness, community feeling, etc.)

Where I'll spend much of my time_____
    (indoors, outdoors, what area of home?)

I'll spend much of my time in this area doing what? _____

My top budgeting priority is _____

I absolutely refuse to have _____

Who will be visiting/living with us and where? _____

What rooms are essential for us to have? _____

Where will we entertain? _____

Are we willing to spend a little more initially for our home to be healthy, comfortable, energy-efficient and have lower operating costs? _____

Where do we plan to be in 5 years? 10 years? _____

Gather Clues from Your Current Home

Activity	Room/area in current home	Hours per week
SAMPLE: Work at home business	Extra bedroom	30

New Home Smart Spaces

- Are there spaces you currently don't have but feel you need? Fill them in below.
- Are there rooms that are rarely used per day? Can you combine activities in one location?
- In addition to cost savings, avoiding a sprawling home adds to its coziness and ability to bring the family together.
- List all activities that will be part of your lifestyle when living in your new home.

Activity	Room/area of new home	Hours per week

For custom buyers who plan to work with an architect, creating articulate answers to these questions will help your architect to draw schematics and blueprints that will reflect your needs and wishes.

If you haven't reached agreement about something significant, the best time to resolve it is before committing to anything. See page 93 for strategies that can help you to focus on what is most important to you.

Creating Your Budget

If you will be applying for a mortgage, obtain pre-approval as soon as possible. Too often, buyers *assume* that their loan approval will go smoothly, only to have a problem show up just as the builder is ready to begin construction.

Information you'll need to bring to a lender

- 30-day pay stubs (2 most recent)
- Monthly bank statements (2 most recent)
- W-2 statements (2 most recent years)
- Annual income tax returns (if self-employed) (2 most recent)
- Statements for 401K, stocks, etc. (most recent)
- Anything else you are asked to bring (when making appointment)

Many homebuyers feel uncomfortable sharing all of this private information with a stranger. Lenders are professionals who are trained to take your numbers, run them through several formulas, and come out with a numerical answer to your question

How much can I borrow? $_____

Your budget should include:

Down payment (0-30%) $_____

Loan amount (70-100%)   + $_____

Contingency factor* (5-20%)   + $_____

Total home budget   = $_____

For more details about Financing see page 223.

After you have looked through this workbook and have selected a builder and home design, complete your budget below, and enter information on the worksheet on page 241

Your total budget $_____

Less builder's base price   - $_____

Budget for upgrades = $_____

*An optional contingency in addition to your upgrade budget can cover items that you *forgot* to include at contract signing.

Getting a good idea of how much you will be spending on home and land allows you to do your shopping in the right price range and to really *enjoy* it.

Who Should Be On Your Team?

REALTOR can locate
- Land
- Builder

Builder will
- Build on your land/his land
- Take responsibility for project

Architect
- Unique design
- Customizes to your lifestyle
- Creates blueprint
- Should match to budget

Structural engineer
- Evaluates structural soundness

Lender
- Provides/shops for best loan for you

- Advises about credit scores, etc.
- Ensures that monies are present at closing

Arborist
- Selects trees to keep/eliminate
- Determines health of specific trees

Landscape designer
- Can create total outdoor plan
- Responsible for maintaining proper slope of ground for positive drainage

Interior designer
- Can create total indoor plan
- May affect early decisions

Structured wiring (See page 102)
- Creates/installs wiring plan
- Plans for future electronics needs

Self-contracting (See page 103)

How To Choose A Good...

REALTOR
- Experienced with land/new construction
- Knowledge about green/high performance
- References/good listener
- Extensive local resource
- Buyer broker/transaction broker

Builder (general contractor)
- Good homeowner references
- Finances/years in business
- All required current insurance
- Uses sustainable materials and building practices (certified green program)
- Good listener/communicator
- Flexible (within reasonable limits)
- Compatible working style
  - hands-off (leave builder alone)
  - involved (work together closely)
- How often on building site
- Organized/written policies
- Willing to work with architect
- Credentials/professional associations

Architect
- Good homeowner references
- Good listener/communicator
- Experienced with green design
- Willing to work with you and builder
- Can alter existing plan
- Charges by hour/percentage of total
- Will design or just consult

- Worked with builder previously

Attorney
- Experienced in new home real estate
- Available for questions/closing

Structural engineer
- Experienced with residential building

Lender
- Attention to detail and service
- Experienced with new construction
- Knows about energy-efficient loans and tax credits available
- Able to explain options clearly
- Checks closing papers thoroughly

Landscape designer/Arborist
- Past work that you like/references
- Can plan for passive solar/shade
- Good listener/communicator
- Able to design all or part
- Will design or just consult

Interior designer
- Credentials/experience
- Knowledgeable about green design
- Good listener/communicator
- Able to design all or part
- Expert shopper
- Will design or critique yours

Private inspector
- References/credentials
- Trained to appraise energy features
- Experienced with new construction
- Impartial

Shopping for Land

Private Sale Essentials

- Soils report
  - problems affecting construction
  - septic/well locations
- Current zoning restrictions
- Future zoning restrictions
- Location/availability of utilities

- Site check by expert for any hidden problems
- Good drainage
- See Defining Land Needs below
- Mortgage shopping
  - acquire construction loan approval

Working with a REALTOR

- Knowledge of land requirements
- May have exclusive access to some land/developments
- Excellent local resource
- Customized search

- saves valuable time
- able to locate hard-to-find properties
- knows the right questions to ask
- understands market value of area

Defining Your Land Needs

Who owns land

- Buyer
  - owns existing land
  - takes out construction loan on new land

- Builder takes out construction loan
- Developer/ subdivision
  - choice of participating builders
  - builder may own land until closing

Traffic patterns

- Traffic noise
  - how much is acceptable
  - prefer windows open frequently
- On or near a busy corner
- At the end of a cul-de-sac where headlights will shine in

- Safe for children and pets
- Easy access to
  - main roads
  - work/school/stores
- Future municipal plans for area
  - traffic lights/future development

Structures in this area

- School/bus route
- Stores/commercial buildings
- Gravel pit/water treatment plant
- Power lines

- Highway (check audibility distance)
  - visit at various times of day
- Airport flight pattern
- Agricultural/farm animals

Taxes/zoning/covenants

- Taxes/tax rate after improvements
- Architectural/district covenants or building requirements
  - height/width dimensions
  - distance from street
  - style restrictions
  - exterior paint colors
  - home price max./min.
- Homeowners association
  - covenants (see page 105)
  - annual/monthly fees
  - personal/association liability

- association "politics"
- Commonly owned areas
  - pool/grass/golf
  - playground
  - tennis courts
  - community room
  - alleys
- Zoning of abutting/nearby land
- Zoning of total area of development
- Future building affecting this area

Municipal services

- Location/quality/special programs of schools
  - pre-school
  - elementary
  - middle/junior high
  - senior high
- Fire station
- distance
- how it affects homeowners insurance
- paid/volunteer
- Police station
  - distance

Street/utilities

- Street
  - is or will be paved
  - at what cost/who is responsible
  - future assessments/improvements
- Impact fees (see page 106)
- Tap fees
  - water/sewer
  - gas/electric
- Driveway curbs
  - city/builder expense
  - owner's expense
  - able to "normalize"
- Utilities/wires
  - installed by builder
  - potential installation problems
  - those you must install/pay for

- ‣ cost of installation
- Cable/DSL available
- Satellite
  - land line phone for remote updates
- Municipal
  - water/sewer available
  - restrictions
  - future planning of utilities
- Water rights (if not municipal)
  - existing well
  - cost of digging well
  - necessary depth
- Septic system
  - soils test results (see page 125)
  - distance from home
- Location of easements (see page 204)

Soil/terrain

- Soils and "perc" tests done (see page 125)
  - by whom/results
  - any special construction due to
    - ‣ expansive/sandy soils
    - ‣ underground water
    - ‣ other
- Drainage capabilities/problems
- Area drainage plan available from
  - developer
  - municipality
- Location for leach field/septic system
- Location for well
- Level/hilly terrain
  - cost to level or slope land
    - ‣ for home only
    - ‣ for entire homesite
  - suitable for walkout/garden level
  - hills are safe for children on bikes
- Radon/other noxious gases
  - special building considerations
  - passive radon piping can be laid (see page 156)

Orientation of your home on this land

For optimum comfort/energy savings from sun, wind and summer breezes
- Consider side of home facing
  - north (least sun, may offer wind)
  - south (best for overhang to shade overhead summer sun)
  - east (morning sun and sunrise view)
  - west (lingering afternoon and evening summer sun, sunset view)
- Location of patio, porch or deck
- sun for morning warmth
- shade for coolness
- protection from unwanted wind
- access to cooling breezes
- Location of driveway
  - south/southeast to melt snow
  - south/southwest if garage protects living areas from sun's heat
- See page 105 to help determine optimum orientation

The Road to Contract

Shop for Land

- With REALTOR
- With builder
- Private sale
- Buyer's existing property
  - equity may be available to use for construction loan

Consider Floor Plans

- Visit model homes
- Peruse magazines
  - study home plans
  - cut out favorite photos
- Work with an architect (custom)
- Ask friends and neighbors about features they like/don't like about their floor plans
- See page 109 to "try on" floor plans

Prepare Questions to Ask Builders

- Read through checklists
- Create and prioritize questions
  - what you must have (see Core Priorities on page 10)
  - what you'd like, depending on price
  - what is least important/can live without
  - builder's policies and procedures
  - homeowner references
    ‣ willing to arrange appointments

Interview Builders

- Check builder's
  - floor plans (if production/semi-custom)
  - design/drafting capabilities
  - relationships with local architects
  - attitude about working cooperatively
  - contract form, if any
- See page 13 for How to Choose...
- Bring prepared questions from worksheet on page 79

Determine Your Available Shopping Time

- Unlimited
  - heavily involved in planning
  - will visit site daily
- Moderate
  - will do some customizing
  - will visit weekly
- Very little
  - minimum number of decisions
  - existing floor plan and limited options
  - required visits only

Sign a Solid Contract, Resulting In

- A clear understanding of what materials will be used or installed (specifications and materials list)
- A schedule for
  - start/completion
  - contingencies if needed
- Good communication with builder and staff (see page 84)
- A legal "blueprint" for success
- See page 86 for contract details

Section 2
The Building Process

Acquiring Land
Selection of Floor Plan
Foundation Design
Excavation/Foundation/Insulation
Framing
"High Performance Home" HVAC
Insulation/Air Sealing
Roof
Exterior Wall Siding
Plumbing
Electrical
Interior Walls
Flooring/Carpet
Cabinets
Appliances
Countertops
Finish Carpentry
Exterior Design

Construction Timeline Example

An example of a typical construction timeline is shown on the following pages, to give you an overview of the details and sequence of the actual construction process. The timeline for your home will probably differ somewhat from this one both in sequence and in inspections that are required by your local municipal authorities.

░ = construction activities
█ = building Inspections (subject to local building codes)

Activity	Weeks																
	1	2	3	4	5	6	7	8	9	10	11	12	13	14	15	16	17
Stake lot	░																
Temporary construction power	░																
Excavate foundation	░																
Footers formed	░																
Footing inspection	█																
Foundation wall set		░															
Foundation wall inspection		█															
Poured foundation walls/insulation		░															
Strip form from foundation walls		░															
Install water and sewer laterals		░															
Water service inspection		█															
Waterproof foundation		░															
Underdrains system installed		░															
Sewer inspection		█															
Backfill foundation			░														
Rough-in underground plumbing			█														
Prep basement, garage floors				░													
Install gas and electric laterals				░													
Pour basement, garage concrete				░													
Deliver lumber, trusses, I-beams				░													
Framing work					░												
Rough-in HVAC						░											
Rough-in plumbing						░											
Gas line air test inspection							█										
Start siding								░									
Start roofing								░									
Order cabinets								░									
Start brickwork								░									
Install fireplace								░									
Plumbing top-out and water test								█									
Electric energize inspection								█									

Activity	Weeks																
	1	2	3	4	5	6	7	8	9	10	11	12	13	14	15	16	17
Rough heating inspection									█								
Electric rough-in inspection									█								
Fireplace inspection									█								
Install batt insulation										░							
Install electrical, gas, water meters										░							
Frame and roof inspection										█							
Insulation inspection										█							
Install and tape wallboard											░						
Install gutters											░						
Paint exterior												░					
Exterior concrete work												░					
Deliver & Install cabinets												░					
Start interior trim												░					
Paint interior													░				
Install floor vinyl, tile													░				
Install countertops & backsplash													░				
Deliver & install grout, lights														░			
Install electric trim														░			
Start plumb. & HVAC trim															░		
Install shower doors & mirrors															░		
Punch (check) wallboard															░		
Clean windows															░		
Sweep and install carpet															░		
Install cabinet hardware																░	
Final clean and test fireplace, HVAC																░	
Test air tightness, combustion safety																░	
Paint touch-up																░	
Start construction punchlist																░	
Final building inspection																█	
Buyer's walkthrough																	░
Punchlist corrections																	░
Closing																	░

Which Type of Builder?

Production Builder

- Existing floor plans
  - models often available for viewing
  - popular features
- Pre-determined base price
- No changes in floor plan
- Options from builder's list only
- Builder owns construction loan
  - may reduce buyer access to site
- Involves minimum decisions/time
- Usually lowest price per square foot

Semi-custom Builder

- Existing floor plans
  - models often available for viewing
  - popular features
- Pre-determined base price
- Structural changes before blueprints
- Options list/additional options
  - can be added/deleted (per contract)
- Change orders after contract
  - varies with builder
- Builder or buyer owns loan
  - access to site per contract policy
- Quantity of decisions/time required is proportionate to buyer quantity of options/upgrades/changes
- Customization and personal service varies with builder

Custom Builder

- Floor plan
  - custom drawn by architect
  - purchased by buyer (adjust if necessary)
  - builder's plan
  - existing homes may be available to view
- Price
  - "cost plus" (materials, time)
  - fixed
- Change orders after contract
  - structural usually accepted with additional charge
- Construction loan taken by
  - buyer or builder
- Maximum customization
  - quantity of decisions/time proportionate to choices/changes
  - maximum personal service

Self-contracting

- Have total control over project
- Provide floor plan
  - selected and purchased by buyer
    ‣ adjustments if necessary
  - drawn by architect
- Obtain
  - financing (may have special qualifications as individual)
  - all required insurance
  - all permits/required tests
- Set budget
- Purchase products
  - create "take down" list of materials
  - supervise daily pick-up/delivery
- Schedule and supervise "trades" determining that they
  - aren't overcharging for single job with no promise of future work
  - will work together as needed
  - have done all work correctly
- Ensure that all materials are on site for day's work
- Manage all paperwork
- Deal with typical construction issues
  - delays
    ‣ weather
    ‣ product defects/mis-orders
    ‣ trade absenteeism
  - re-scheduling of trades
    ‣ can be "domino effect"
    ‣ trade availability for single job
  - correction of work improperly done
  - timely payment to trades
    ‣ bank inspection before payment
  - budget overruns
  - daily extended site visits
    ‣ morning to get work started
    ‣ evening to see that work was done
    ‣ mid-day to check as needed

Section 3
Choosing the Right Floor Plan

Model Homes

Know what is important

Walking through model homes is fun. You can feel the excitement. All brand new, so many luxurious features. Read through the following checklists to educate yourself about what to look for in a floor plan. This includes features that you will absolutely want and features that will make you cross a particular model off your list. This is the largest purchase you'll ever make. You'll want to know what to look for before you buy.

Ask questions

Whether you're gathering ideas for your custom home or will be selecting a builder's model, use the information in this book and from any other sources to help you choose the right builder. Create a list of questions to ask of the builder or sales representative (worksheet on page 79.) If you need further information, either put your questions in writing for the builder to research, or visit another builder, or both.

What's included?

Models are loaded with upgrades. While this practice showcases options which may be of interest to many, they make it more difficult to picture what the base price really buys. Avoid "falling in love" with a model until *after* you've checked it out with an educated eye.

Floor Plans from Magazines

In addition to visiting model homes, have fun looking through some of the many magazines that are available in retail stores. This is a way to more easily focus on floor plan basics, since upgrades aren't present to dazzle you. Magazines enable you to look at many floor plans in one place, and to compare features that serve your lifestyle needs.

What magazines cannot do, however, is simulate three-dimensional reality. They look small on a page in a magazine, making it more difficult to determine what size of home they represent. It's strongly advisable to determine if the floor plans have been checked by an engineer for structural soundness. Also keep in mind that stock plans may need alteration to fit on your land, probably incurring additional cost.

Home Style

- One-story (ranch-style or rambler)
  - all necessary areas on one level
  - handicapped-accessible
  - cozy "togetherness" of one level
  - traditional skylights (sky view)
  - sufficient land required
  - more expensive per square foot to build *out*
- Multi-level
  - living space/bedrooms upstairs
    ‣ separate level privacy
    ‣ necessity of stairs
  - architectural flair of levels
  - maximum home size for homesite
  - less expensive to build *up*
  - one-story may not fit on land
- Special construction (see page 106)
  - modular
  - log
  - timber frame
  - solar

- Ceilings
  - standard 8 feet
  - 9-12 feet
  - two-story (16 feet)
  - vaulted
- Basement raised
  - may require engineering approval
- Room/door sizes
  - will furniture fit in rooms and through doorways

Curb Appeal

- Entryway
  - sheltered from rain/wind/sun
  - fully visible from street
  - attractive and inviting
- Windows
  - balanced appearance
  - shapes/sizes complement style of home
- Visible outdoor living space
  - front porch/terraces
- Garage
  - front mount does not dominate (fortress-style)
  - side mount allows easy in and out
  - rear mount allows safe entry to home
- Siding and roof materials/style complement style of home
- Yard setback at attractive distance

Whole-house Traffic Patterns

Traffic pattern from entrances

- When I go from garage to kitchen (carrying groceries)
  - distance to kitchen
  - rooms I must cross
  - any carpet on this path
  - any stairs to climb
- When I enter home with keys/mail/briefcase/backpack
  - "welcoming area" place to
    ‣ put everything down
    ‣ store items conveniently
    ‣ dry boots/shoes
      · see Finish Carpentry on page 201
- View upon entering from the front door
  - formal rooms
  - kitchen
  - powder room
  - staircase
- General feeling of
  - spaciousness
  - coziness
- Entrance hallways
  - narrow/wide
  - short/excessively long
- Traffic pattern
  - to staircases
  - to kitchen
  - to mud room
  - any carpet on these paths
  - through any room to get to another
- Entering from other doors
  - traffic pattern within home
  - special purpose entrance from outside

Traffic patterns between rooms

- All rooms have hallway access
- Hallways- length and width
- Kitchen in relation to other rooms
  - opens to family room
  - view of
    ‣ television
    ‣ fireplaces
    ‣ children playing
  - convenient to dining room
    ‣ doorway
    ‣ butler pantry
- Noise level between kitchen and other rooms
- Convenient arrangement for entertaining
- Quality of outdoor views
- Natural light from size, location, quantity of windows
- Reversing floor plan (see page 108)
- Principles of Feng Shui (see page 108)

Universal design/ Handicapped-accessible

- Zero-step entrance (less than 1/2") for
  - baby stroller
  - wheelchair/walker
  - mobile visitors who have difficulty with steps
- 36"-42" wide doorways
- Staircases with
  - low rise
  - wide tread
  - handrails on each side
- Elevator
  - location
  - sufficient size for wheelchair
  - remote control of interior door
  - spring-closure of exterior door
- Closet rods with adjustable height
- Cabinet height adjusted
  - raised for less bending
  - lowered for handicapped access
- Bathrooms
  - at least one bathroom on main level
  - toilets 18" high (chair height)
  - tub grab bar
    ‣ accessible getting *in* and *out* of tub
    ‣ can be matched to other hardware and beautiful!
  - shower grab bar
  - adjustable hand-held sprayer
  - "zero-step" shower entry

- fold-down seat in shower
- 3/4" plywood behind walls wherever grab bars may be needed (blocking)
- under sink recessed pipes (to clear knee space)
- Kitchen
  - zero-step entry from garage to kitchen
  - dishwashers/ovens at raised height
  - cooktops with accessible knobs
  - variable height countertops
  - accessible
    ‣ switches
    ‣ outlets
    ‣ thermostat
- Lighting
  - high levels without glare
  - skylights
  - undercabinet
  - recessed under stair step edges
  - footlights on staircase wall
- Hardware
  - lever handles throughout home
    ‣ doors
    ‣ sink/tub faucets
    ‣ cabinets
- Wall switches
  - rocker
  - touch
  - remote control

Floor Plans by Room

Within the kitchen floor plan

- Location of sink
  - room to stand when dishwasher is next to sink and open (see drawing on page 114)
  - distance to refrigerator
  - distance to stove unit/stovetop/wall oven(s)
  - view when standing at sink
  - traffic pattern that accommodates two cooks
- Location of refrigerator
  - to nearest countertop
  - to opposing countertop
  - refrigerator doors can open more than 90° to allow bin removal
  - opposing countertop allows refrigerator door swing clearance
  - away from entryway (does not block traffic when open) see page 114
- Location of stove unit/stovetop/wall oven(s)
  - distance to nearest countertop or heat-resistant surface
  - distance to refrigerator
  - sufficient standing room when oven door is open
  - away from entryway (does not block traffic when oven door is open)
- Counter space
  - main work surface
    ‣ central location
    ‣ at least 24" width and depth
    ‣ depth is reachable for cleaning
    ‣ desirable view
  - usable surfaces at least 18" wide
- Pantry closet or cabinets for storage of groceries/paper supplies
  - supported every 18" or less to support weight of cans and bottles
  - shallow enough to access items against wall
- Storage of plates/glasses/flatware/utensils
  - convenient to dishwasher and serving area
- Storage of pots and pans/lids
  - convenient to stovetop

- sufficient height/depth for large items
- Location of island/peninsula
  - doesn't block traffic patterns (sink to stovetop to oven to refrigerator)
  - if it includes eating bar overhang
    ‣ sufficient room to sit/pull out stools
    ‣ seating
      · shoulder-to-shoulder
      · opposing or perpendicular
    ‣ overhang sufficient depth to avoid bumping into knobs and handles
  - if it includes stovetop/grill
    ‣ safety issue
      · hot surface
      · spattering
  - if it includes sink/wet bar
    ‣ water splashing above/around
- Washable flooring under eating overhang
- Counter level
  - one level/multi-level
  - mixed countertop materials
- Location of separate kitchen eating area has
  - sufficient room for
    ‣ table size and shape
    ‣ chairs to pull out
    ‣ traffic pattern to exterior door
  - lighting centered over table
  - light switch convenient to table
  - open or cozy feeling
- Kitchen keeping room/sitting area
  - sofa/chairs
  - fireplace
- Butler pantry
  - area sufficient width to maneuver
  - cabinets
    ‣ base for storage/drawers
    ‣ wall for storage/decorative inserts
  - sufficient work surface
  - wet area/sink
  - appliances
- Natural light from windows

Family room/great room floor plan
- Open to other rooms for spaciousness
- Convenient entrances to other rooms
- Use of half walls for room definition
- Use of ceiling finishes or colors for room definition
- Walls accommodate furniture arrangement
- Fireplace well-located for
  - view
  - seating
  - furniture arrangement
- Entertainment area accommodates
  - television dimensions
  - convenient for viewing
  - conversation grouping
  - parties
- Built-in cabinets
  - sufficient for electronic items
  - includes necessary wiring/outlets
- Indoor and outdoor views
- Natural light from windows

Dining room floor plan
- Convenient to kitchen
- Closed room
  - large enough for your table and chairs
  - sufficient wall space for furniture
- Open area
  - dining area within larger room
  - able to accommodate an occasional crowd
- Convenient to other entertaining areas
- Built-in cabinets needed/desired
- Potential "flex area" for other uses
- Indoor and outdoor views
- Natural light from windows

Flex rooms floor plan
- Rooms that can serve several purposes
  - dining room/study area
  - exercise area/sewing room
  - office/guest room
  - guest room/gaming area
  - open computer area/home management
  - laundry/pet dining and bathing/plant care

Living room floor plan
- Function of formal living room
  - haven from noise for visiting/reading
  - wasted space that should be eliminated
- Closed/open room
- Sufficient wall space for furniture
- Piano or other items that must fit
- Indoor and outdoor views
- Natural light from windows

Study/office floor plan
- Location isolated from home noise
- Potential for commercial office
  - separate exterior entrance
  - check zoning restrictions
- Indoor and outdoor views
- Potential for his/hers offices
  - side-by-side or angled desks
  - opposite-sides-of-room desks
  - noise control when on phone
- Natural light from windows

Powder room floor plan
- Location
  - on main floor
  - convenient access for guests
  - affords some privacy
- Sufficient size for spaciousness
- Window that affords light and privacy

Master bedroom floor plan

- Sufficient privacy from
  - within home
  - windows
- Sufficient size for existing furniture
- Sufficient space for
  - sitting area/exercise room
- Vaulted/raised ceiling for spaciousness
- Outdoor views
- Natural light from windows
- Closed room (doors at each entrance)
- Open to master bathroom

Master bathroom floor plan

- Closed to other living areas
- Open areas prevents control of
  - temperature
  - light
  - sound
  - odors
- Shower/tub
  - height/width/depth allows comfort
  - sitting bench
  - shelf/niche for shampoo, etc.
  - grab bar to enter/exit tub
  - glass enclosure/shower curtain
- Toilet(s)
  - separate room
    ‣ sufficient clearance when door swings *in*
    ‣ can door swing *out*
    ‣ pocket door
    ‣ sufficient space and light
  - located next to tub
    ‣ serves as "seat" when bathing children
    ‣ may be unwelcome if reclining in tub
  - washable floor around toilet
  - toilet paper holder located for convenient reach

- Vanity area
  - sitting area requires proper counter height
  - light for makeup/contact lenses/shaving
    ‣ wall lighting best
  - access to water while sitting

- Sufficient counter space at sink
- Organized storage under sinks
- Linen closet size/location
- Flooring
  - carpet
    ‣ provides soft and warm feeling
    ‣ color to match décor
  - tile/vinyl
    ‣ toilet area
    ‣ non-skid in front of shower entry
    ‣ entire bathroom
- Towel bars
  - convenient when exiting shower/tub
  - sufficient quantity

- Windows for natural light
- Privacy with window placement
- Special features (see page 167)

Master closet(s) floor plan

- Sufficient size for
  - clothing and storage
  - dressing/mirrors
  - dresser/chest
- Adjustable rods/shelves
- Storage bins
- Window/skylight
  - affords natural light
  - guard against fading
- Special features (see page 118)

Additional considerations for other bedrooms floor plan

- Conveniently located
  - near master bedroom
  - away from master bedroom
- Sufficient size for
  - occupants
  - furniture
- Window placement for safety
  - high/low for small children
- no bunk beds near windows or ceiling fan
- Jack and Jill (see page 120)
  - shared bathroom between bedrooms
  - alternate designs to "dueling doors"
- See Plumbing on page 167

In-law quarters floor plan
- Traffic pattern for privacy
- Separate bathroom
- Separate exterior entrance
- Stairs/no stairs
- Separate heating/cooling zone/system
- Structured wiring
- Natural light from windows

Laundry room floor plan
- Location convenient for
  - time of day that washing is done
  - location of dirty clothes storage
- Noise isolated from other rooms
- Mud entrance for wet shoes
- Not a preferred entrance
- Appliances will not block doorway or traffic pattern (see page 121)
- Washer next to laundry sink
- Dryer exhaust lined up directly with exterior wall vent (see page 170)
- Ability to install laundry chute
- Natural light from windows
- Pet eating/bathing area

Separate mud room
- Hooks for coats/hats
- Bench
- Storage bins for shoes/boots
- Shelf for
  - mail/keys
  - laptop
- backpacks
- Closet for
  - sports equipment
  - broom/vacuum
- Floor drain
- Pet eating/bathing area

Garage floor plan

- Sufficient width/depth/height for
  - oversized vehicles
  - bicycles
  - sports equipment
  - yard equipment
  - toys/trash cans/tools
  - baby carriage/stroller
- Hinged door to outside conveniently located to
  - side yard/back yard
  - purpose of door dictates location
- Hinged door into home (walking from car through entry door)
  - convenient placement in garage
  - "welcoming" area
    ‣ pleasant environment
    ‣ place to put belongings down when arriving home

General storage floor plan
- Sufficient total quantity of
  - clothes closets
  - linen closets
  - kitchen cabinets/pantry shelving
  - garage storage
- additional storage rooms/areas
  ‣ under staircases
  ‣ niches in angled walls (if dead space exists behind walls)

Outdoor living spaces
- Defined areas
  - sitting/conversation
  - dining
  - food preparation
  - solarium/greenhouse
- Fireplace
- Water feature
- Sheltered from sun/wind/water
- See Exterior Design on page 203

Worksheet For Favorite Features From Models

Feature	Builder / model	Cost	Comparison of features

Process for Buying a Production Home

- Financing
  - locate quality lender who can
    - explain loan options in easy-to-understand language
    - help you to determine appropriate loan amount
    - possibly help to increase your credit rating, if desired
  - acquire pre-approval for mortgage (if financing)
- Shop
  - look in Section 2 for how to evaluate selected model homes and floor plans
  - consider neighborhoods using checklists (page 14) and detail (page 104)
  - select a REALTOR or shop on your own to evaluate
    - land
    - neighborhoods
    - builders/models
    - lending options
  - visit models and floor plans with an "educated eye"
  - examine builder's option list and prices, comparing them to your budget
- Do some investigating
  - create questions to ask builders on form located on page 79
  - make appointments to interview builders/sales agents
  - read Homeowners Association covenants that apply to your homesite
  - request a referral list of buyers with similarly priced and styled homes
    - request the builder to arrange for you to visit referrals (very important!)
    - bring list of questions to ask fellow buyers
  - request a copy of the builder's contract
- Select
  - a builder and model
  - a homesite - consider home's orientation to sun and wind (page 105)
- Contract (your roadmap for success)
  - read through Section 5 before signing a contract
  - read through all of builder's literature for policies and procedures
  - sign a contract that you understand, and have had your attorney examine
  - have payments put in escrow account
- Organize your selections process
  - write all decision deadlines on calendar pages in back of workbook
  - allow time to shop for each item well in advance of decision deadline
- Learn about options
  - refer to checklists beginning on page 32 before shopping
  - read more in Section 6 when questions about checklist items arise
  - know why each selection is the right one for you
- Submit decisions in writing before deadline to avoid late charges
- Visit site and take notes
- Have construction inspected if agreed to in contract (see page 212)
- Lock in mortgage rate at some point during construction (if applying for mortgage)
- Bring pre-closing walkthrough list and make punchlist notes prior to closing
- If builder has a second walkthrough, check that punchlist items are fixed
- Closing
  - request a preview of all paperwork
    - check that all charges are correct and not duplicated elsewhere
    - read through fine print
  - confirm with lender that money will be available at closing time

Process for Buying A Custom Home

The chronological order of tasks may vary, depending on individual situation.
- Prepare before shopping for land
  - peruse checklists for items of special importance to you
  - detailed information in Section 6
- Purchase land
  - use existing property or shop privately for land
  - contact REALTOR
  - contact builder directly
  - obtain copy of Homeowners Association covenants, if any
- Obtain pre-approval for a loan amount (if applying)
- Create blueprints
  - learn how to evaluate floor plans and design features, starting on page 106
  - visit models homes or look through floor plan magazines
  - clip photos of preferred design features
- Interview and select architect
  - create list of questions for architect (see page 101)
  - read, understand and sign architect's contract
  - preliminary schematic before blueprints
- Interview and select builder
  - create list of questions for builders (see page 79)
  - determine who takes out construction loan
  - agree on pricing model
    ‣ fixed bid with allowances
    ‣ fix bid with specifications defined
    ‣ cost-plus with a fixed fee
    ‣ cost plus a percentage
- Schedule meeting with builder and architect
  - builder creates written budget estimate
  - architect or builder/designer creates blueprints
  - study blueprints carefully for necessary changes
- Have attorney or builder create contract
  - review and sign contract (see page 209)
  - determine if monies will be placed in escrow account
  - determine if buyer and builder will "approve" monthly invoices before paid
- Obtain construction loan/financing, if necessary
- If architectural review committee, must approve blueprints
- Builder
  - acquires all required permits and tests
  - breaks ground and schedules "trades"
- Plan for enjoyable, efficient shopping
  - fill in decision deadlines on calendars in back of workbook
  - use checklists beginning on page 32 to prepare for shopping decisions
  - make timely decisions at each phase of construction
- Visit site regularly (as agreed) and take notes
- Schedule desired inspections
- Bring list for each walkthrough
- Lock in mortgage rate at some point during construction (if applying)
- Bring pre-closing walkthrough list and make punchlist notes prior to closing
- Conduct additional walkthroughs to assure that punchlist items are fixed
- Execute closing, including
  - certificate of occupancy
  - lien waivers

Section 4
Customizing Checklists

Watching Your Budget

Except for low-cost or no-cost options, be aware that *most options add significantly to the price of your home*. It is therefore important to get accurate written costs for all items. Ask builder's references if this process worked well for them.

Some options will save you money in the long run, and are difficult or impossible to add or change after the home has been completed. These include adding more windows, choosing higher quality or tinted windows, additional or higher quality insulation, structured wiring, enlarging a room or raising ceilings.

$$\$ In some regions, building off-season can save you money. In all but the hottest southern climates, most building occurs in the spring, summer and fall. If you are able to plan your project so that building can be done in the winter, you may be able to get the same work done for less. Where scorching summers are the least popular time, prices may be lower then.

Shoppers, be wise: know where to spend and where to save.
Also see page 94 for ways to identify needs and wants.

Impossible/very difficult	Expensive or disruptive to change	Relatively easy to change/add later

• Basement/lower level room size, ceiling height, additional windows
• Exterior brick/stone
• Fireplace
• "Behind the wallboard" materials s
  - wiring
  - rough-in plumbing
  - heating system
    ‣ duct tightness
    ‣ quantity/size
  - insulation
  - air sealing
• Change window
  - size
  - shape
  - location
• Expand walls
• Expand doorways
• Raise ceiling height
• Plumb for central vacuum
	• Replace windows
	• Door swing (left or right)
	• Bathtubs/sinks
	• Wall tile
	• Roof/siding
	• Concrete patio/walkways
	• Interior paint
	• Wood or tile flooring
	• Wall trim
		• Faucets/sink accessories
		• Light fixtures
		• Appliances (most sizes)
		• Decorative glass inserts
		  - front door sidelights
		  - cabinet doors
		  - transom windows (non-weight bearing)
		• Paint/wallpaper by room
		• Carpet
		• Countertops

Foundation Design

For areas of the country that have basements or crawlspaces.

- Land remediation, if required
- Survey/stake land
- Soils report and evaluation
  - special construction
    ‣ poor drainage
    ‣ expansive soils
    ‣ noxious gases
- Drainage plan
- Plot plan evaluation
- File permits
- Any foundation changes
  - slab-on-grade
    ‣ improve frost protection
    ‣ increase/decrease size
  - crawlspace
    ‣ included in "envelope" (see page 125)

- basement
  ‣ increase/decrease square footage of foundation
  ‣ raise ceiling height
- Add/enlarge/eliminate windows
  ‣ enlarge window wells for light
  ‣ add/change location of doors
  ‣ relocate heating/cooling system (while maintaining effective HVAC design)
  ‣ move/add rough-in plumbing
  ‣ add wine cellar
  ‣ add media room
  ‣ change grade of land for a walkout basement

Excavation/Foundation

- Prepare site
- Dig hole (basement/crawlspace)
- Footers formed and poured
- Foundation
- Lateral pipes (if municipal services)
- Radon pipes (if desired/required)
  - radon pipe route to wall/roof
  - passive system (see page 156)
  - active system
    ‣ fan installed to exhaust fumes
- Waterproof foundation
- Exterior insulation of foundation walls for additional
  - warmth
  - protection from moisture
- Install underdrains system if necessary

- Retaining walls (if necessary)
- Backfill foundation/compaction (see page 129)
- Install underground plumbing
- Install gas and electric lateral pipes (if gas connection)
- Prepare and pour foundation and garage floors
- Install foundation sub-floor
- If not on municipal utilities
  - well
    ‣ required/desired depth
    ‣ cost to drill
  - septic tank
    ‣ required distance from home
    ‣ cost to dig/install

Framing Walls, Floors and Openings

Exterior Wall Construction

- 2 x 4 walls
- 2 x 6 walls
- Insulated concrete forms
- Structural insulated panels
- Special foundation-level framing in expansive/sandy soils
- Porch
  - front door shelter
  - full/partial
  - wrap around
  - provides shade for passive cooling
  - potential to screen-in
- Terraces
  - outside of any room(s)
  - safety factor (upper levels)
- Matching "lean to" for storage

Sub-Floor Construction

- OSB (oriented strand board)
- Plywood
- Pre-fabricated joists (non-squeaking)
- Sub-floor for radiant floor heat

Garage

Garage size

- Double/oversized double
- Triple/quad or more
- Tandem
- Sufficient height for SUV/camper/truck
- Sufficient width/depth for
  - size/quantity of cars
  - teenager/in-law cars added later
- Sufficient space for
  - tools/lawn mower
  - sporting equipment/toys
  - workbench

Garage style

- Attached
  - ease of entrance to home
- Detached
  - sheltered access to home
  - exposed steps subject to rain/snow
- Integral (lower level)
- Service door(s) (see Garage doors)
- Windows for light/safety
- Place for basketball backboard

Garage doors

- Single or double combinations
  - solid
  - window inserts (shape/style)
  - "carriage" and other décor styles
- Automatic door openers
  - installed with convenient opener
  - pre-wire opener for extra doors
- Keyless pad entry
  - Install at height for children's use
- Hinged service door(s)
  - locate at side/back of home
  - swings left or right
  - can swing open with cars in garage

Garage finishing

- Separate circuit breaker for added security
- Insulation, air barrier, foam or caulk on
  - walls common to home
  - ceilings with living space above
    - ‣ insulation (blown-in or foam) properly fills entire cavity
- Door to home carefully air sealed
- Walls
  - paint/texture
- Floor
  - stain/seal
  - paint a sports floor (see page 132)

Driveway (see Exterior Design, page 204)

Windows

Window allowance $_____

Upgrade amount (add on page 241)

Where to Shop (list on page 240)

Looking out of home through windows

- Change/add/eliminate windows for
  - privacy
  - street noise
  - natural light
  - views
  - excessive solar heat gain
  - ventilation
  - furniture placement/built-ins
- Balanced look on each side of home
- How sizes and shapes of windows affect curb appeal (see page 137)
- Will windows

- prevent privacy
- always need to be covered
- Shutters block
  - cold or high winds
  - hot sun
  - light
- Shutter detail
  - shape/cutouts
  - sufficient exterior space on each side
  - storm safety potential

Popular window styles

- Casement (see drawing on page 134)
- Picture (fixed)
- Picture/awning combination
- Double-hung
- Horizontal slide
- Bow/bay

Creative window locations

- Two perpendicular walls
  - increases light and ventilation
- Where they won't prevent furniture arrangement
- Transom (over doorways)
- Sidelights (sides of front door)
- Kitchen
  - over backsplash on exterior wall

- over cabinets
- high on wall (with raised/vaulted ceiling) for skylight effect
- Sides of fireplace or above it
- Master closets
  - avoid direct sunlight on clothes
- Laundry room
- Dormer (see page 162)

Window frame material

- Wood with vinyl or aluminum cladding
- Vinyl
- Fiberglass
- Aluminum

Window quality

- Energy efficiency rating of frame and glass
  - U-value (see page 136)
    - lower number is better
- initial cost vs. energy savings/comfort
- Price vs. quality
- Ease of operation

Window installation quality

- Windows aligned with each other (proper height and squared)
- Window unit tightly sealed in opening
- Properly installed to drain moisture

- Builder/window specialist's opinion of
  - manufacturer
  - installer

Window glass
- Double/triple pane
- Argon-filled
- Spectrally-selective
  - low-E$_2$ or higher (low emissivity)
  - tinted
    - west/southwest orientation
    - reduces heat/fading from direct sun
- Laminated
  - reduction of sound transmission
- strength for storm safety
- burglar-resistant
- reduces fading (ultraviolet rays)
- Tempered/plexiglas® (safety code)
- Self cleaning (water *sheets* instead of spotting)
- Screens
  - quality
  - safety

Window size
- Standard per plan
- Larger
  - increased heat/cooling loss or gain
  - how to access for cleaning
  - ease/cost to cover unusual size
  - increased view/light/glare
  - may decrease usable wall space
- Smaller
  - reduced heat/cooling loss or gain
- reduced view/light/glare
- may increase wall space
- may decrease cost of windows/window coverings
- Windows low to the floor
  - pet/child viewing level
  - safety factor for children
- Windows high or narrow
  - for privacy/security

Window shape
- Rectangular
  - vertical/horizontal
- Square
- Radius
  - half round/archtop
- Oval
- Trapezoid/triangle
- Bay/bow
- Garden box
- Glass or acrylic block (various shape)

Window orientation challenges
- Sun/solar heat
  - south – within 30° of due south
  - southwest/west – low sun is challenge to shade
  - southeast – morning/early afternoon sun and heat
  - north – light without sun
- Wind/prevailing breezes
- identify area's direction of prevailing summer breezes
- identify direction of strong, cold wind- often north/northwest
- Solar screens
  - alternative to tinted windows
  - reduces visibility and light
- Overhangs (see page 138)

Skylights
- Quantity/location
- Properly insulated/sealed
- Rectangular full size
  - style
    - fixed
    - vented
    - remote control
    - sensors
    - programmable
  - material
    - tempered/laminated glass
    · solar heat reflective
    · argon-filled
    · laminated best for storm safety
    - plastic
      · less energy efficient
      · subject to scratching
- Tubular (see page 138)
  - 10" - 21" diameter
  - for light without heat or view
  - can be used in "tight" spaces

Exterior Doors

Exterior door allowance $_____

Upgrade amount (add on page 241)

Where to Shop (list on page 240)

Exterior door style

- Hinged single
  - swings left or right
  - glass insert for light/style
    ‣ stained/cut glass inserts
    ‣ textured/clear
    ‣ special shape
- Hinged double (French)
  - solid doors
  - glass inserts

- Sliding glass
  - is direction important to traffic flow
- Front door sidelight
  - one/both sides
  - half/three-quarter/full length
- Transom (over door)
- Storm/screen door(s)

Exterior door material

- Wood/type
- Fiberglass

- Metal

Exterior door size

- Width
  - standard 36" (front)
  - standard 32" (other exterior doors)
  - double doors for width or elegance

- Height
  - 7 feet (6'8")
  - 8 feet (7'8") or higher
  - should match home's proportions

Exterior door location

- Sheltered from rain, wind and sun
- Convenient
  - access to walking paths
  - entrance to preferred location

- Proximity to neighbors
  - your /their outdoor entertaining areas
  - your/their quiet area

Pet door

- Type (see page 141)
- Size
- Location for

  - pet access
  - home/pet security
  - wind resistance

Exterior door hardware

- Lockset (handle and lock)
  - finish
    ‣ interior side matches other interior hardware
    ‣ exterior side matches other exterior hardware
  - style
    ‣ doorknob with lock
      · easy to "lock and go"
      · easy to get locked out
    ‣ doorknob without lock/with deadbolt

  - lever door handle without lock/with deadbolt
    ‣ must use key
    ‣ can't get locked out
- Doorbell button outside
  - style/finish/matches lockset
  - lighted
  - location
- Doorbell mechanism inside home
  - location/volume level

Interior Doors

Interior door allowance $_____

Upgrade amount (add on page 241)

Where to Shop (list on page 240)

Interior door style
- Flush (hollow core)
- Solid material
- Louver
  - closed (decorative)
  - open (allows ventilation and noise)
- Double
- solid doors
- with glass inserts
- Saloon (swinging half/full)
- Dutch (divided for each half to operate separately)
- Pocket (slides into wall)

Interior door material
- Wood
  - solid
- hollow
- Painted particle board

Interior door size
- Standard 32" or less
- Oversized 36" or more for
  - laundry room (washer/dryer width)
  - basement (furniture width)
  - wheelchair-accessibility throughout home
- Double doors for
  - style
  - occasional handicapped-access

Interior door location
- Swings left or right
- Allows convenient furniture placement
- Door will be in the way when open
- Door blocks another door

Interior closet doors
- Single hinged
- Double hinged
- Bypass
- Bifold

Interior door hardware
- Hinges
  - quantity (two or three)
  - type
    ‣ standard
    ‣ ball bearing
- Door hardware style
  - knob
- lever
  ‣ straight/curled/other
- Door hardware finish
  - brushed, antique, polished
  - nickel, chrome, copper, brass, others

Laundry Chute
- Feed (to deposit clothes)
  - central location
  - in someone's bedroom closet
    ‣ privacy issue
- End (clothes' destination point)
  - laundry room location
    ‣ can be left in closed tube until wash day or removed for sorting
    ‣ door spring adjusted to allow clothes to dump into basket

Staircases

Location

- Open to interior of home
- Against exterior wall
  - window

- bench seat if two-stage with landing

Stair finish

- Closed-carpeted (wrapped ends)
- Open-carpeted (wood showing on one or both ends)
- Wood
- Tile
- Marble

Stair shape/style/features

- Style
  - two-stage (in two parts with landing)
  - single-stage
  - curved (one or two staircases)
  - open on one side
  - open on both sides
- Finish/trim on outside walls
  - wood
  - wallboard
  - other

- Railing/spindles
  - wood/iron/other
- Railing end cap style
- Steps have
  - width for traffic/comfort (42"+)
  - depth for safe foothold
  - height low enough for safety
- Distinctive stair shape
  - flaired at bottom (increased width)
- Footlights (see Staircase lighting on page 175)

Fireplaces

Where to Shop (list on page 240)

Fireplace locations

- For heat
- For style
- Between rooms
  - master bedroom/bathroom
  - main floor master/common room

- eating area/family room
- Centered/cornered in room
- Basement/lower level
- Outside locations

Fireplace style

- Single (wall or corner)
- Multi-sided/see-through
- On floor
- Raised hearth

Fireplace mantle (shelf) and surround

- Wood
- Stone
- Cultured stone
- Tile
- Marble
- Granite
- Other material/trim

Fireplace construction

- Direct-vent sealed glass (gas)
  - electric starter with switch for gas
  - remote control/timer regulated
  - electric blower with
    ‣ wall switch
    ‣ remote control
- Atmospheric/"B" vent/open hearth
  - wood

- gas
- convenient location of
  ‣ gas shut-off
  ‣ flue control
- Insulation/air sealing of exterior wall behind fireplace
- Separate hearth
  - location/function

• Free-standing stove (see page 151)

Attic

- Height
- Flooring potential (see page 146)
- Attic hatch (pull-down stairs)
  - insulating above hatch is challenging
- Staircase
- Ability to finish as living space
  - heating/cooling of sealed attic
  - rough-in plumbing
  - wiring

Add/Change/Remove Interior Walls

- Cannot change/remove structural walls
- Add extra wall or half wall
- Remove wall for larger room
- Extend wall to expand room when
  - eating area cramped for table and chairs
  - dining room too small for table and guests
  - any room too small for furniture/living needs
- Add a window box/window seat
  - less costly than extending full wall
  - requires insulation and air sealing care
- Add interesting shape to wall
  - arch
  - niches/insets
    ‣ mirrored back
    ‣ lighted
  - plant shelves
  - open areas
  - "dead space" behind walls allows niches (check blueprint)
  - locate central flue (see page 156)
    ‣ cannot build into wall behind it
- Decorative columns
- Closets
  - Add/enlarge/delete/relocate

Ceilings

- Standard 8 feet
- Raised (8½ ft +)
- Vaulted
- Two-story
- Coffered (tray)

HVAC (Heating, Ventilation, Air Conditioning)

What is the High Performance Home?

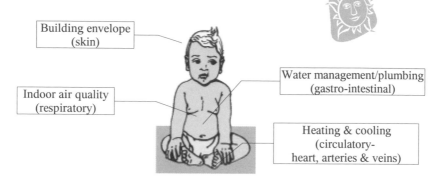

The home's HVAC system can be compared to a baby's body:
1. Building envelope (baby's skin)
2. Solar-smart design (maximize sun's heat in winter, shade in summer)
3. Heating and cooling (circulatory)
4. Indoor air quality (respiratory)
5. Water management, interior and exterior (gastro-intestinal)
6. Energy-efficient lighting and appliances (nervous system)
7. Performance testing (doctor's checkup)

1. *Parts of the Building Envelope*

- Foundation (see page 126)
- Exterior walls (see page 130)
- Windows and doors (see page 136)
- Skylights (see page 138)
- Insulation and air sealing (see page 157)
- Roof (see page 161)

2. *Elements of Solar-Smart Design*

- Orientation of homesite (see page 105)
- Natural shading
  - overhangs
    - ‣ depth to shade varies by region
    - ‣ typically 1-2 feet of overhang shades 8 feet of house height
  - ‣ most effective within 30° of south
  - covered terraces
  - strategically-placed trees and shrubs
- Quality windows to keep heat/cooling in or out (see page 136)

3. *Heating and Cooling*

- Benefits of the High Performance Home
  - lower operating costs
  - healthy indoor air
  - combustion safety
  - comfort
  - low maintenance/durability
  - storm safety
  - higher resale value
- See Questions to Ask on page 80
- See Energy Efficiency Checklist on page 43

Type of heating system

- Forced-air
  - induced-draft
  - sealed-combustion/direct vent (see Special exhaust venting, page 42)
- Baseboard hot water
  - quieter than air
  - adds moisture to air
  - zoned temperature control
  - smaller duct system needed for fresh air circulation
- Radiant floor
  - costly

- comfy on the feet
- quiet
- smaller duct system needed for fresh air circulation
- Heat pump
  - mild climates (see page 150)
- Electric baseboard
  - clean (no exhaust fumes)
  - traditionally an expensive fuel
- Free-standing stove (see page 151)

Fuel

- Natural gas/propane
- Electric
- Fuel oil

- Solar thermal (active or passive)
- Wood

Size/design of system

- Correctly sized to match heat/cooling loads (see page 150)
- Minimal duct leakage for even draw of return air (see Ducting page 153)
- Separate zones (of one system)
  - heating

- cooling
- Separate heating/cooling systems
  - large square footage
  - in-law apartment
  - living space over unheated space
  - basement/lower level

Location of heating system

- Basement location that is
  - optimal for efficiency
  - convenient for room planning
- Crawlspace
  - optimal for efficiency

- sufficient access for maintenance
- Closet on main/upper floor
- Garage closet (warm climates)
  - doesn't interfere with storage/cars
- Attic (with sufficient access)

Creative cooling options

- Conditioned attic cavity (see page 157)
  - maintains even attic temperature
  - absence of exterior venting prevents
    ‣ wind
    ‣ rain
    ‣ animals/bugs
  - increases storm safety
- Unconditioned attic cavity
  - requires adequate exterior venting
  - variable attic temperature
    ‣ hot in summer
    ‣ cold in winter
- Radiant barrier roof materials
  - reflects heat
  - popular in hot climates
- Light color roof material reflects heat
- Central air conditioner

- correctly sized for cooling loads
- SEER 13 or higher (see page 152)
- location of exterior unit
- Central humidifier/dehumidifier
  - convenient control
  - drain located near system
- Evaporative cooler (see page 153)
  - dry climates
  - check energy efficiency for climate
- Whole-house fan
  - central location
  - properly sized to draw cool air in
  - control
    ‣ thermostatic
    ‣ timer
  - winterize in cold climates
    ‣ cover fan/insulate above
- Ceiling fans
  - 5-paddle/4-paddle

4. Indoor Air Quality

Central ducting and venting of heated or cooled air

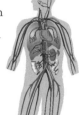

- **Supply** ducting (arteries) delivers conditioned air to each room
  - sheet metal ducting
    ‣ connecting joints sealed with mastic
  - sheet metal or flexible ducting
    ‣ avoid unnecessary turns/kinks
    ‣ locate within conditioned space
    ‣ won't be blocked by furniture
    ‣ style/finish of vent cover
- **Return** ducting (veins) draws used air out of rooms
  - connecting joints sealed with mastic
  - return vents in each room
    ‣ won't be blocked by furniture
  - centrally located return vent in common area with transfer grilles over doors (see page 154)
- Each duct end has a vent opening (not accidentally covered with flooring!)
- Thermostat
  - location
    ‣ eye level/accessible
    ‣ best area for temperature reading
  - programmable for setbacks (one or multiple)
  - part of structured wiring

Air circulation of heated or cooled air

- Fresh air exchanger (forced air fan)
  - provides fresh air to tight house
- Filter types
  - HEPA
  - MERV rating
  - electrostatic – requires wiring
- Filter removes
  - dust
  - pollutants
  - allergens
- Energy/heat recovery ventilator
  - purifies air
  - captures energy
  - reduces humidity

Special exhaust ducting and venting

- Furnace and tank water heater
  - high efficiency sealed-combustion
    ‣ 90-93 percent efficiency
    ‣ toxic fumes safely exhausted to exterior
    ‣ fresh air supplied to furnace
  - atmospheric
    ‣ toxic fumes rise and exhaust if there is no backdrafting
    ‣ 80% efficiency
    ‣ furnace must find fresh air
- Kitchen stove
  - exterior - vented to outside
  - type of exhaust fan
    ‣ updraft
      · built into microwave
      · in stove hood
      · remote (at roof level)
    ‣ downdraft
  - efficiency
  - noise level
- Bathroom
  - exterior – vented to outside wall
  - high-efficiency fan
    ‣ more effective
    ‣ quieter
  - fan control
    ‣ separate – direct control
    ‣ operates with light switch
    ‣ humidity-controlled
      · operates until excess humidity has been removed
- Radon/other noxious gas
  - passive pipes installed (see page 156)
  - active (power fan)
- Carbon monoxide detectors on each level
- Propane gas sensor and alarm
- Central vacuum system (see page 178)

5. Water management – interior and exterior

- Interior
  - homerun plumbing (see page 165)
    ‣ dedicated pipes to each destination
  - hot water systems (see page 164)
- Exterior
  - proper grading and backfill (see page 129)
  - sprinkler systems (see page 207)

6. Energy-efficient lighting and appliances

- Types of lighting (see page 173)
- Energy-efficient appliances (see page 198)

7. Performance testing

- Blower door
- Duct blaster
- Infrared/thermography (see page 160)

Certified "green" home

- National green organizations
  - see Website directory on page 234
- State/local search engine keywords
  - green + built + (your state)
- Building waste recycled
- Your high performance home meets organization's criteria
- documentation (for you to keep) of how certification was met on your home
- ask for an attractive label to display!

Energy Efficiency Checklist

- Insulation
  - walls
  - attic
  - foundation/crawlspace
- Air sealing
  - all seams between insulated areas
  - cantilevered areas (bumpouts)
  - behind
    ‣ fireplaces
    ‣ dishwashers
  - skylights/all cutouts in walls
    ‣ around outlets/switches
    ‣ around exhaust fan openings
- Windows
  - low-E (most climates)
  - tinted glass (to block direct sun rays)
  - quality frames/glass/installation
- Water heater
  - ENERGY STAR rated
  - tankless
  - sealed combustion tank
- Furnace/heat pump
  - ENERGY STAR rated
  - sealed combustion
  - properly-sized
- Well-sealed ducting sections
- Ducting through conditioned space only
- Heating/cooling loads calculated
- Cooling
  - orientation best for solar gain/shade
  - a/c properly-sized, ENERGY STAR rated, SEER 13+
- Positive drainage (to keep foundation dry)
- Fresh air exchanger operates
  - automatically
  - intermittently
- Humidifier/dehumidifier
- Lighting types (coolest)
- Appliances ENERGY STAR rated
- Testing of all systems to work together
- Cost comparison
  - additional cost to build
  - savings in
    ‣ energy costs
    ‣ health
    ‣ comfort
    ‣ resale value

Figuring Payback

	Example	Your actual cost
Cost of high efficiency appliance	$810	$ _____
Minus cost of low efficiency appliance	-$600	-$ _____
EXTRA COST	=$210	= $ _____
Annual estimated cost of operation for **low** efficiency appliance (from label)	$64/yr	$ _____
Minus annual estimated cost of operation for **high** efficiency appliance (from label)	$34/yr	-$ _____
ANNUAL SAVINGS Divide extra cost by annual savings to get years until payback	=$30/yr	= $ _____
	$210-$30/yr= 7 yrs	$ _____

Insulation

Tight building envelope

- Insulation and air sealing for
  - roof
  - exterior walls
  - windows
  - skylights
  - doors
- Foam/caulk around other openings
  - outlets
  - pipes between floors
  - pipes through exterior walls

Types of Insulation

- Blown-in
  - fiberglass
  - cellulose
- Sprayed-on foam
- Fiberglass batts

Attic Insulation

- Conditioned space
  - attic cavity filled with foam or
  - roof interior filled with foam
  - storm resistant
- Unconditioned space
  - sufficient exterior venting
- Radiant roof decking (hot climates)

Exterior Wall/Ceiling Insulation

- Housewrap (see page 158)
  - protects against wind/sheeting rain
- Exterior rigid board
- Basement walls/crawlspace
  - included in conditioned space/no exterior venting
  - insulated/air sealed
- Special care exterior walls
  - behind bathtub/shower
    ‣ backer board (water resistant)
    ‣ insulation/air barrier/foam
  - washer and dryer
  - dishwasher
  - cabinets (any room)
  - fireplaces
  - garage walls and ceiling
- Vaulted ceilings

Interior Wall Insulation

- Around bathtubs
  - wrap fiberglass insulation around and under outside bathtub base
    ‣ keeps water warm
    ‣ muffles noise
- Locations for noise reduction
  - media room with surround sound
  - powder room
  - laundry room
  - teen bedroom
  - master bedroom
  - study
  - in-law quarters
  - all bathrooms
- Resilient channel, any wall (see page 159)

Performance Testing

- Sight check before wallboard installations
- Blower door test
- Duct blaster test
- Infrared/thermography

Roof

Shape/Pitch/Overhang

- Shape/combinations
  - gable
  - hip
  - gambrel
  - gambrel/hip gambrel
  - flat
  - shed
- Pitch for
  - style
  - snow shedding
  - shade (overhang)
- Roof details on page 161

Style/Material/Color

- Asphalt
  - three-tab
  - dimensional
- Concrete tile
  - barrel
  - shake
  - slate
  - reflective (hot climates)
- Cedar shake or shingle

- Natural slate
- Metal
  - sheet
  - shingle
- Check any covenants for
  - fire resistance
  - color
  - material
  - cupola/other decoration

Chimney

- Functional
  - within interior walls
  - on external wall
- Decorative only
  - location

Dormers

- Functional
  - enlarge room
  - add light
  - create interesting exterior
    architectural shape/dimensions
  - require extra care when insulating
    and air sealing
  - finishing potential
- Decorative
  - create interesting exterior décor

Gutters/Drainage

- Gutter material
- Full perimeter coverage
- Painted/natural
- Extensions
  - to keep water away from
    foundation
  - located under driveway/paths

Worksheet for Roof

Item (brick, stone, etc.)	Style	Color

Exterior Wall Siding

Siding Material

- Type of wood
  - stain
  - paint
  - combination of stains/paint colors
  - type of seam cover
- Stucco (color)
- Composite (engineered) material
  - looks like wood/stucco/brick/stone
- Stained concrete
- Brick (color/size/pattern)
- Stone/cultured stone
- Combination

Decorative Accent/Location

- Brick (one color/varied colors)
- Stone (color/pattern)
- Wood (stain/paint/color)
- Tile (color/pattern)
- Stucco
- Address plaque
  - engraved concrete
  - glazed tile
  - lighted (requires wiring)
  - location (coordinate with lighting)
- Shutters (size/style/color)
- Attachments to siding/brick/stone
  - basketball backboard
  - decorative wall hanging
  - flag holder
  - check covenants for each

Exterior Paint

- One color/varied color pattern
- Trim color
- Third color for accent
- Paint color is LIGHTER than sample

Worksheet for Siding and Insulation

Item (brick, stone, etc.)	Style	Color

Plumbing

Water Heaters

Type

- Tank type (stores hot water)
  - gas atmospheric
  - gas sealed-combustion
  - electric
  - oil
- Tank size
  - standard 40 gallon (gas or oil)
  - standard 50 gallon (electric)
  - oversized 50-127 gallon
  - two heaters
- Determine efficiency rating
  - EF (energy factor)
    - ‣ electric .75-.90
    - ‣ gas 0.5-0.7
- Tankless type (heats on demand)
  - gas
  - electric
- Tankless size
  - 1-13+ gallons per minute
- Circulating system
  - loop with sensor or push button pump
- Determine water usage needed
  - FHR (first hour rating 43-90)
- Figure payback (see page 44)

Piping

- Size (may affect pressure)
- Material
  - PEX (flexible plastic)
  - copper
- Configuration
  - homerun plumbing (see page 165)
  - loop

Other hot water features

- Surge-protected shower mixing valves (see Glossary)
- Shut-off valves at each end point (sink, washer, toilet)
- Shut-off at
  - central location only
  - entrance and exit of water heater
- In-sink instant hot water

Location of water heater(s)

- Tank
  - basement location that is
    - ‣ optimal for efficiency
    - ‣ convenient for room planning
  - first/second floor closet
    - ‣ safety (avoid backdrafting)
    - ‣ noise
    - ‣ convenient for room planning
  - garage (non-freezing climates)
    - ‣ doesn't interfere with storage
  - attic
    - ‣ sufficient access for maintenance
    - plumb for floor drain near hot water
- Tankless
  - determine quantity needed
  - exterior and interior models
    - ‣ venting required for gas models
  - place centrally or near destinations

Kitchen Plumbing and Fixtures

Upgrade amount $ _____ (add on page 241)

Where to Shop (list on page 240)

Plumb for appliances
- Plumb for dishwasher(s)
  - proper exterior wall insulation and air sealing
- Plumb for sinks
  - in-sink hot water
  - built-in water softener
  - built-in water filtration system
- Plumb for refrigerator
- icemaker/water filtration
- recessed box
- recessed wall for entire refrigerator
  ‣ refrigerator at counter depth
- Plumb for garbage disposal(s)
  - location(s) left/center/right sink
- Plumb for gas (if gas stove/stovetop)

Kitchen sinks and faucets
- Sink bowl quantity/function
  - single/double/triple
  - vegetable/wet bar
- Sink installation (see page 166)
  - drop-in (self-rimming)
  - under-counter
  - tile-in
  - integrated with counter material
- Sink material
  - porcelain-enameled-cast iron
  - stainless steel
  - polymer composite
  - granite/marble
- cultured marble
- quartz resin composite
- enameled-steel (chips easily)
- Built-in sink accessories
  - soap/lotion
  - instant hot water
  - water filter/reverse osmosis
- Faucet finish
  - one/two handle
  - pull-out spray
  - side spray
- Pot filler faucet/drain

Bathroom Plumbing

Bathtubs and faucets
- Tub style/size
  - soaking
    ‣ length/width/depth
    ‣ contour of back for comfort
    ‣ apron (outside wall of tub)
      · tile/marble/other
  - jetted
    ‣ location of jets for therapy/comfort
    ‣ location of access panel
    ‣ overflowing
      · tub within a tub
      · changing colors
- Tub material
  - acrylic
  - porcelain-enameled-cast iron
  - marble/granite
- fiberglass
- enameled-steel
- Tub faucets
  - located within convenient reach when standing outside tub
  - style/finish to match hardware
- Wall above tub/enclosure material
  - tile
  - granite/marble
  - fiberglass/acrylic
- Shelf for storage/books/candles
- Grab bar
  - accessible when getting in and out of tub
  - necessary for safety of all bathers
  - wood "blocking" required

Showers and faucets

- Bath/shower combination
  - material on floor/walls
    ‣ tile
    ‣ granite/marble
    ‣ fiberglass/acrylic
    ‣ glass enclosure
- Shower style/size
  - shower dimensions
  - built-in shower seat(s)
    ‣ stationary
    ‣ fold-down seat
  - built-in shelving for shampoo, etc.
    ‣ sufficient height/width/depth
    ‣ cultured marble
    ‣ tile

- Shower faucets
  - one or two handles
  - uniform/variable pressure
  - push/pull or circular handle
  - separate hand-held shower spray
  - separate body sprays
  - steam enclosure
    ‣ drain size sufficient
- Shower wall/floor material
  - non-skid tile
  - granite/marble
  - fiberglass/acrylic

Shower door

- Width of door opening
  - hinged left or right
    ‣ swings out (and drips)
    ‣ swings in (if sufficient room)
  - bypass (need 42" min. width)
  - oversized walk-in/step-in
    ‣ no door needed
- Shower wall/door frame

- material/color/finish
  ‣ coordinate/contrast with other bathroom hardware
- custom towel bars on door or wall
- Style of glass
  - clear/tinted
  - textured
  - color-coordinated with hardware

Toilets

- Style
  - one or two piece
  - standard or low tank
- Flush options
  - gravity
  - pressure or vacuum-assisted
  - two modes of flush
- Research quality of brands
  - ensure that it flushes well
- Toilet seat shape

- round (standard height only)
- elongated (standard or "chair" height)
- Toilet height
  - 15" (standard)
  - 18" (chair height)
- Bidet
- Urinal

Bathroom sinks and faucets

- Sink style
  - drop-in
  - integral (one piece with counter)
  - under-counter
  - pedestal
  - tile-in
  - one hole, 4" or 8" on center
- Sink material
  - porcelain-enameled-cast iron
  - cultured marble

- polymer composite
- marble/granite
- vitreous china
- enameled-steel
- fiberglass
- stainless steel
- Faucet style/finish
  - brushed/antique/polished
  - nickel, pewter, copper, chrome, brass

Laundry Room Plumbing

- Location of washer and dryer
  - washer next to laundry sink
  - washer or dryer won't block nearby
    swinging door (e.g. garage door)
- Plumb for washer
  - box recessed
    ‣ high enough for proper drainage
    ‣ hidden by washer if possible
- Plumb for dryer

- wall cutout should align with
  dryer's exhaust pipe (see page 170)
- location of vent on outside wall
  ‣ good air flow (no kinks)
  ‣ short enough for good pull
- Plumb for gas (dryer)
- Plumb for floor drain for
  - wet shoes and boots
  - washer
  - second floor laundry

Other Plumbing Needs

- Plumb for gas (interior/exterior)
  - stove
  - BBQ
  - fireplaces
- Rough-in plumbing
  - basement
  - *casita*/granny flat/carriage house
- Plumb for
  - drains
    ‣ near tank water system

‣ mud room
‣ pool/changing area
‣ garage
‣ sump pump (or rough-in)
- fire sprinklers
- sprinkler system stub
- hose bibb (water spigot) locations
- garage floor drain
- pool/spa/fountain

Worksheet for Kitchen and Laundry

Room	Brand	Style	Color	Dimension/ Location	Material	Special features	Cost
Kitchen							
Main sink							
Main sink faucet							
Main sink accessories							
Vegetable sink							
Vegetable sink faucet							
Veg. sink accessories							
Wet bar sink							
Wet bar faucet							
Wet bar accessories							
Garbage disposal #1							
Garbage disposal #2							
Trash compactor							
Refrigerator ice maker water filter							
Laundry							
Sink							
Faucet/ accessories							
Washer							
Dryer							

Worksheet for Master Bath and Powder Room

	Brand	Style/ color	Dimension /Location	Material	Quantity	Glass/color texture	Cost
Master bath							
Sinks							
Faucets							
Accessories							
Bathtub							
Bath faucet							
Bathtub accessories							
Shower style							
Shower faucet							
Hand-held spray							
Other accessories							
Towel bar on shower							
Toilet							
Bidet/ urinal							
Powder room							
Sink							
Sink accessories							
Faucet							
Toilet							

Worksheet for Additional Bathrooms

Room	Brand	Style/ color	Dimension /Location	Material	Quantity	Glass/color texture	Cost
Bath #2							
Bathtub							
Shower							
Bath/ shower							
Sink							
Faucet							
Sink accessories							
Toilet							
Bath #3							
Bathtub							
Shower							
Bath/ shower							
Sink							
Faucet							
Sink accessories							
Toilet							
Bath #4							
Bathtub/ shower							
Sink							
Faucet							
Sink accessories							
Toilet							

Lighting

Lighting allowance $_____(See page 173)

Upgrade amount (add on page 241)

Where to Shop (list on page 240)

Specifications
- Manufacturer
- Style/finish/glass
- Model #
- Locations

Lighting design
- Ambiant (general/mood)
- Task (concentrated for work area)
- Focal (spotlight on object)

Types
- Energy-efficient, cool (see page 173)
  - compact fluorescent
  - dimmable fluorescent
  - LED
- Halogen
- Xenon
- Incandescent

Light styles
- Flush-mount
- Hanging
- Wall mount
- Track
  - monorail
  - standard
- Cable
- Recessed can
  - flush
  - eyeball (directs light to one area)
- Sconce/indirect
- Under-counter
- Ceiling fan light

Interior lighting locations
- Kitchen
  - over
    ‣ eating areas
    ‣ cabinets
    ‣ sink
    ‣ island/peninsula
    ‣ main work area
  - under
    ‣ wall cabinets
    ‣ base cabinets
  - inside cabinets
- Bar/entertainment area
- Dining room
  - coffered/tray ceiling
  - chandelier/where to center
  - over artwork
- Family room/formal living room
  - switches/outlets for table lamps
  - over artwork/photographs
- Study/hallways/foyer
  - lighted art or photo gallery
- Over staircases
  - where to center
- Inside of staircase walls
  - footlights on wall next to stairs
- Master bedroom
  - overhead/switched outlets
  - recessed dimmable cans
- Master bathroom
  - heat lamp in front of shower
  - shower/tub
- Master closets
- Toilet room on
  - wall
  - ceiling
- Additional
  - bedrooms
  - closets
  - bathrooms
- Linen closets
- Laundry room
- Garage ceiling/walls
- Attic/basement/crawlspace

Exterior lighting locations

- All entrances to home
- Garage overhead lighting
- Over/in front of garage exterior
- Patio/porch/driveway
- Post lights
- Low-voltage path lights

- Landscaping
  - to enhance natural night lighting
  - to create mood
- Security lights
- Holiday (wiring behind eaves)
- See Exterior Design (page 203)

Worksheet for Lighting

On your blueprint or floor plan, include furniture or cabinets in each room before determining where lights should be placed. Recessed cans gather little dust and spotlight an area below. Hanging lamps can be an important part of your décor. How should they be centered? Where will you want table lamps (switched outlet or not) and where will you want built-in lighting?

See How to Read a Blueprint on page 123 and About Outlets and Switches on page 175. Work with your electrical blueprint or create your own sketch for planning purposes. Imagine, one room at a time, where light will be needed, and of what type.

Room	Ceiling height	Location	Manufacturer style #	Quantity	Cost

Worksheet For Additional Lighting

Room	Ceiling height	Location	Manufacturer / style #	Quantity	Cost

Interior Outlets

- Family room
  - entertainment area
- Kitchen/eating area
  - horizontally-or
    vertically-mounted
    outlets placed low on backsplash
  - behind appliance garage
  - 240v for electric range
  - microwave
- Island/peninsula
- Dining room
- Formal living room
  - floor outlets for
    seating areas
    away from walls
- Study
  - floor outlets for desk areas away
    from walls

- switched outlets
  - ▸ full (two gangs)
  - ▸ half (one gang)
  - 4-gang outlets
- Master bedroom
- Master bathroom
- Master closets
- Toilet room
- Hallway(s)
- Each bedroom
- Each bathroom
- Other_____
- Laundry
  - 240v for dryer
  - 120v for clothes iron
  - 240v/120v for freezer
- Tamper-resistant, any room

Exterior Outlets

- GFI (see page 177) for
  - any outdoor electrical appliances
  - workbench/tools
  - garage
    - ▸ 240v/dedicated 120v for freezer
    - ▸ on ceiling for each garage door
      opener
    - ▸ on walls/quantity
  - patio/deck
  - porch
  - soffits (for holiday lights)
  - future landscape lights
  - pool/spa

Interior Switches

Switch style/color
- Standard
- Rocker
- Dimmer
- Touch/sound
- Multi-scene preset control

- Switch color
  - white
  - ivory
  - decorator
- Switchplate covers
  - standard
  - screwless
  - decorator

Kitchen switches and locations
- Single pole (one switch per light)
- Two/three/four pole (switch at each
  entrance/desired location)
- Switch/location for
  - under cabinet/desk lighting
  - inside cabinets
  - ceiling/over cabinets

- over sink/stove
- Over eating area
  - within reaching distance of table
- Garbage disposal
  - within reaching distance of sink
  - out of children's reach
- Trash compactor

Bedroom/bathroom switches

- Bedrooms
  - light fixtures (may have dimmers)
  - switched outlets for lamps
  - ceiling fan
    ‣ separate for fan/light operation
    ‣ switch near bed for easy on/off
- Bathrooms
  - light fixtures
  - dedicated exhaust fan
  - exhaust and light combination
- Toilet room
- Sitting area
- Hallway(s)
- Staircase(s)
  - top of each staircase
  - bottom of each staircase
- Closets
- Other

Switches – other locations

- See Interior lighting locations on page 55
- Ceiling fan, any room
  - separate for fan/light operation
- Dimmer, any room
- Fireplace starter/blower

Exterior Switches

- See Exterior lighting locations on page 56
- Garage overhead lighting switches at
  - entrance to service door (to back or side of home)
  - entrance to home from garage
- Garage door opener
  - installed with convenient operating button
  - pre-wire operating button for future doors

Structured Whole-House Wiring

- Communications
  - wiring for ports throughout home for
    ‣ phone
    ‣ LAN infrastructure (computer wiring)
    ‣ intercom systems
  - satellite systems
  - central control for all systems
- Video and home theatre
  - satellite/cable systems
    ‣ requires land line nearby for updates
  - security cameras
  - HDTV
  - DVD
- Audio systems
  - multi-source/zone distribution
  - speaker configuration
  - baby/teen monitoring
- Home automation
  - multiple system control
  - remote access to all systems
  - central touch control panel
  - smart appliances
  - central vacuum system
    ‣ rough-in pipes
    ‣ install full system
    ‣ broom-vac in kitchen
  - motorized window treatments
  - remote care of pool/spa
  - security systems
- Lighting control
  - complete home control
  - vacation mode
- Climate control
  - sensors and thermostats
  - multi-zone heating/cooling
  - in-floor radiant heat
  - climate safety
    ‣ smoke/carbon monoxide detectors
- Wireless
  - Infrared
  - WiFi
  - Zigbee
  - Bluetooth
  - WiMax
  - UWB
  - UHF

Interior Walls

Wallboard (Drywall, Gypsum Board, Sheetrock®)

Wallboard quality

- Types
  - standard wallboard
  - backer board
  - paperless wallboard
- Thickness
  - 1/2"
  - 5/8"
- Seams not visible between wallboard
  - sections
  - at ceiling line

Wallboard styling

- Rounded corners (bullnose)
- Bulkheads (enclosing open areas)
- Fancy cutouts
- Plant shelves
- Niches
- Texturing
  - orange peel
  - knockdown
  - stomping
  - other popular style

Plaster

- Style/finish/texture
- Color
  - mixed in/on surface
- Ceiling finish

Paint/Wallpaper

Allowance $_____

Upgrade amount (add on page 241)

Where to Shop (list on page 240)

Interior Paint

- Type of finish
- Quality
  - coverage/washability
  - low/no VOCs
- Color selection availability
  - walls/ceilings
  - accent paint/location
- Walls primed (2 coats of paint in total)
- Sprayed/rolled
- Special treatment/application
  - specific wall in accent color
  - interior molding in accent color
  - stenciling/sponging
  - faux paint finish
- Interior colors are DARKER than sample

Other Wall Treatments

- Stained wood (see page 75)
  - paneling
  - molding
  - area/style #/color
- Wallpaper
- Glued fabric
- Decor stucco/brick
- Faux plaster/faux finish
- Wainscoting (treat lower part of wall)
- Mirror
  - bathroom walls
  - medicine cabinets
  - closet doors
  - bar/entertainment
  - exercise room wall
  - back of decorative niches

Wall Tile

Upgrade $_____per sq. ft. x _____sq. ft. = $_____

Upgrade amount (add on page 241)

Where to Shop (list on page 240)

Specifications
- Style #
- Material
- Color name and #
- Sizes of tile
- Patterns
- Grout color and color #

Bathroom tile locations
- Tub/shower walls built-in
  - grab bar (requires blocking)
  - shampoo/soap niches
- Tub wall apron (horizontal border around tub exterior)
- Wall surrounding top of tub
- Steam tile enclosure
- Tub backsplash
- Painted/decal tile inserts
  - quantity/locations
  - cost per tile or decal
  - sizes fit/can be ordered to fit (see page 182 under Tile cost-saving)
- Create pattern with standard tiles

Kitchen tile locations
- Backsplash
  - partial/total
- Painted/decal tile inserts
- Create pattern with standard tiles

Laundry tile locations
- Sink backsplash
- Sorting counter/decorative wall

Fireplace tile locations
- Walls/floor area
- Painted tile inserts

Worksheet for Wall Tile

Area	Size of tile	Style #	Color name	# of tiles	Grout color	Special/ deco

Interior Wall Finishes Summary

Place a ☑ in each row where type of wall finish will be used.

Room	Paint	Wall-paper	Stained wood		
Kitchen					
Foyer					
Living room					
Dining room					
Family room					
Office/Study					
Master bedroom					
Bedroom #2					
Bedroom #3					
Bedroom #4					
Bedroom #5					
Bedroom #6					
Bathroom #2					
Bathroom #3					
Bathroom #4					
Bathroom $5					
Bathroom #6					
Lower level					

Carpet

Carpet allowance $_____ total OR $_____ per sq. ft.

Upgrade $_____additional per sq. ft. x _____sq. ft. = $_____

Upgrade amount (add on page 241)

Where to Shop (list on page 240)

Specifications

- Brand, style #
- Color name and #

- Fiber
- Quality, weight

Suggested locations for carpet

- Dining room
- Family room
- Living room
- Bar area
- Powder room
- Bedrooms

- Bathroom
  - avoid toilet/shower entrance area
- Exercise room
- Playroom
- Exterior deck
- Basement

Carpet material

- Nylon
- Corn
- Olefin

- Polyester
- Wool
- PET (see Carpets on page 185)

Carpet padding

- Rebond
- Urethane foam
- Fiber
- Rubber
- Density (weight)
- Thickness (depth)

  - 1/2"
  - 7/16"
  - 3/8"
- Heavy duty density/depth on staircase

Worksheet for Carpet Selections

Area	Style #/ name	Color name/ #	Padding/ type wt./ depth	Sq. footage	Cost (incl. labor)

Flooring

Flooring allowance $_____ total OR $_____ per sq. ft.

Upgrade $_____additional per sq. ft. x _____sq. ft. = $_____

Upgrade amount (add on page 241)

Where to Shop (list on page 240)

Wood/Tile/Cork/Vinyl/Linoleum/Stone/Concrete

Specifications
- Brand, style #
- Color
- Size
- Dark colors show dust/pet hair

Wood flooring
- Locations
- Type of wood/stain
  - eco-friendly (sustainable wood)
    ‣ cork
      · warm feeling
      · "self heals" if dented
    ‣ bamboo
      · unfinished/can be stained
      · hardness varies
    ‣ eucalyptus hybrid
    ‣ engineered wood
      · many types of wood over fiberboard
      · cross-laminated layers (for stability)
  - standard wood
    ‣ beech/cherry/hickory
    ‣ maple/oak/pecan
    ‣ red oak/walnut/exotic imports
- Style
  - strip/plank/parquet
- Tongue-in-groove/nailed/glued
- Protective finish
  - glossy/semi-gloss/matte finish
  - pre-finished
  - applied after installation
    ‣ number of coats

Tile/stone flooring
- Locations/patterns
  - interior
  - exterior
- Accent/focal point
  - foyer
  - center/focal point of any room
- materials must be uniform height to avoid guests tripping
- Grout color
- Protective finish
  - product/number of coats
  - glossy/semi-gloss/matte finish

Concrete flooring
- Locations
- Stain/texture
- Pattern
- Protective finish
  - product/number of coats
  - glossy/semi-gloss/matte

Linoleum/vinyl/laminate
- Natural linoleum
  - no VOCs (see page 185)
  - environmentally-friendly
  - can be used over radiant floor heat
- Standard linoleum
- Vinyl
- wide range of price/quality
- variety of colors/patterns
- Laminate
  - decorative coating with look of wood/tile/stone
  - underlayment of fiberboard/wood

Suggested locations for flooring
- Foyer
- Kitchen
- Dining room
- Family room

- Living room
- Bar area
- Powder room
- Laundry room
- Shower entry
- Bedroom(s)
- Bathrooms (non-skid)

- toilet area
- shower entrance area
- entire bathroom
- Exercise room
- Playroom
- Exterior deck
- Basement

Worksheet for Flooring Selections

Area	Type of flooring	Style/pattern# /name	Color name/ #	Grout color/name	Sq. foot/total cost (incl. labor)
Foyer					
Foyer					
Kitchen					
Kitchen					
Dining room					
Dining room					
Family room					
Living room					
Bar area					
Powder room					
Laundry room					
Shower entry					
Toilet area					
Bathroom					
Bathroom					
Bathroom					
Bathroom					
Exercise area					

Carpet and Flooring Summary

Place a ☑ or other notation in each row where type of covering will be used.

Room	Carpet	Vinyl	Wood	Tile			
Kitchen							
Foyer							
Living room							
Dining room							
Family room							
Office/Study							
Master bedroom							
Master bathroom							
Bedroom #2							
Bedroom #3							
Bedroom #4							
Bedroom #5							
Bedroom #6							
Bathroom #2							
Bathroom #3							
Bathroom #4							
Bathroom #5							
Bathroom #6							
Lower level							

Cabinets

Cabinet allowance $_____

Upgrade amount (add on page 241)

Where to Shop (list on page 240)

Cabinet Materials

Door material
- Wood
  - type of wood
    - raised panel
    - flat one-piece
  - stain color name and #
  - glaze, protective finish
- Laminate (plastic coated)
  - finish/texture
  - brand/style #
  - color name/ #

Box (walls and back) material
- Solid wood
- Particle board
- Laminate

Cabinet Style
- Box frame/frameless, no mullion
- Country-style
  - doors cover frame completely/partially
- Craftsman-style
- Box with central mullion
- Decorative molding
- Area above cabinets
  - open space
  - closed with wallboard (soffits)
- See page 190 for Cabinet details

Cabinet Hardware
- Hidden hinges (European style)
- Hinges showing
- Handles
- Knobs
- Finger pulls
- None (beveled edges)

Kitchen Cabinets

Cabinet height/width
- Height of wall cabinets
  - 36"
  - 42"
  - other
- Height of base cabinets from floor
  - standard 24"
  - higher/lower
- Width of wall and base cabinets
  - 1½" or 3" increments (24"/27"/30")
- Height according to special needs

Island/peninsula cabinets
- Base cabinet height
  - standard 24" or 30"
  - higher/lower
  - multiple heights

- Countertop shape/dimensions (see Countertops on page 199)
- Island/peninsula front wall
  - wallboard
  - wood laminate (skin)
  - solid wood

Cabinet drawers

- Material
  - particle board
  - solid wood
  - laminate
- Shelf supports
  - adjustable
  - fixed
  - locations
    ‣ front/back/sides
- Drawer types
  - swing out/pullout
  - adjustable/supported
  - potential to add extra shelves
- Drawer slides
  - full extension
  - under-mount
  - side-mount
- Size of drawers
  - depth/width
- Construction
  - dovetailed
  - doweled
  - dado (notched)
  - stapled/glued
  - "self-close" when near base

Special cabinets/drawers

- Dividers for
  - silverware
  - plastic/foil wrap
  - plastic ware bowls/lids
- Cookie sheet cabinet
- Linen drawer
- Tall item cabinet (cereal box height)
- Bread keeper
- Spices

Special locations for cabinets

- Over and under the
  - raised dishwasher
  - wall ovens
  - microwave
  - bar sink
  - desk area

Pantry closet/cabinet

- Location convenient to food preparation area
- Sufficient space for storage needs
- Pantry shelving
  - quantity
  - depth
  - material
    ‣ wood
    ‣ laminate
    ‣ wire
  - strong shelf supports for weight
    ‣ at least every 18"
  - adjustability
  - potential to add shelves
  - special (bins, pullout, etc.)
- Separate closet
  - shape of room
  - closet door
    ‣ solid
    ‣ glass insert (solid/decorative)
  - closet light
    ‣ switched
    ‣ automatic
- Pantry cabinet
  - height allows contents accessibility
  - depth allows contents storage

A few cabinet options

- Lazy Susan
  - wall corners
  - base corners
  - extra shelf
- Glass inserts
  - clear
  - stained
  - textured
  - single piece
  - multiple pieces
- Wine rack
- Wet/dry bar

- Interior lighting
- Tilt-out tray in front of sink
- Recycle/trash bins
- Appliance garage/charging stations
  - rolltop/double swing-out
- Linen hanger drawer
- Desk (built-in with cabinets)
  - keyboard pullout
  - file drawer
  - structured wiring nearby
- Ready-made desk to match or complement cabinets

Master Bathroom/Master Closet Cabinets

- Base cabinet height
  - standard 24"
  - raised for less bending
- Drawer style/depth/width
  - must not block sink bowl beneath
- Dual vanity areas
  - two sinks
  - vanity trays/drawers
- Storage
  - countertop garage
  - under sink dividers/half shelves
  - separate cabinet for towels, etc.
- Medicine cabinet(s)
  - location(s)
  - door
  ‣ wood
  ‣ mirrored
  ‣ edge finish
- Wall mirror(s)
  - flat
  - angled/hinged
  - edge finish
- Towel closet
- Master closet(s)
  - dressers
  - drawers/jewelry
  - open cabinets/shelving
- Hamper/location
- Safe/vault cabinet/door

Powder Room Cabinets

- Vanity cabinet
  - furniture style
  - standard base
  - drawers
  - storage
  - hidden area for trash

Hall Bathrooms Cabinets

- See bathroom details above
- Base cabinets
  - raised for less bending
  - lowered for children
- Storage area for bath toys
- Recessed toe kick for footstool storage
- Jack and Jill bathroom
  - double cabinets/sinks
  - sufficient counter space for all
  - sufficient under-sink/closet storage

Laundry Room Cabinets

- Wall cabinets
- Base cabinets
  - under laundry sink
- Cabinet for ironing board
  - iron and outlet
- Open shelving
- Gift wrap center
- Rod for hanging clothes
- Pet supply cabinet

Worksheet for Cabinets

Room/location /function	Dimensions	Style/color	Hardware and special features	Cost (incl. labor)

Appliances

Appliance allowance $_____

Upgrade amount $ _____(add on page 241)

Where to Shop (list on page 240)

Specifications

- Brand
- Model #
- Style

- Color
- ENERGY STAR rating for energy efficiency (excludes stoves)

Kitchen Appliances

- Stove unit
  - electric
  - gas
  - gas top/electric oven
  - oven size sufficient
  - single/double oven
  - drop-in
  - slide-in (provides surface over "crack")
- Stovetop
  - electric
    ‣ number of coils per burner
  - gas
- Venting to outdoors (see page 155)
- Wall oven
  - oven height from floor
  - single/double
  - electric/electric convection
  - gas
  - size sufficient
- Microwave/microwave convection
  - over wall oven
  - over stove/stovetop
    · built-in exhaust fan
    · over all burners
    · over back burners only
- Dishwasher(s)
  - standard height
  - elevated height
  - double drawer
  - in-sink
  - good rack configuration for dishes
  - racks vinyl or nylon
  - "hard" internal garbage disposal
  - built-in soap supplier
  - amount of water used (part of energy rating)

- Garbage disposal
  - ¼, ½, ¾ and 1 horsepower
  - upgraded models less likely to clog pipe
- Trash compactor
  - savings from reduced trash volume
  - lingering odor
  - location
- Refrigerator
  - dimensions to fit opening
  - depth of refrigerator
    ‣ flush
    ‣ depth of protrusion
    ‣ wall cut-out for flush to countertop
  - clearance for each hinged door to open fully (more than 90°) (see page 114)
  - custom built-in
  - finish (color/texture/to match cabinets)
  - plumb for
    ‣ icemaker
    ‣ filtered water
- Refrigerated wine cooler
- Separate ice maker
- Coffee/cappuccino bar
  - plumbed for continuous water supply
- Bread warmer drawer
- Food steamer tray
- Check store for latest available appliances

Worksheet for Appliances

Item	Brand	Model #	Color	Dimensions	Features	Cost
Stove/oven stovetop						
Microwave						
Dishwasher						
Garbage disposal						
Trash compactor						
Refrigerator/freezer						
Other						

Countertops

Countertop allowance $_____

Upgrade amount $_____ (add on page 241)

Where to Shop (list on page 240)

Kitchen Countertops

Specifications
- Material brand/style # /color name/#
- Backsplash tile
  - full
  - partial
- Counter edge finish
  - rounded
  - squared
  - if laminate
    - beveled
    - trimmed with accent material

Countertop materials
- Engineered stone (quartz surfacing)
  - high percentage of natural quartz
  - small percentage of plastic/resin
  - environmentally-friendly
  - emulates look of granite but more uniform
  - antimicrobial agent throughout
  - highly durable/requires no sealing
  - usable as cutting surface
  - seams not visible
- Granite/granite tile (see page 199)
  - unique patterns
  - porosity depends on grade
  - should be sealed as necessary
  - bacteria-resistant
- Solid surface
  - plastic (resin)
  - emulates look of solid marble/stone
  - seamless
  - environmentally-friendly
  - can be sink/countertop combination
- Laminate
  - new styles have
    - color/texture of natural stone
  - styles in glossy or matte finish
  - can have decorative edging
  - usually requires drop-in sink
  - some models have integrated sink
- Ceramic tile
  - can have tile border
  - decorator accent tiles
  - creative colors of standard tiles
- Recycled glass in resin
  - environmentally-friendly
  - non-porous
  - especially heat-resistant
- Stainless steel
  - non-porous
  - shows scratching
- Marble/onyx
  - veined/elegant
  - porous
- Concrete/soapstone
  - porous
  - should be scaled
  - especially heat resistant
  - usable cutting surface
- Wood
  - porous/should be oiled regularly
  - usable as cutting surface

Bathroom Countertops
- See Countertop materials (above)
- Sufficient workspace for sink areas
- Vanity area lowered for sitting
- Banjo counter (countertop extending over toilet tank)
  - must have sufficient space over tank for toilet maintenance

Laundry Room Countertops
- Countertop for sorting/folding
- Countertop over front-load washer/dryer
- Workspace for gift wrap/hobbies
- Pet counter for private dining

Worksheet for Countertops

Room/location Function	Material	Style/ Color	Sink mount	Back-splash	Edge Finish	Cost. (incl. labor)

Finish Carpentry

- Molding
  - type of wood
  - color name and # of stain/paint
- Baseboards
  - height
  - style
- Toe kicks (on cabinet against floor)
  - wood to match woodwork
  - vinyl/color
- Crown molding
- Chair rails
- Paneling
  - full wall
  - partial wall
- Staircases (see page 144)
  - spindle width
    - 1 ⅜"
    - 1 ¾"
  - outside wall(s)of staircase
    - solid paneling
    - stacked planks
- Built-in cabinets
  - dining room
  - entertainment/bar area
  - hallways
  - corners
  - loft/open areas
  - master bedroom
  - closets
    - split shelving

- wood/metal
  hardware
- adjustable
  shelving
- raised platform
  - for shoe storage
  - step-up for reaching top shelf
- Built-in shelving/any room
  - open
  - closed (with doors)
    - wood doors
    - glass doors (allow remote operation of electronics through glass)
- Laundry room shelves
- Built-in bench seats
  - near exterior entrances
    - with hinged seat for storage
    - fixed seat without storage
  - in laundry room
    - for storage and sitting
  - under windows
  - in bedrooms
    - for toys/extra clothing
  - other location for seat/storage
- Office area built-ins
  - desk/file drawers
  - keyboard
  - computer/tower cubbies
  - charging stations

Worksheet for Finish Carpentry

Item	Stain/paint	Color	Style	Location	Cost
Woodwork (baseboards, doorways, sills)					
Chair rails/ Room molding					
Crown molding ceilings					
Other special molding					
Built-in cabinets					
Built-in cabinets					
Built-in desks					

Exterior Design

Design Planning

- By landscape architecth/designer
- By homeowner

First decisions to make

- During **framing phase**
  - driveway
  - deck/screened porch potential
  - collapsable folding glass walls
- During **electrical phase**
  - location of
    ‣ designated power for sprinkler system controller in garage
    ‣ GFI outlets (see page 177)
    ‣ integral wiring for
      · outdoor sound system
      · all current/future outdoor lights
- During **plumbing phase**
  - location of
    ‣ sprinkler stub
    ‣ gas stub for barbeque
    ‣ gas fireplace(s)
    ‣ hose bibbs (water spigots)

Hose Bibbs

- Quantity/locations
- Convenient for car washing/gardening, etc.
- Type (to prevent freezing)
- Access won't be blocked by fencing

Land Parameters/Easements

- Locate lot pins periodically
- Verify location of lot pins before closing
  - spray paint nearby sidewalk/landmark
- Locate easements on blueprints
- Check with municipal authority or attorney for regulations about
  - building on easements
  - use of easement land

Grading and Drainage

- Backfill is correctly compacted
- Final grading
  - positive grading keeps water draining away from home/foundation dry
  - negative grading drains water (sometimes imperceptibly) toward home
  - positive drainage should be maintained/not altered
  - licensed land surveyor can determine correct re-grading
- Retaining walls if hilly terrain
- Drainage plan available for viewing
- In expansive soils
  - maintain even moisture level to avoid severe cracking
  - build foundation on piers to avoid introducing excess moisture to foundation and walls

Driveway

- Length/slope
- Extra width for additional vehicles
- Concrete finish
  - brushed
  - smooth
  - stamped/decorative
- Brick/stone/crushed rock/blacktop
- Heated elements to melt snow
- Shape
  - straight/circular/curves/cutouts
- Ease of entry and exit from garage
- Sufficient exterior wall space for a basketball backboard over driveway

Walkways

- Best traffic patterns
- Concrete/brick/stone/crushed rock
- Paths abutting home foundation
- Paths separating landscape from home
  - allows *dry* landscaping next to home
- avoid adding moisture near foundation
- Creative shapes
- Multiple levels/stairs
- Decorative slopes/bridge
- Recessed channels for gutters beneath

Patios

- Foundations
  - concrete/brick/stone/crushed rock
- Location convenient for lifestyle
- Dimensions/shape
- Sufficient area for table, chairs, BBQ
- Fireplace
- Pergola/gazebo
  - creates natural shade
  - attached to home
  - free-standing

Decks

- Material
  - engineered decking
    ‣ recycled plastic/wood mixture
    ‣ environmentally-friendly
    ‣ no splinters
    ‣ no maintenance
  - pressure-treated wood
  - cedar/redwood
- Location convenient for lifestyle
- Dimensions
- Decorative shape
- Sufficient area for table/chairs/BBQ
- Stairs/exit
- GFI outlets
- Railing
  - spindle height/width
  - decorative pattern
- Under deck area (if enough height)
  - screwed-in play equipment
  - hammock anchors
  - storage
  - spa
- Potential to add deck later

Play Areas for Everyone

- Grass/sand area for swing set
- Safe area for trampoline
- Sauna
- Pool/spa
- Basketball court
- Tennis court

Garden Areas

- Consider sun/rain/wind orientation
- Flower/vegetable/herb planting beds
- Ground level/elevated
- Xeriscaping (see page 207)

Dog Run Area

- Consider orientation
  - full sun
  - some shade always available
- Grass area
- Location/dimensions
- Entrance/exit
- Pet safety
- HOA restrictions

Exterior Storage

- Items to store outside
  - trash cans
  - tools
  - sports equipment
  - other
- Shed/lean-to/storage facility
- location
- dimensions
- HOA restrictions
- Compost farm (food scraps become loam)

Landscaping

- Allowances
  - sod/trees/shrubs
- Amount/depth of topsoil
  - rototilled into existing dirt
  - sprinkled on top
  - none
- Total design planned
- Positive grading restored (see page 204)
- Location of
  - sod/seed
    ‣ type/square footage
  - trees/shrubs
    ‣ identify fast growers
    ‣ size/shape when mature
    ‣ provide natural shade/cooling
- Decorative beds

  - location/material
- Xeriscaping®
  (water-conserving)
  - group plants
    with similar
    watering needs
  - choosing native plant varieties
  - finding creative alternatives to all-grass yards
- Traffic path through landscaping
  - flagstone/brick/stamped concrete
- Mulch
  - crushed rock/wood chip
- Retaining wall
  - decorative/functional
  - material/construction/strength
  - drainage plan

Sprinkler System

- Blueprints/plans
  - location of sprinkler stub
  - system within property lines
  - sprinkler head/tubing
    ‣ number/type/location
- Type (see page 207)
  - sub-surface/pressurized/self-drain
    ‣ drip areas
    ‣ quick coupler locations

- Sprinkler controller type
  - programmable
    ‣ scheduled times
    ‣ soil moisture sensors
    ‣ smart controllers connected to
      satellite weather data
  - avoids over-watering

Water Features

- Architectural fountains

- Waterfall/ponds

Outdoor Lighting

- Locations/type
- Light shines out/down/up

- Switch locations (structured wiring)
- See page 56

Exterior Sound System

- Type/locations outside

- See Electrical on page 178

Fencing

- Material/style/color/height
- Access through/around on all sides
  - number/location of gates

- Check HOA restrictions
- Within property lines

Sketch Your Exterior Design

- Roughly sketch outdoor areas
  - backyard/sides/front
- Picture yourself spending evenings
  outside
- Review Exterior Design section to
  include items

  - place any planned fencing
  - include proximity of neighbors
    ‣ privacy/activity areas as
      planned

General Questions for Builder

Builder's Name	Phone/ website
Question	Response
REFERRALS Do you have a list of referrals? Do you arrange for buyers to visit them?	
SELECTIONS Where do I shop? What kind of support do you offer in helping me to make decisions?	
INSPECTION What access do I have to the construction site? Can we put in writing that I am entitled to private inspections?	
CHANGE ORDERS What is your policy for making changes after decisions have been submitted? After materials/labored have been ordered? After work has been completed?	
COMMUNITY Are there legal covenants for the entire community? Are there requirements for specific homesites?	
WARRANTY What is your average number of service calls per home after closing? Do you regularly send out customer satisfaction surveys to your homeowners?	
WHY YOU? What makes you a superior builder? Do you have any signature features?	

Questions For Builder and/or Architect About How They Ensure a High Performance Home

SYSTEMS APPROACH What steps do you take to ensure that the parts of my home work well together for comfort, health, safety and energy-efficiency?	
SOLAR-SMART DESIGN How will the effects of sun, rain and wind be considered in the design of my home on my land?	
WINDOWS Will all windows effectively control ultraviolet rays, solar gain, high wind and noise, as needed?	
INSULATION How can I be sure that insulation will be installed to deliver its rated performance?	
INDOOR AIR QUALITY How do you balance tight construction and the need for fresh air year 'round?	
MOISTURE CONTROL What steps do you take to keep exterior water out of your homes?	
ENERGY-EFFICIENT COOLING Will my home be comfortable in the summer without a large air conditioner?	
TOTAL HOUSE COMFORT What steps have been taken to ensure that each room receives the amount of fresh conditioned air that it needs to be comfortable year 'round?	
OTHER ENERGY-EFFICIENT FEATURES What other energy features can my home have?	
GREEN CERTIFICATION Do you participate in a certification program for which my home will qualify?	
RECYCLING What percentage of construction waste do you recycle?	

Questions For Builder

Builder's name	Phone/website
Question	Response from builder

Questions For Builder

Builder's name	Phone/website
Question	Response from builder

Questions For Builder

Builder's name	Phone/website
Question	Response from builder

Section 5
Contract, Construction, Communication

Congratulations on your upcoming marriage...

Contracting with a builder is, in some respects, like getting
married. For the custom home process, planning for and
building a home takes many months of working together. With
every builder, because there are so many people, so many
details and such crucial timing involved, challenges may arise.

Buyer preparation is crucial

Your "partner" in this relationship has the advantage of knowledge and
experience. Because homebuyers are usually "amateurs," we can unwittingly
cause problems for ourselves and our builder. The preparation you receive from
this workbook will help to optimize the productivity and enjoyment of this
relationship.

Choose wisely

As with marriage, choosing the right partner is the most important ingredient
for success. It will be well worth your time to research any builder you are
seriously considering. In trying to determine if he (or she) is a good match for
you, ask his previous clients how he was to work with, how happy they are with
their home and about the quality of service they've received since closing.

Contract and communication

Use the information in this workbook and guidance
from professionals to ensure that a solid, thorough
contract is created and agreed to by all parties.

Also remember that, while you are a 21st century,
educated consumer, the building industry is still
working to accommodate greater homebuyer
participation.

Why is this important to know? Many semi-custom builders and almost all
production builders are accustomed to using their own legal documents that
are written in language that they understand, but that the average homebuyer
may not.

Custom builders may provide a contract but are usually accustomed to having
the homebuyer's attorney create the document (this practice varies by builder
and region.) In any case, homebuyers are strongly encouraged to consider the
enormity of this project and give all of the contract's details due attention.

Honor thy partner

If you are working with a spouse or partner, it is in both of your interests to
treat each other respectfully throughout the homebuying process. Because this
project requires so much money and so many decisions, communication can
break down. This does not have to happen to you! Let this workbook and your
support system be your guides.

Extend the honeymoon

To use a metaphor within a metaphor, timing is very important to the builder because he is like an orchestra conductor; many hands will be needed to put this home together

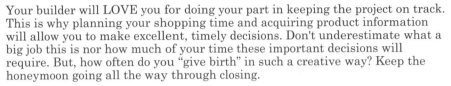

In addition to scheduling, the weather may throw a monkey wrench into the best-laid plans. It's a BIG problem to change your window order after the framing's been done because it throws off not only the framing schedule, but also the scheduling of each "trade" that follows framing.

Your builder will LOVE you for doing your part in keeping the project on track. This is why planning your shopping time and acquiring product information will allow you to make excellent, timely decisions. Don't underestimate what a big job this is nor how much of your time these important decisions will require. But, how often do you "give birth" in such a creative way? Keep the honeymoon going all the way through closing.

Stay in the solution

You need not accept others' mistakes nor shoddy workmanship. Learn when to speak up and to whom. Speak to the problem and avoid attacking people. Remaining *positive and reasonable* will make room for the effective communication that will get you the results you want faster and more effectively than confrontation and anger.

Rely on your thorough contract and scheduled meetings with your builder to address any concerns. If both sides of this partnership do their part, this story should have a happy ending. See page 84 for communication strategies that are available to use if you need them.

Custom Contract

Your contract is a legal document. An *experienced* real estate attorney is your authority on its thoroughness and quality. **The following description is general in nature and should not be considered complete for any building project.**

- Homeowner name, address, phone
- Architect name, address, phone number
- Builder/contractor name, address, phone number
- Job location address/lot #
- Expected date of start and completion
- Signed blueprints (# of dated pages)
  - front, rear, side elevations
  - floor layout for each level
    ‣ cabinets/plumbing/dimensions
    ‣ windows/mirrors/fireplace, etc.
    ‣ electrical
- Legal description/plot plan
- Specifications and materials list
- Cost of project (fixed/cost plus)
  - include all allowances
  - itemize each upgrade/change
- Payment schedule with
  - items and date for each to be completed
  - payment terms
- Change order policy
  - cost of change orders (in addition to materials and labor)
  - schedule of deadlines
- Site visit policy
- Contingency clauses
- Signatures of all parties

A semi-custom contract begins on page 214. As you interview builders, ask to examine a sample contract that they use. Question any area of the contract that you don't understand. Remember that you are paying for "the whole shebang" and ask questions about anything that you don't understand.

Specifications and Materials

Some items listed here may be indicated on blueprints, which are usually considered legal documents. Where appropriate, specific brand name, style name and #, color name and # and size for all of the following should be listed on specifications and materials list.

Framing/windows/doors
- Framing stud sizes
- Windows (brand, style, sizes, U-value, special coatings)
- Skylight(s) (brand, style #, size, location)
- Doors (type, size, hardware, R-value)
- Garage door(s) (brand, style, size)
- Garage door opener(s) (brand, style, quantity)
- Keyless pad entry (brand, style)
- Fireplace(s) (brand, style)
- Any option from checklist on page 33

HVAC
- Mechanical equipment (heat and a/c) (type, brand, energy efficiency, ENERGY STAR rating)
- Whole-house controlled ventilation system/fresh air exchanger
- Ducting (size, location, sealing material)
- Thermostat(s) (brand, style, location)
- Whole-house fan (brand, size, location)
- Humidifier/dehumidifier (brand, style)
- Radon vent piping
- Exhaust fans -bathrooms, kitchen stove- (brand, style, open/closed, location of vent)
- Any option from checklist on page 40

Plumbing
- Water heater(s) (type, brand, size, energy efficiency rating, ENERGY STAR rating)
- Faucets- kitchen/bath/laundry/other (brand, model #, color)
- Fixtures- kitchen/bath/laundry/other (brand, material, style, color)
- Glass shower/tub doors (brand, material, size, style, color)
- Piping (material, size)
- Any option from checklist on page 48

Electrical
- Light fixtures (brand, style #)
- Wiring for HVAC/plumbing needs
- Switches, outlets (brand, style, color)
- Structured wiring components (brand/style/locations/blueprint)
- Any option from checklist on page 55

Roof
- Roofing dimensions/height/slope
- Roofing material (brand, style #, color)
- Gutters (brand, type, location)
- Any option from checklist on page 46

Insulation/air barrier/air sealing
- Insulation (type, R-value, locations, installation measures)
- Air barriers (wallboard, plastic sheeting)
  - not needed with foam insulation
- Air sealing (type, foam/caulk)
- Backer board behind bathtubs/showers
- Housewrap (type, brand)
- Exterior rigid foam (brand, type)
- Any option from checklist on page 45

Exterior walls
- Siding material (brand, type, seam cover)
- Trim material/location (brand, type, color)
- Integrated address plaque (type)
- Any item from checklist on page 47

Interior walls
- Wallboard (thickness)
- Tile (brand, style #, size, color, location)
- Special (niches/medicine cabinet)
- Paint/primer (brand, quality, # of coats, spray/brush)
- Any item from checklist on page 60

Flooring/carpet
- Tile/wood/vinyl/linoleum/concrete
  - brand, style #, size, color, location
- Protective finish on wood floors (if not pre-finished)
  - brand, quality, # of coats
- Carpet
  - brand, style #, color, location
- Padding
  - material, weight, thickness
- Any item from checklist on page 64

Cabinets
- Brand, style name and #
- Dimensions, quantity
- Hardware (style #, finish color)
- Protective finish (sealer) on cabinets (brand, quality, # of coats)
- Any option from checklist on page 67

Appliances
- Brand name, model #, color, size, ENERGY STAR rating (except stoves)
- Stove/hood
- Stovetop/wall oven(s)
- Microwave
- Dishwasher
- Garbage disposal

- Trash compactor
- Additional built-in appliances
- Refrigerator
- Washer/dryer
- Any option from checklist on page 71

Countertops

- Brand, style name and #
- Material (brand, style #, color, location)
- Counter edge (material, style)
- Backsplash tile (full/partial)
- Any option from checklist on page 73

Finish carpentry

- Woodwork (type, stain, locations)
- All built-in items
  - type of wood/hinges
  - location
  - dimensions
- Any option from checklist on page 75

Exterior design

- Hose bibbs (brand, type, quantity, location)
- Driveway/paths (material, dimensions)
- Patio/deck (material, style, layout)
- Outdoor lighting
- Sprinkler system/sprinkler stub
- Fence
- Sod/landscaping allowance
- Any option from checklist on page 76

Performance testing

- "Green" certification/label/documents
- Tests to be performed
  - blower door
  - duct blaster
  - infrared/thermography
- Maximum leakage percentage
- Type of remedies (if necessary)

Payment Policy

Reaching agreement about how much and when to pay varies a great deal. If you have questions about this, see your attorney. Some options include:

- Payments
  - for change orders
    ‣ administrative fee
    ‣ materials/labor costs of change
  - for costs over allowances
  - for scheduled payments
  - administered from **escrow account** for materials and labor per invoice (see page 209)
  - administered **by builder** for materials and labor per invoice

Change Order Policy

Lack of planning too often results in many change orders. This is where costs and conflicts can arise unnecessarily. *Careful homebuyer planning* reduces the number of change order requests, which will benefit you and your pocketbook. Be sure that you are in complete agreement with your builder about this policy. *The sooner the better for any changes; late changes cost money and create headaches all the way down the line.*

- Get builder's policy, in writing about
  - who to contact/level of authority
  - approval process
  - cost basis
  - change order fee
    ‣ per item
    ‣ per phase
    ‣ charged at any time after contract deadline
- Change order deadlines (specific date, when known)

- foundation/framing
- HVAC/plumbing
- electrical/structured wiring
- roof/exterior walls/siding
- wallboard/tile/paint
- cabinets/countertops
- finish carpentry/exterior wiring/plumbing
- When change orders not possible
  - written policy for resolution of conflicts

Construction Schedule/Supervision

- Projected
  - start date
  - completion date/each phase
- Decision deadlines for each phase
- Projected completion/closing date
  - written definition of "completion"
- Approval authority (who, when)
- Frequency of your communication with
  - builder
  - superintendent

- Method of communication
  - office/site meetings
  - email/phone
  - dedicated website/webpage
- Frequency of construction site visits by
  - builder
  - superintendent
- Daily work ethic standards
  - daily clean-up/trash control
  - noise level/proper language

Contingency Clauses

- When closing is delayed
- When your house doesn't sell

- Termination procedure
- See page 211 for details

Site Visitation Policy

- Safety rules/protective wear required
- Limited/unlimited access to site
  - anytime unsupervised
  - after workers have left
  - receive key/lockbox code

- At private inspection appointment
- With appointment only, accompanied by builder representative
- Only at scheduled walkthroughs
  - see page 211 for details

Inspection Policy/Walkthroughs

- Inspection
  - per homebuyer request
  - within builder policy guidelines
  - by homebuyer only
  - by homebuyer's agent
    ‣ *qualified* private inspector
    ‣ structural engineer

- Walkthroughs
  - at the end of each "jurisdictional" phase (foundation design, excavation, etc.)
  - at the end of certain phases only
  - pre-closing only
- See page 212 for details

Builder's Warranty Policy

- Length/type
  - 1 year "bumper-to-bumper"
  - 8-10 years structural
  - what is/is not covered
- Builder warranty
- Additional warranty may be available
  - extra cost
  - builder/outside provider
- System for warranty calls
  - builder calls periodically
  - owner must call (per procedure)
- See Contract on page 213

Product Warranty Policy

- Retain documentation for each product
- See Contract on page 213

Contract Inspection (by your attorney)

- Specifications and materials list complete
- Standards and testing to be completed before closing
- Plan for contingencies
  - house doesn't sell by agreed time
  - trades get hurt or put a lien on home
  - the home isn't completed by move-in date
  - can't get clear title on this property
  - the builder runs out of money
- What else could go wrong?
- Is there a mandatory arbitration clause?

Financing

- Pre-approval for loan (as early as possible)
  - construction
  - final
  - combination (rollover)
- Lender shopping
  - product/level of service provided by
    ‣ mortgage broker
    ‣ bank
    ‣ Internet lender
- Coordinate construction completion with best time to close, if possible
- Become familiar with current rates
- Investigate builder incentives
- Agree with builder on closing date
  - who will/will not attend closing
- Loan options
  - fixed/variable rate
  - loans with/without points
  - government associates
- Policy for locking in mortgage rate
  - ability to extend locked-in rate if necessary
- Settlement costs
  - Truth-in-Lending form
    ‣ mandatory/additional fees
- Title search (if necessary)
  - by REALTOR
  - by attorney
- Insurance
  - title
  - mortgage
  - homeowners
  - flood
  - other
- REALTOR's fee
- Other fees

Worksheet for Coordinating with Builder's Timetable

Remain current about deadline dates. Missing them may throw off the construction schedule and cost you MONEY.

Date entered	Phase	Deadline date	Item to be decided/changed	Noted on calendar
Example: Th 6/26	Framing	Tu 7/15	Submit relocation of patio door	☑

The Building Process

Builder/General Contractor's Role

- Estimate all costs
- Create and/or sign contract
- Obtain permits
- Order all materials
- Schedule trades (workers)
- Set deadlines for each phase of construction
- Provide a copy of blueprints
  - work with architect as necessary
- Set start and completion dates

- Provide product information and cost
  - standard items
  - upgrades
  - change orders
- Execute change orders, as agreed
- Maintain communication with buyer
- Accept responsibility for overall quality and performance of completed home
- See page 225 for details

Superintendent's Role

- Ensure onsite that construction matches
  - specifications and materials
  - blueprints
- Oversee correction of errors
- Oversee trades/quality of work
- Communicate with buyer as needed

- See that site is left reasonably clean
- Covering/protection on
  - vent openings
  - tubs/showers
  - appliances
  - floors and carpets

Buyer's Role During Construction

- Research each phase of construction before blueprints to
  - choose design features/options that serve your lifestyle
- Obtain telephone numbers to call with questions
- Set budget for
  - allowances
  - upgrades
- Begin shopping
  - gather useful information

- stay within your budget
- make decisions by/before deadline
- Understand and adhere to builder's policies in your contract
- Visit site as needed for
  - checking on progress
  - checking for errors that haven't been corrected since last visit
  - enjoying the progress you see
- Keep yourself focused on success (see page 93)

Problem Prevention and Solutions

Problem Prevention

- Select a quality builder
  - see page 13
- Create a clear, detailed contract
- Use workbook to get/stay organized
- Promote harmony
  - get educated about
    ‣ your role as buyer
    ‣ builder's role
  - feel part of a good team
    ‣ express appreciation
- Make all decisions on or before deadlines
- Avoid late change orders
- Prepare for meetings with builder
  - bring notes/lists
  - write down
    ‣ items discussed
    ‣ decisions
    ‣ explanations received
- Visit site as needed/desired

Problems that Typically Occur

- Materials/product
  - information from builder
  - costs from builder
  - availability
  - late delivery
- Labor
  - work/installation done poorly
  - work not done
  - labor behind schedule
- Communication
  - understanding builder's schedule
  - executing change orders
  - having errors corrected
  - disagreement/mis-communication
    ‣ between buyers
    ‣ with builder

Stay Focused on Solutions

- Remain calm and reasonable, focused on solutions, not blame
- For issues with builder, focus on
  - everything that's been done correctly (see Core priorities on page 94)
  - how to
- ‣ correct "mistakes" you've made
- ‣ accept mistakes that can't or shouldn't be corrected
- ‣ accept builder's mistakes you can live with
- ‣ have builder mistakes corrected effectively and calmly

Strategies for Success

It may help you to know the scope of this project:

- 250-1000 decisions
- 100-300 suppliers
- 300,000-700,000 parts
- 50-250 workers

With this magnitude of detail, give your fledgling home the flexibility to vary a little from what you have in mind. You'll be allowing the process to be dynamic and creative while giving yourself a "perfection relief valve" that will reduce stress and let you sleep at night.

Make Time for Games

Some of this may initially seem silly to you. Consider that over the many months that buyers live with this project:

- 75% will experience some conflict with
  - each other
  - their builder
  - both
- 65% will experience sleepless nights
- 20% will wish they never started this project
- 15% will have legal issues with their builder
- 5% will get divorced

These statistics are the product of anecdotal information from many building professionals. Homebuyers do their best to work through differences and issues that arise, often *without* adequate information or guidance. Avoid being a statistic by using communication strategies whenever needed.

Identify core priorities

- Each decision-maker lists
  - Two MOST IMPORTANT features (must-haves)
  - benefit you'll get with each feature
- Re-define values as needed
  - if new information becomes relevant
  - if partner's values become a priority

Tweak your priorities

- Use the exercise below to
  - come to agreement
  - spend building dollars wisely
  - stay within your budget

Partner A Core Priorities (must have)	Partner B Core Priorities (must have)
1.	1.
2.	2.

Partner A "Wish List"	100 pts	$$ cost	-$ saving	#	Partner B "Wish List"	100 pts	$$ cost	-$ saving	#
1.					1.				
2.					2.				
3.					3.				
4.					4.				
5.					5.				
6.					6.				
7.					7.				
8.					8.				
9.					9.				
10.					10.				
11.					11.				
12.					12.				
13.					13.				
14.					14.				

Core priorities are those items that contribute significantly to lifestyle needs and desires. The "wish list" contains desired features. Include all desired items that you might be willing to pay for.

- **Points:** with a total of 100 points each, "spend" your points on each item.
- **Budget::** under **"$$"** write approximate cost next to each item
- **Cost savings:** "-$" column
  - put a check mark next to any item that
    ‣ reduces the total cost of your home (purchase price or lower annual operating costs)
    ‣ increases value of home (by more than cost of item)
    ‣ increases projected resale value (adjusted for cost of item)
- **Benefit to occupants**: "#" column
  - indicate how many home occupants will be affected by this feature, and whether positively or negatively, with a "+" or a "-."
- Include any other criteria that are important to you

Evaluate individual lists, considering all criteria.
- Ask each other questions to
  - show interest in his or her desires
  - understand his or her viewpoint
- Merge lists, resulting in a total of 100 points and ultimately, total budget
  - eliminate items until
    ‣ *combined* lists equals 100 points
    ‣ total does not exceed budget
    ‣ partners are each satisfied
    ‣ if "stuck," switch lists, "spending" 50 points or 50% of budget on each other's list
- Adjust this list as you learn more about design and products

Ask a buddy

Finding someone with whom you can share your ideas and frustrations can help you to process as you talk and possibly gain a new perspective. Your buddy should be a good listener and *non-judgmental:*

- Friend
- Relative
- Coach

- Inner reflection through
  - meditation
  - journal

Box listening

Box listening is simply paraphrasing your partner's words but this can be a powerful, eye-opening exercise. We often don't hear as well as we speak. It is important for each partner to have a turn to talk and to listen.

- One partner gets five uninterrupted minutes to talk
- Other partner responds with
  - "What I heard you say was..."
  - Is that correct?
  - Partner clarifies, if necessary
- Process is reversed
- If mutually agreeable, the round is repeated
- Identify any new understanding gained

Sticky notes with colored dots (for family decisions)

- Each person creates list of priorities (from exercise above or elsewhere)
- Determine total house/land budget and cost of each item being considered
  - each person can be given a budget for their priorities, or
  - budget can be determined as a group
- Each person writes priorities on separate sticky notes
- Place large white poster board in visible area
- Obtain sticky dots in several colors or dots with numbers 1-10

- assign each color with a value (red-1pt, orange-2pts, yellow-3pts, etc.)
- each person is given a supply of each color or number on dots
- Walk around and examine all notes
  - put one colored/numbered dot on each note
  - most points wins
  - re-vote any tied priorities
  - check each person's satisfaction level

Separating needs from wants

- Use exercise on page 10 to
  - identify items not related to values
  - items excessively expensive
  - items not supported by both/all
- See page 31 for some guidance on
  - identifying practical needs
  - items to include in post-closing budget

Flip a coin game (to be played alone)

For when you can't agree with yourself!

- List your priorities
  - select two at a time
  - flip a coin
- The winner is ...

- when coin was in air, which were you *secretly hoping would win*?
- you've just identified your preference

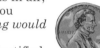

Reverse the roles

- You assume role of your partner or builder
- Your partner will become you or your builder
- Review the other's position on issue
  - ask for clarification if necessary
- Each gets five minutes to state their *partner's* case (not their own!)
  - listener must react from *partner's* perspective

- Have fun doing this while you...
  - gain new perspective on the other viewpoint
  - experience feeling understood
  - come closer together on issue

Worksheet for Time Management

At the end of the book, on page 246 are blank calendars for your use. Fill in each month's days and all deadline dates. Plan backwards from each deadline. Gather information, go shopping, talk with your partner, MAKE INFORMED DECISIONS.

Making solid decisions by construction schedule deadlines provides peace of mind to you and is likely to save additional costs related to change order requests.

Month_____

Sun	Mon	Tue	Wed	Thu	Fri	Sat
1	2 study plumbing section in workbook	3 plan where to shop for plumbing	4 make appt. with plumbing salesperson	5 visit plumbing showroom	6 bring Madge to showroom for ideas	7 go through showroom notes/shop online
8	9 determine plumbing budget	10 revisit plumbing showroom	11 study electrical section in workbook	12 make appt. with builder-plumbing changes	13 final decisions on plumbing fixtures	14
15	16 meet with builder-plumbing changes	17 plumbing changes **deadline**	18 mark changes in electrical plan	19 make appt. with builder	20 discuss electrical changes	21
22	23 shop for electrical fixtures	24 work on fixtures budget	25	26 revisit fixtures store	27 final decisions on electrical fixtures	28 electrical changes **deadline**
29	30					

This example is an accelerated version of a typical custom shopping schedule. Its purpose is to illustrate how much research may be desired on specific items. Don't run out of time! Begin your shopping earlier than you think necessary.

Also notice that you may need to focus on more than one area at a time.

The Closing

Pre-Closing Walkthrough Items to Inspect

Every electrical item is in working order

- All appliances working and undamaged
- Jetted tub filled and working
- Ice maker/chilled water flowing
- All light fixtures (interior/exterior)
- Structured wiring
- Fireplace starter/blower
- Exhaust fans
- Outlets and switches
  - firmly installed (shouldn't wiggle)
  - working and installed straight and even
- Ceiling fan paddles balanced
  - silent and smooth when running

Wood

- All doors installed
  - no "play" in closed door when shaken
  - doors not warped at top and bottom corners, no gaps
  - door hardware with/without locks as ordered
- Staircase banisters/spindles solidly installed
- No molding missing

Cabinets

- All as ordered or acceptable
- Cabinets not damaged
- Drawers slide smoothly
- All shelving included

Walls/floors

- No major cracks
- Paint job acceptable
- No tile chipped/cracked

Heat/air conditioning

- Heating/cooling systems
  - have good air flow
  - respond to thermostat
- All vent covers fit correctly
- Exhaust fans properly installed
- Drains installed where
  - necessary
  - functional

Windows

- All as ordered or acceptable
- Operate smoothly
- Hardware (handles/locks)
- All screens included/undamaged

Exterior

- Paint/siding/brick/stone not damaged
- Nails flush/no nails missing
- Roof shingles/tiles in place
- Paint job acceptable
- Patio/driveway acceptable
- Grading/compaction next to foundation

Other items before or at closing

- Refer to workbook checklists
- Items that *must* be corrected before closing
- Create a punchlist notebook or use Pre-closing walkthrough/punchlist form on page 245
- Certificate of occupancy or written municipal approval
- Unconditional release from all liens
- Warranty notebook
  - dated product information, each item
  - name/phone # of workers to contact (if your responsibility)
- Test results on systems/products
  - itemized remedies, if necessary
  - systems perform within maximum leakage percentage
- Consider buying extended warranty (see page 213)

Moving In

Plan Your Move

Severing ties

- Notify all publications and friends about address change and date
- File change of address with current post office for forwarding
- Close bank accounts
- Gather records from doctors, dentists, vets, lawyer, broker
  - ask for referrals in new community
- Arrange disconnection of utilities
- Request refunds of partially-used
  - homeowner's insurance
  - pre-paid cable/satellite/other
- Arrange for school records transfer

Obtain utility information

- Telephone/cable/satellite
- Electricity/gas
- Water and sewer
- Trash collection
- New address/mailbox key (from P.O.)
- New address on new driver's license

Make new connections

- Open bank accounts
- Contact schools
- Make medical connections for continuous care issues

Organize the packing

- Written inventory list of all belongings being moved
- Moving company estimates/contract
- Reserve moving date based on closing date
- Obtain cartons, and label
  - contents/room number
  - NOT "miscellaneous"
- Pack items not immediately needed
- Number and label boxes
- Obtain special transport for
  - irreplaceable items
  - pets/plants
- Plan new kitchen cabinet storage in advance (to unpack efficiently)
- Determine storage area for boxes that won't be unpacked immediately
- Keep toilet paper/paper towels handy

Before the movers arrive

- Have lawn mower and any tools emptied of oil and gasoline
- Dispose of all toxic chemicals
- Empty the freezer and refrigerator
- Check carpets/flooring for jewelry
- Self-addressed, stamped envelope for belongings that were left behind
- Hire babysitter for moving day

Protect Floors/Appliances/Fixtures on Moving Day

- Tarps or mats along traffic path (floor and carpet)
- Supervision to guard walls, furniture, appliances

Long-term protection measures

- See page 229 for more information
  - floors/carpets
  - wood cabinets/staircase railings
  - showers/tubs
  - foam/caulking/grout
  - appliances/cabinets/countertops
  - water heater/furnace
  - driveway

Follow through with your punchlist

- Add items as needed
- Call, call, call
  - politely but resolutely until all punchlist items are corrected
- Follow through with product manufacturers until satisfied
- Send "Thank You" letter to the builder
- CELEBRATE!

Section 6
Learn More About It

Who Is On Your Team?

Builder

The checklists on page 20 suggest some characteristics of quality builders or general contractors. Good investigative shopping includes asking for and then contacting references.

You may want to request that the builder arrange appointments for you. It seems to be human nature to resist actually checking references; it takes effort and we hate to bother people.

The reality is that we often do considerable research on much less expensive items such as sound systems and automobiles. Isn't this investment worth at least as much effort? Good builders thrive on their high quality referrals. See page 84 for more information on this very important relationship.

REALTOR®

If you don't own land, you may want to begin with a REALTOR who should know what questions to ask when evaluating a piece of property, as well as what is currently available. You may find land that is owned by a builder or private party but be sure that all relevant issues have been addressed before buying.

Look through Shopping for Land checklists, beginning on page 14, for questions you'll need to ask before making this important decision.

In addition to knowing what potential problems to look for and what questions to ask, working with a REALTOR is an efficient way to shop. Equipped with important information supplied by you, he or she can "zero in" on the land you are looking for.

A Special Piece of Land

Having lived in a forested area of New Hampshire and the countryside of Pennsylvania where deer ran through the expansive backyard hills, we knew that when we moved to urban Fort Collins, we would want some open space behind our home.

Our REALTOR spent several weekends showing my husband existing properties. None was suitable, which let us quickly know that we'd have to build. When I arrived in town, she showed us several attractive parcels so that we would have some choice. There was no contest; she had shown us land that backed up to a 15-acre park and afforded a full view of the beautiful Rocky Mountains, and I was in love. This land was part of a development that worked exclusively with REALTORS.

When interviewing REALTORS, ask about their training and experience with new construction and the high performance home. This should include some knowledge of financing, floor plan evaluation, design and product expertise including green building practices, and local building practices. REALTORS should also be knowledge about local information, such as climate, neighborhoods, school districts, and shopping.

REALTORS are often paid by the seller, as a cost of marketing. In determining REALTOR value to you, ask *their* referrals about help received (saved them money, suggested specific design or products, avoided a potential problem, etc.)

REALTORS build a successful practice by referral business. They want you to have the best experience possible and are in a position to be of great help to you. They know that if you are pleased with your building experience, you'll recommend them to your friends, and call them back when it's time for you to move.

Architect

For an idea you'd like to "see on paper," consider hiring an architect, who can match a custom design to your lifestyle. Architects charge by the hour, at a flat rate or as a percentage of the final cost of the project but may be well worth the cost to get the basic plan for this whole project, the blueprints, as close to what you want as possible. The more specific the blueprints, the more accurately the bid or budget can be determined.

Is the architect able to draw plans to match your budget? How well does this architect work with builders, and who do they think should be "in charge" of the project?

Structural Engineer

Architects and engineers differ, in that the architect wants to build something artistic as well as functional; the engineer would be very happy with a box because he or she is responsible for its structural soundness. Some municipalities require their engineer's stamp of approval on blueprints as part of the building permit process. In some areas, less or no regulation exists.

Keep in mind that, while the architect/engineer is a new degree in some colleges, most architects are not engineers. The complexity of your design or the building challenges of your land may be your best guide of what is needed.

Attorney

The role of an attorney who has *knowledge and experience with new construction* varies according to locality and type of contract. Custom contracts are often written by attorneys while production builders typically work only with their own contract forms. The attorney may be involved in the closing and title examination processes. Contracts for construction services (the building) may differ from contracts for the real estate (the land) and attorneys are often involved in the former, or both.

Arborist

If there are trees on your property, the uneducated eye may not be able to determine which trees are healthy and best to retain or discard. Consider hiring an expert to have this important part of your landscaping, and perhaps part of the cooling and sheltering of your home, done right.

Landscape Designer

For a planned exterior, a landscape designer that is knowledgeable about green building principles can provide blueprints that include desired features, aesthetic considerations and practicality. Depending on the size and scope of your yard projects, an interview with this professional will give you a better idea of how to proceed. This is a tangible art, and a visit to yards that this landscaper has done for others will give you an idea of his or her work, and possibly some new ideas you would like to incorporate in your yard design.

Interior Designer

An interior *designer* can be a part of your architectural plan, while a *decorator* works with an existing room. If you want a particular style or mood for parts or all of your home, consider shopping for a designer who will listen to your ideas and respond with an experienced eye for style, shape, color and *budget*.

Because they can incorporate your ideas into a total home design, it can be advantageous to involve them before blueprints are drawn. Interior designers can also serve as consultants who review your existing plans. Some of the many decorating themes that are classically or currently popular include traditional, Old World, modern, country, southwestern, and mission, to name only a few. Because of their increasing popularity, a very brief description of Feng Shui principles is given on page 108.

You may want the opinion of a professional before you begin shopping. Depending on the scope of your project and your level of interest, you may want this professional to be in charge of some aspects of your shopping.

Structured Wiring Systems Specialist

A structured wiring specialist can showcase the latest devices and systems that are designed to make your home safer and more enjoyable. This is an area where expertise is essential; if the wiring or its installation is not done correctly, it is likely to be very difficult to remedy later.

Self-contracting

Home construction involves knowledge of the latest building practices, designs and products. The home must or should be able to pass local building inspection. All of the "red tape" falls on you: tests, permits, excavation irregularities and so on.

High-quality workers or "trades" are in high demand and are usually busy working for professional contractors. Even if you have friends in the trades, they may not be available when you need them because your construction has been delayed by a late materials shipment, or the weather didn't cooperate, or problems occurred on other jobs, preventing them from starting your home on time. Coordinating subcontractors will feel like a full-time job. You'll want to be sure to have workers compensation insurance. If not, any damages from injuries on the job will come out of your pocket.

One advantage to being the boss is that you have exclusive control over how all construction is done. As with most custom homes, you own the construction loan (which may be an additional challenge to obtain if banks consider you to be a higher risk) and can withhold payment until work is done to your satisfaction. You may save money by doing this job yourself but builders generally have more "clout" with merchants and subcontractors. They qualify for builder discounts, and they assume very considerable risks of both time and money. They carry expensive insurance whose cost is spread over many projects.

If you are considering this route, thoroughly investigate what you are getting into, and be sure you have the time, patience and expertise necessary to run this project.

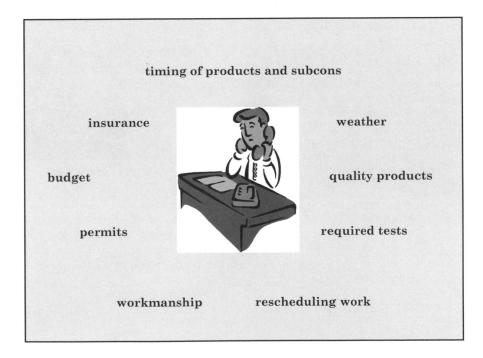

Shopping for Land

Shopping on Your Own

For people who like to spend their weekends looking around  for available land, and will buy when the right parcel appears, shopping on their own may be their choice. Since there are so many factors to consider when evaluating land, use of the checklists beginning on page 14 will give you a good start, but is not complete.

Another option is to shop directly for a piece of land that is owned by a builder. In this case, you would be purchasing the land from the builder and probably taking out the construction loan, although another common practice is for the builder to carry the land and financing until the closing. Research the land, the builder and his references just as you would any other property owner.

For information on working with a REALTOR, see Who Is On Your Team, on page 100.

Regional Climates

Discussion about orientation of the home on its site, energy efficiency and building practices requires local climate information, which is available from your local team. Since this workbook is general in nature, its scope includes raising issues and suggesting some of the right questions to ask. Homebuyers can then address issues that exist in their local climate.

Social Climates

In today's high-tech world, many people tend to go home to their computers or television, and rarely visit with neighbors. There is a growing trend toward planned communities that are designed with front porches and quiet, narrow streets to encourage neighbors to get to know each other.

Do you want total privacy and to be left alone, or a community in which you can fully integrate, or neighbors that you just wave to and with whom you can have an occasional outdoor chat? This is where you will be living every day, so your environment should feel comfortable.

Consider Sun and Wind

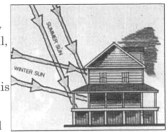

This can be a "chicken and egg" issue: do you buy land because of its favorable orientation potential, or choose a floor plan that takes advantage of whatever land is available?

In this drawing, the porch on the south side of this home (to the left) will shade the rooms behind it from *high* summer sun and allow *lower* winter sun and its heat in. The sides facing the east and west (front and back in this drawing) will still get some heat in the summer. Porches serve as useful overhangs but will make room they shade darker.

Deciduous trees on the east, and especially on the west side of the home are ideal because they offer welcome shade in the summer, and let in the winter sun's warmth through the bare branches. Some evergreens work well on the east and west, and when planted to the north, can effectively block cold winter winds. Sketch how sun and wind will affect rooms in your new home with a specific orientation.

Homeowners Associations

Homeowner associations exist to maintain the property value of the neighborhood. Some people are happy to live by these rules and others are not. Homeowners may be legally responsible for common ground such as green space, swimming pools and a community center. All members of the association share the cost of maintenance. Find out if the association operates with a budget and a cash reserve, if there are dues, and who runs the association. Membership in the association is probably mandatory.

If a REALTOR is involved in the purchase of this land, he should have this information, or consult the developer, builder or your attorney. It may be a legal requirement that you receive this information at closing but that is too late! Investigate the HOA's rules to see if they match your values *before* you "fall in love" with the community.

Covenants

Your homeowners association or local jurisdiction may have a set of legally enforceable covenants. The focus is usually on what is visible from the exterior. Some of the items listed as covenants may include:

- Building dimensions
  - height/width/length
  - elevation from ground level
- Building style
- Price
- Plot plan (home placement on land)
  - angle
  - setback from street
- Exterior paint colors (lot #2 = dark red)
- Antennas/flagpoles
- Fences (height/material/not allowed)
- Address plaques
- Siding and roof styles/materials
- Outdoor lighting

- Mailboxes
- Clotheslines
- Pets
- Landscaping, yard maintenance, flower and vegetable gardens
- Building additions
- Street and driveway parking restrictions
- Parties or other large gatherings
- Home businesses
- Outdoor barbeques
- Pools/hot tubs
- Gazebos
- Swings or playsets
- Permanent signage

Architectural Review

If your land is part of a development or is subject to specific municipal building codes, your plans may have to pass an architectural review which may be administered by the homeowners association or municipal authority. These are important details to investigate before purchasing land to be sure this parcel of land is suitable for the home you want to build.

Typical requirements may include minimum or maximum home dimensions, height limits, plot plan restrictions, and cost of house but are not likely to be concerned with many of the "finer details" listed above. Find out from your architect, builder, REALTOR or attorney if you must obtain approval from any authorities.

Impact and Tap Fees

Municipalities often charge impact and tap fees to home builders, which in turn, get passed on to you. Impact fees go toward the building of streets, neighborhood parks, new schools or other civic projects related to the neighborhood while tap fees contribute to start-up and maintenance of utilities including water and sewer, gas and electric. Remember to budget for these significant chunks of money.

Choosing the Right Floor Plan

See floor plan checklists (page 109) to identify features you may want to include in your design or wish list.

One Story/Multi-level

Match your lifestyle (the way you really live) to floor plans to help you find one or two that best meet your needs. A one-story eliminates stairs but often requires a larger homesite. Some people prefer the coziness of everything on one floor. A garden level one-story or multi-level can take advantage of sloped land to have a lower level that is above-ground and therefore has less of a "basement feel," and may be more desirable living space.

A two-story home is generally less expensive per square foot and can afford more living space on a smaller homesite. Upstairs bedrooms are out of sight and therefore more private. Also popular is a first-floor master bedroom with other bedrooms on the second floor or lower level.

Multiple floor levels add dramatic architectural flair: a sunken great room, a defined dining area or a "tower-like" feel of a few steps up to the master suite or children's hideaway.

Special Construction

Modular

Watch for modular construction to grow significantly. Luxurious homes are being constructed is this manner, with more to follow at all "price points." Custom modular homes are built in major pieces in a quality-controlled, dry, indoor environment. After the foundation is prepared on-site, five to nine modules that have been built to order are transported to the site and carefully mated together much faster than conventional construction.

Only a builder would be able to identify modular from "stick-built." In addition to more efficient labor and therefore lower costs and less time required, your home under construction is not subjected to the weather. Modules are subject to strict quality control measures, from which you benefit.

Log

If your desire is for a log home, see page 234 for website sources. Floor plan, design and product considerations in this book will be useful but log homes have specific issues that should be researched. Pay particular attention to log wall thermal performance.

Timber frame (post-and-beam)

The modern post-and-beam home is made of beautiful wood. Instead of dimensional lumber that is hidden behind wallboard, timber frame wood serves as the home's framing from *inside* the walls. Its rich and rustic feel is often popular for luxury and vacation homes. Page 234 lists suggested websites for learning more about this special construction.

Solar

Using solar collectors, as either a sole or supplemental energy source, is becoming a popular practice everywhere the sun regularly shines. Standard solar collectors are usually placed on the roof, facing south. Newer solar collectors are integrated into roofing material (typically metal but can be other materials.) They are currently less efficient than the separate solar panels, but including them as an integral part of the roof creates sufficient surface. Because this technology is changing rapidly, check the website directory on page 234 for information sources.

Courtyard

Because outdoor living is gaining in popularity, the courtyard is part of many home designs. It allows enjoyment of the outdoors with both privacy and shelter, and is no longer limited to warm climates. Collapsable glass doors can provide a disappearing wall between indoors and out in almost all climates.

Courtyards can include barbeques, fireplaces and anything else that imagination and budget allows. Also note that a central courtyard will break up the traffic flow between rooms and may necessitate more walking.

Universal design/wheelchair accessibility

$$$ If you choose a one-story home to avoid stairs, consider 36" wide doorways throughout the home. Even if you never need a wheelchair, this measure could be very attractive at resale time to someone who does, making this a low-cost option that could have an attractive payback. See checklist on page 23 for universal design items to consider.

Universal design is not just for the elderly. Having one entrance to the home that has no steps is user-friendly for strollers and for anyone recovering from an accident. Wider hallways and better lighting may be pleasing to all occupants. Having an accessible grab bar at the entrance to every bathtub and shower provides safety to all users.

Floor Plan Traffic Patterns

Does this floor plan feel welcoming to you? What impression do you get when you step through the doorway? Where will guests enter the home? Is the entryway protected from wind gusts? Where will your children (and all their friends) enter the home, and through which rooms will they travel?

How do the room sizes and shapes feel to you? Do you want a conversation area for a cozy feeling or do you want spaciousness? Who generates noise and who is not noise-tolerant? Does anyone love the solitude of a study and if so, is there one, and does it have the potential to be a quiet space? Will your furniture fit?

Reversing Your Floor Plan

Would an existing floor plan suit you better if mirror-reversed? This is not difficult for builders to do. If you know what will be built on each side of you, is your master bedroom better on one side than the other? If your home will face south, which side of the home should face east? Consider the views from each room to see if "flipping" the floor plan is a better choice for you.

Feng Shui

Feng Shui (pronounced *fung shway*) is the Chinese art of placement. It uses information about energy to determine where particular living spaces (i.e. kitchen, entryway, bedrooms) should be located, based on corresponding principles, to achieve maximum harmony with nature. If this interests you, meet with an expert in this field who can interpret the relationship between you and your home using compass directions, birthdates, or other information.

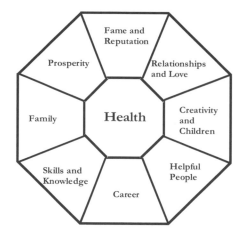

"Try-on" Floor Plans

Have some fun trying on the floor plans on the next few pages.

- Garage entry "welcoming" area
  - shelf/bench/hooks/closet
- Distance from garage to kitchen
  - carrying groceries
  - sheltered above/dry floor if outdoors
  - any steps
- Curb appeal
  - warmth from visible living areas
    ‣ porch
    ‣ terrace
  - balanced/proportionate windows
- Front entrance
  - open/closed
  - view when entering
- Kitchen traffic patterns
  - stove/stovetop to sink to refrigerator to pantry
  - dishwasher to sink and storage cabinets
  - room for two cooks to function at once

- Room flow
  - entrance to main living areas
  - kitchen to dining room
- Quiet area with door for privacy/noise control
- Views from favorite work/living areas that
  - are pleasing
  - you'd rather avoid
- Natural light
  - from two perpendicular walls
- Patio area sheltered from wind/hottest sun
- Powder room for guests
- Multiple use rooms
  - extra bedroom/study
  - laundry room/hobby center
  - media room/exercise area
- General storage/closets
- Garage space sufficient for
  - car doors swinging open
  - necessary storage

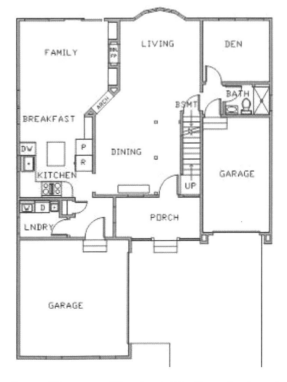

What do you like or not like about this floor plan's main level?

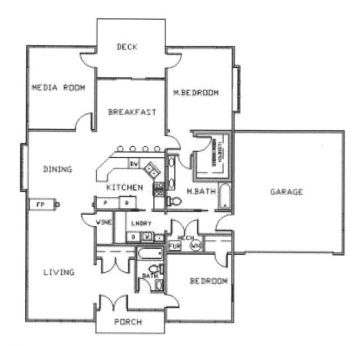

Above, a side mount garage requires sufficient land width. This plan features a master bedroom closet/storm room, wine room and media room. The deck has two entrances.

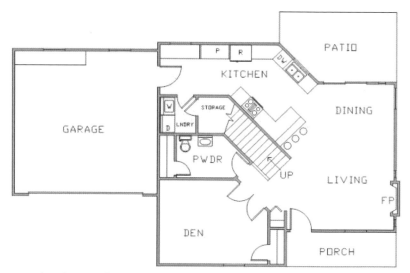

Above, notice that angles create architectural interest throughout main floor.

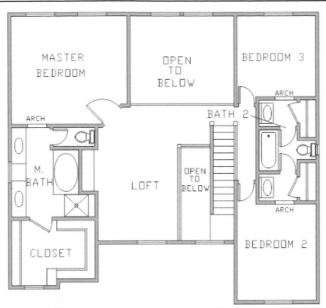

Notice the "Jack and Jill" bathroom on this second floor. The toilet/tub area has doors for privacy, allowing access to individual sink areas.

This plan features a front-load garage that dares visitors to enter- even to find the front door. Notice the "his and hers" bedrooms (master and #2.) If one partner SNORES, the other can slip into the spare bedroom without leaving his or her *boudoir*.

Kitchen Floor Plan

Getting to your kitchen

Since real life means lugging groceries from the car to the kitchen, how far will this trip be? Must you walk back and forth on stairs or over carpet? Does this journey disturb others unnecessarily?

Kitchen's neighboring rooms

Do you want to see the family television or hear the entertainment system from the kitchen while cooking? Is noise from kitchen or family room a problem for occupants of either one? How will this arrangement work when you entertain? Will people gather in the kitchen or elsewhere?

Is the dining room convenient to the kitchen? Larger homes sometimes feature a butler pantry for storage, counter space and final meal preparation between kitchen and dining room.

Kitchen design and flow

The kitchen is usually the most important room in a home design. It will cost the most to equip, you will spend more waking hours in it than in any other room, and "rearranging the furniture" is difficult and expensive.

Imagine yourself in this room as it is designed. Checklists of what to look for in a kitchen floor plan begin on page 24. Consider the location of appliances in relation to each other and the distance between them. Important work areas that are located in room corners can cause unnecessary congestion. In this version of the "L" will spattering grease and a hot surface be dangerously close to anyone sitting at the overhang?

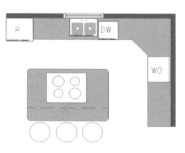

"L" shape

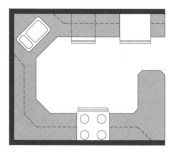

"G" shape with peninsula
creates narrow traffic area

Island/peninsula placement

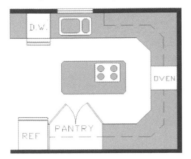

"U" shape with island not blocking appliances and sink

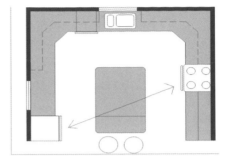

"U" shape with island blocking stove to refrigerator

Does the island or peninsula break up the traffic flow from one important area to another?

Is there sufficient room for people to sit at the eating bar overhang without blocking traffic? Does this area have flooring or carpet (or a break between the two) under it? Carpet is usually impractical in casual eating areas, especially if you have small children. How will this area be used? When a friend drops by, is this a comfortable seat in a preferred location?

An interesting alternative to sitting next to each other is to have the eating bar seating at the end of the island or peninsula, allowing people to face each other or sit at a 90° angle instead of feeling like they're eating at Joe's Diner.

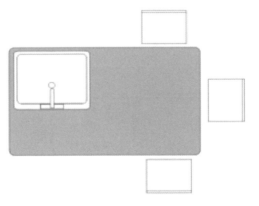

Island with leg room for opposed or perpendicular seating

Refrigerator placement

Where will the refrigerator be? You'll want to be able to open its doors fully (more than a 90° angle) in order to open and remove bins. Is there clearance for your refrigerator doors?

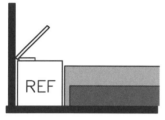

Is the area height and width sufficient to accommodate your refrigerator? Is there a countertop nearby to use as you empty or fill the refrigerator? When refrigerator doors are open, is the traffic path blocked? Which way should the door swing?

This island is too close to allow clearance, but an opposing surface is handy when properly located

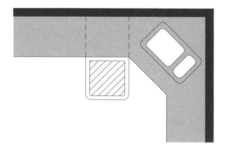

Can't open door fully

Dishwasher

Dishwashers are most convenient when very close to the sink and reasonably close to the dish storage cabinet. How far must you travel to load the dishwasher and put clean dishes away? Notice that in the diagram on page 110, there is probably a narrow base cabinet between the sink dishwasher that is on an angle, which is a far better design than the one illustrated below.

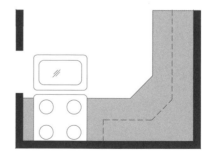

Dishwasher on angled island leaves no room to stand

Range or wall oven door too near doorway

Stove ranges

Stove ranges allow the cook to check the stovetop and oven in one spot, adding convenience and reducing traffic. This oven does, however, always require bending.

Stovetop

Is the stovetop in a convenient place for you? A hot stovetop should be reaching distance only for the cook. Is the area behind the stovetop accessible for frequent cleaning? Will you be able to store pots and pans near the stove or stovetop? How is the traffic pattern from stovetop to serving area?

Wall oven(s)

This can be one oven, a combination oven and microwave, or two ovens. The main oven can be on top, which would require no bending. Is the oven in an area where opening and closing its door will be safe for those passing by? Is there a safe place to put items hot out of the oven?

Microwave

Is the height of the microwave convenient for all users, not just the main chef of the home? If this is a stretch for someone, pulling a hot dish out of the microwave over one's head can be dangerous. Microwaves placed in an island are too convenient for small children who should not be operating a microwave oven, and too low for most adults' comfort. Would a microwave located very near the eating area be appreciated?

Trash compactor

Is the trash compactor and its contents located far enough away from all eating areas ?

Cabinet placement

Are cabinets conveniently located for storage of plates, glasses, flatware, utensils and all food supplies that don't belong in a pantry closet? Notice the distance to the eating area. Are there enough cabinets for your storage needs?

Kitchen dining placement

Where will all meals be served? Will you have an area that accommodates a table and chairs *and* room to pull the chairs out without banging into something or blocking someone's path? Is there a door that, when open, will interfere with chairs?

Keeping room

Larger kitchens may include a sitting area, possibly with a fireplace, hearth and sofa or easy chairs. This concept has grown out of the undeniable fact that the kitchen is the heart of the home, and where family and visitors congregate.

Butler pantry

Larger kitchens and larger budgets may allow for an area between kitchen and formal dining room that can be used for serving and storage. It may include cabinets, a sink, a warming drawer, a towel drawer warmer...as much as imagination and budget allow.

Ceilings

How high should your ceilings be? Higher ceilings are more expensive but add spaciousness. The higher they are, the more potential for sound to bounce off of bare walls, creating echoes. Would you like dramatic cutouts and angles in walls or arched doorways? These architectural considerations add cost and style.

Family Room/Great Room Design

Family rooms are designed to be casual and often feature a television and entertainment area. They are often referred to as "great rooms" when they are open to the kitchen and casual eating area. Decide where your furniture will go and where people will watch television or sit in a conversational group. Does the wall, door and window placement fit your family's way of living? If windows allow glare on the television or on people's faces at any time of the day, must they be covered? Are they well-placed?

Dining Room

You'll want the dining room to be convenient to the kitchen, which is not always the case. If you occasionally have large gatherings but would rather not spend a large amount of your square footage on this room, consider a dining room that is open to another area, such as the living room or family room. With this arrangement, you can extend the table and accommodate additional chairs, spreading into an adjacent room as needed.

Multiple Use/Flex Rooms

Many homebuyers are discovering that bigger is not always better. Instead of a home that sprawls, you may want to build smarter by having fewer rooms that can serve more than one purpose. Can you combine a crafts/sewing room with a spare bedroom, or the den with a media room? Consider creating flex rooms using space in a clever, attractive and practical way.

Living Room

What is the function of this room? Is it a special place for company and your most elegant furniture? Is it the place to listen to music? Will your piano fit in it? Will this room be used or just gather dust? Plan your furniture in the room to see if you have sufficient wall space and light. What is the traffic pattern to and from this area?

Study/Office

You may want a first-floor study, which is usually a room with a door to provide a quiet space. Will you have sufficient light? Is this a good place for a skylight? Should this room have an elegant look? You may want built-in bookcases. If this is a "technology center" of the home, ensure that it is properly wired for today and tomorrow. If the desk will be away from the wall, does this area require a floor outlet to avoid wires to trip over?

If this room is planned as a home office, do you need a separate entrance? If so, it should look as residential (not commercial) as possible. This may or may not be allowed by legal covenants. Is the study designed to accommodate multiple desks, and if so, how should they be configured?

Media Room

Does your budget allow for a room dedicated to wide screen television with surround sound? Should this be in the main living area or on the lower or upper level? Should this room have no windows and are there building code egress (exit to outside) requirements? Are there other electronic devices that belong in this room? Because this technology is changing rapidly, seeking the advice of a wiring specialist is advised.

Powder Room

Where is the powder room in relation to other rooms? Is it visible from the front entrance? Is it convenient for guests? Does the location allow for sufficient privacy without compromising ease of access? Is it large enough for guests to not feel cramped? Would a window or skylight make it feel more spacious? Consider having the walls of the powder room insulated for added sound control.

Master Bedroom

The purpose of today's bedrooms is to sleep and to lounge. It no longer is the primary dressing area, which has been moved to the enlarged master closet (see Master Closet.)

If this describes your lifestyle, then the size of the closet may be more important than the size of the bedroom. If not, determine if all of your furniture will fit in the bedroom.

Sitting area

Is there sufficient space for a sitting area or a desk? Do you want this room to have an atmosphere of elegance, and how might you achieve that feeling? If this is an important consideration, an interior designer can create a theme and assist in shopping.

Orientation

What view will you have with various furniture arrangements? Do you want this room to have an eastern orientation so that you may enjoy the sunrise? Do you want a skylight? If so, will it have an adjustable shade or will the morning light be welcomed at an early hour? If this room faces the street, will this be a privacy or noise issue? Is there sufficient distance from other rooms for privacy?

Plan the room ahead

Deciding where the furniture goes at this early stage may affect the door's location, its width, and which way it swings. How about double doors for a dramatic flair? If this is your choice, check that installed doors close firmly and don't rattle. You'll want the light switch on the wall of the door that opens (the other door usually remains stationary) to be just beyond where the open door blocks the wall (see drawing on page 176.)

Master Bathroom

Does the master bedroom flow into the master bath and yet remain separate? If these areas are open to each other, will one person be trying to read or sleep while the other has the shower radio playing? Will an open bathroom be warm enough while you bathe or shower? Does the location of the bathroom allow the most direct access to the dressing area? Can you safely enter and exit the tub?

The tub

You may want a six-foot tub in which to stretch out your legs, a five-foot tub which uses less water, a triangular tub for two or no tub at all. The absence of a tub may be a drawback when you resell the house, but some of the following options may be more attractive and practical for your lifestyle. If you choose a tub, is there an *accessible* towel bar?

The shower(s)

Showers have become luxury centers, with multiple types and locations of spray and special features, including benches and built-in sound. Walk-in showers may have no door, and contribute to handicapped-accessibility if they don't include a step to climb over. Be sure to have tall, deep niches included for everything you want to store in the shower. Will there be a handy towel bar or rod? For all showers that have a door, what style of door is best?

The toilet(s)

Is the toilet room large enough for you to comfortably close the door? Consider adding a magazine niche for convenient throne reading! Do you need two toilets or a urinal? Do you want a vanity area where you can sit down to put in contact lenses or put on makeup?

Where do you want the soft feel of carpet underfoot? Non-skid tile is a much better idea at the shower and tub entrances and certainly in the toilet area.

$$$ Do you want a towel closet? Open shelves provide storage and are less expensive than closets. These open shelves can have as a shallow wall that serves as a privacy partition for toilet area.

$$$ Angled walls that are non-load bearing and have "empty space" behind them may accommodate a storage niche. (Examine your blueprints for "empty" spaces.) A square or oblong rectangular box niche is a good place to stack clean towels.

Master Closet(s)

Master closets may include adjustable shelves, multi-height handing rods, bins, furniture and a generous dressing area. Split poles, suitable for many clothes, doubles that area of the closet space. A built-in platform along the floor allows easier access to high shelves.

Some closets include jewelry cabinets, a tie rack, a shoe rack and a bolted-down safe. The closet walls can be lined in cedar, which smells wonderful! Visiting model homes will give you some ideas for creative closets.

Will this area be conditioned or might it be uncomfortably hot or cold? If the closet is on an exterior wall, a high privacy window brings natural light, although sunlight can fade clothing. An alternative is a tubular skylight. Sufficient lighting in the closet will be appreciated with or without natural light.

Additional Bedrooms

Standard floor plans frequently provide a spacious master bedroom suite but skimp on the other bedrooms. If you have little use for these bedrooms, they need not be any larger. If people will be living in these rooms, will they and their furniture have adequate room? Are the windows high enough to prevent romping children from falling through windows? If there is an upper level terrace, is this an accident waiting to happen?

$$$ One less expensive alternative to extra bedroom square footage is a window box, in which a wall is extended a foot or so, all around the window. This makes a room look larger and can also provide a hidden storage area and a place to curl up with a good book. A vaulted ceiling also adds volume, giving the room a more spacious feeling.

Bathroom design

$$$ Half walls that help to hide the toilet are less expensive than a separate toilet room and may be more handicapped-accessible.

Where is the toilet located? When the toilet is placed next to the bathtub, the proximity of toilet to someone actually soaking in the tub may be closer than desired. On the other hand, this toilet placement provides a handy "chair" while supervising young children in the tub.

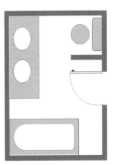

Partially or totally hiding the toilet is a touch of class.

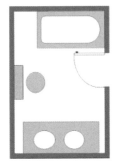

This toilet has a starring role.

Banjo countertops

Banjo countertops have been around for a long time and are still being built. They not only prevent easy toilet tank maintenance but also invite foreign objects that are supposed to remain on the countertop to fall into the toilet. Installing a low toilet or raising the counter height avoids one of these problems.

Banjo countertop

Jack and Jill bathrooms

For a shared bathroom, a smarter alternative
to dueling doors is a single door to the private
area, that includes toilet and shower/tub.

Bedroom Closets

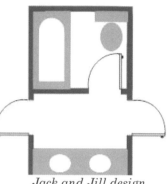

The customizing of closets is most easily and
effectively done during construction. Split
shelves in children's rooms provide a pole and
shelf closer to their level with an extra pole
and shelf above. Do they want mirrored walls
or doors? Mirrored closet doors have a
practical use while making the room look
bigger but are not everyone's fashion choice.
See Closet Doors on page 143.

*Jack and Jill design
without dueling doors*

Linen Closets

Do you want a linen closet in the bathroom for convenient towel and toiletry
storage? Will a central linen closet away from high moisture be best? Where
will everyone's bed linens and towels be stored?

In-law Quarters

Will you want a separate apartment for someone now or later? Plan the traffic
patterns, the size of rooms and the proximity of a bathroom. How will noise
from the rest of the home affect this area? Where is the closest exterior
entrance? Does this design offer optimum use of space, views, and privacy?
This area should be wired for separate electronic connections. Does it need a
separate heating/air conditioning zone for a varied level of comfort?

Laundry Room

The laundry room has gotten larger and become multi-purpose. It can be the
pet center for dining, sleeping and bathing, the sewing and gift wrap center
and the ironing center.

It also tends to be a noisy place. Is it convenient to use and still far enough
away from popular rooms? Doing laundry requires many trips back and forth.
Is it convenient to your favorite living area during laundry time? Or would you
prefer to have the laundry near the dirty clothes?

One advantage to a first-floor laundry is that it often serves as a mud entrance.
When located at an exterior entrance, muddy or wet shoes are usually better on
a washable laundry room floor than on a carpet or wood floor. In climates
where wet shoes and boots are a common occurrence, a floor drain may be
desirable.

If you are looking at an existing floor plan, notice where the plumbing is for the washer and dryer. If there is a laundry sink, is the washer next to the sink?

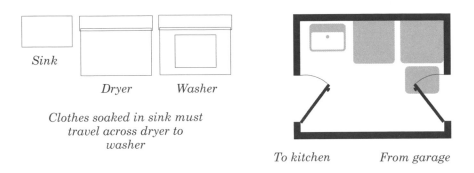

Sink

Dryer   *Washer*

Clothes soaked in sink must travel across dryer to washer

To kitchen   *From garage*

Are the washer and dryer located right next to a doorway? This design has two problems. When you are standing at the washer or dryer, if someone opens the door, will there be a collision? If the dryer is next to the door and has a front-opening door, the door won't last very long.

If your dryer's exhaust doesn't match the cutout in the wall requiring an extension (see page 170) what happens if the dryer must be moved forward?

Laundry Chute

An old-fashioned but practical addition to a home is a laundry chute. This was popular when the laundry area was in the basement and the clothes could travel down the chute and pile high without being noticed. If your laundry is on the first-floor or lower level, you might want to consider having clothes land in a strategically-placed basket, or just gather at the end of a closed chute. Since the passageway is a fire conduit, it must meet local fire code, which will require having both ends of the chute spring-closed.

Studying the Blueprints or Floorplans

Having design details ironed out before blueprints are drawn saves time and money. Your workbook will be indispensable because so much may need to be decided without the visual of a blueprint.

You may find yourself poring over blueprints for hours, planning how you will live in the home, determining if the design will serve your lifestyle well. Significant changes may require drawing up new blueprints for which you will be charged. See page 86 for a checklist of blueprint details.

On the following page is a very simple electrical blueprint. Learning to read this one will help you to be able to read your own. Refer to Electrical, beginning on page 172, to help you evaluate your blueprint. Don't hesitate to ask your builder or architect to help you understand the plans completely.

"Live" in each room of the blueprint as you study the foundation design, framing, HVAC, plumbing, electrical, walls, floors, cabinets, countertops, finish carpentry and exterior design. This is most easily done one construction phase at a time, especially the electrical.

Cutouts to scale, available at large office supply supply stores, are like "furniture Colorforms®" that let you do your arranging without lifting. Having older children draw their favorite rooms to scale and then create furniture cutouts to scale is a fun, practical math lesson. While they have fun arranging their new rooms, you can do the same with other rooms.

Getting the floor plan right

We had our beautiful land abutting what would become an attractive open park, and had chosen an existing floor plan that we planned to modify. Shortly before the architect made our changes to the blueprint, my husband realized that, because the back of our land had a slight angle in the middle, the floor plan we had chosen would have the family room angled away from the mountain view, but if the plan were mirror-reversed, the view would be perfect.

The park has since been built, and the mountain view is beautiful. The only unsettling thought is what could have been: failing to realize that our floor plan should have been reversed and having to settle for something that would have been a daily visible reminder of a big disappointment.

Architectural Electrical Blueprint Symbols

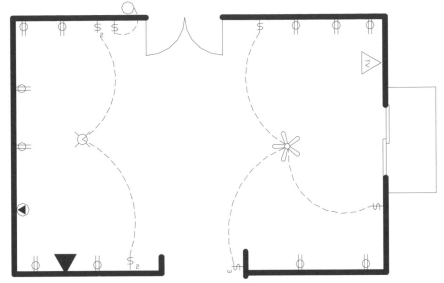

The basic symbols used in the electrical blueprint on page 123 are listed below it. Lights have dotted lines (two lines if on a 2-pole switch for two room entrances, three lines for a 3-pole) leading to the switches that control them. Symbols vary a great deal and those on your blueprint may vary somewhat from those shown here.

 Single pole light on patio (outside)
Switch is just beyond where open door blocks wall

 Double pole (two-way) light in kitchen with switches near interior and exterior entrances

$\dashv$$_{3}$ Three-way light in family room with switches near interior entrance and exterior double doors in back, and door on side

2-gang (standard) outlets at intervals around rooms

240v outlet (range outlet) in kitchen for electric stove

Ground Fault Interrupt (near water and outside)

Switch and duplex outlet (combination of wall switch and 2 outlets)

Cable outlet Ceiling fan

Telephone outlet Flush-mounted light

Cutouts to Scale on Graph Paper

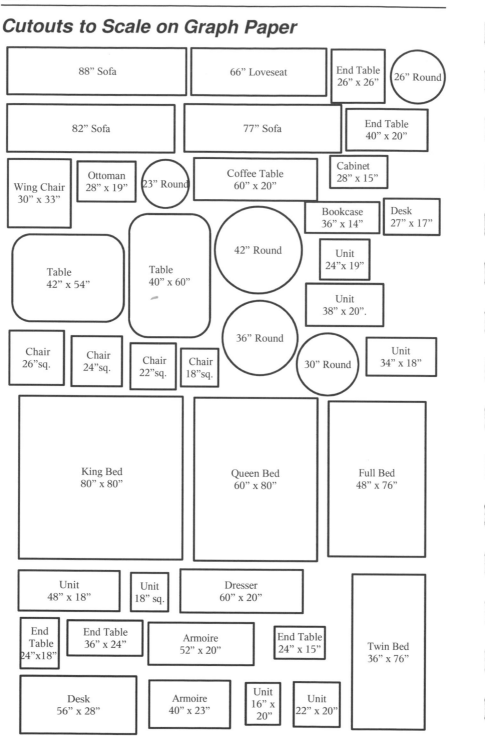

Foundation Design

This section may contain more detail than you need, depending on your degree of involvement in construction but it will allow you to be a better observer as your home takes form, and will be very helpful if you make foundation design changes.

Survey

You or your builder will hire a survey company to stake the homesite. They will hammer metal pins into its corners. These pins define your property lines and let the builder know where he can and cannot build. They will be important to you later when you want to install a fence or sprinkler system and need to know the *exact* location of your property lines. Check them occasionally during construction to make sure they're still visible.

Soils Report Evaluation

It is important and usually required to have a soils report evaluation before excavation. If a problem is found that will affect the stability of your home, it must be addressed before construction begins. To understand the report, a structural engineer is the ultimate expert but builders are likely to be aware of common problems. Municipal building departments should be familiar with local soil problems but are not likely to offer advice about your particular homesite.

Percolation Test Evaluation

The purpose of the percolation test or "perc test" is to determine the soil's ability to absorb moisture. If three inches of rain fall in less than an hour, will your soil be able to absorb none, some or most of it? The results of this test can affect foundation design, sewer pipe or septic installation, well digging and landscaping.

Septic System

If you will not be connecting to municipal water and sewer, pay attention to details about your septic system installation. Soils and percolation reports should be examined by an engineer or qualified technician. Understand the correct order for the leach field and excavation to be dug. Acquire an estimate of the cost of installation, knowledge of any potential problems with locating the septic system or with its future operation.

Any area that may be a future septic field needs to be protected from compaction (see page 129) which can occur when heavy equipment runs over it. Septic fields are dug relatively near the house.

Crawlspace

 Part of the "high performance home" is an unvented crawlspace. It is well-insulated and air sealed, and is included in the conditioned air of the home, helping this area to remain dry year 'round.

Slab-on-Grade

$$$ If your home is built on a concrete slab, insulation (including plastic sheeting) under the slab provides frost protection in cold climates and allows shallower footings, a cost savings measure. If termites are a problem in your area, your builder should be familiar with the best local building practice.

In areas that have expansive soils under slab, cracks can develop from changes in soil moisture level, called a "hinge effect.". One practice is to attempt to maintain an even level of soil moisture but this can result in over-watering, and related moisture problems for the home. An alternate solution is to build post tensioned slab-on-grade or on piers. If you live in an area with expansive soils, discuss best practices with local builders.

The heating and air conditioning systems can be located outside, in the garage, attic or dedicated closet (often depending on climate) but since a concrete slab is cold to the touch, some homebuyers plan their budget to include radiant floor heating. See page 150 for more information.

Beware of second floor placement of water heaters since they occasionally fail and flood. A plan for this possibility is a must.

Foundation Walls

Regional preferences include poured concrete, cement block, pre-formed concrete or wood. The stability, insulation and waterproofing features of each need to be examined according to climate and local soil conditions.

Drainage

The foundation needs to be dug to a specific depth so that the home is at the correct elevation for water runoff. If neighboring homes have been built on ground that is higher than yours, you'll want to find out what the drainage plan is, making sure that those above you aren't draining onto your property. There may be easements through your property to accommodate drainage from properties at higher elevations than yours. Don't *assume* that this important plan exists.

Plot Plan Evaluation

The blueprints will show exactly where your home will sit on the homesite. They also ensure that your home will fit on it within parameters dictated by legal ordinance. What orientation to the sun and wind will each side of your home have with this plot plan? Is it possible to change the angle or reverse the floor plan?

A well-built home won't mind the wind, but you will, if you plan to sit outside. See your notes from page 105. Notice the presentation of the front of the home for curb appeal, placed at this angle and depth (setback) on the land. Check that your property isn't subject to plot restrictions.

File Permits

Your builder should file all necessary permits, which vary by municipality. If you are serving as your own contractor, these are your responsibility.

Changes in Foundation Design

In many parts of the U.S., basements are prohibitively expensive to dig, or impractical due to climate or soil conditions. If your home will have a crawlspace or a slab, most of this section can be skipped. If your design includes a "lower level" which is above-ground but serves as a secondary living area, parts of this section will be important.

Foundation walls and ceiling height

This is the time to be sure that the foundation walls are acceptable as planned. This may be dictated by the size and shape of your land. Reflect on what you've learned about your lifestyle; consider access to daylight, storage needs, extra bedrooms, a pool table, your plans to entertain or the possibility of having an integral garage at basement level.

$$$ A cost-cutting measure is to reduce the size of your basement, or choose a crawlspace, especially if the basement is not considered desirable living space. Estimating your future needs now may help you to decide if this is an appropriate place to spend or save building dollars. If you plan to use the lower level as living space, is it worth the considerable expense to have higher ceilings for a more spacious feel for home office, bedrooms or media room? If they are raised to greater than eight feet, a design review by a structural engineer may be required.

Finishing concrete slab flooring

Today's concrete can be beautiful! Concrete can be stained, stamped, swirled and sealed to an impressive finish.

Foundation sub-flooring

Some foundation designs include structural wood sub-floors, which provides a softer feel underfoot. This design requires that the area beneath the sub-floor is properly ventilated to ensure that it remain dry in all seasons. If this idea interests you, talk with area builders about its advisability and additional cost.

Adding basement windows

If you have the option to add extra basement windows, consider three important features. A functional, attractive basement includes ample light, preferably from two walls, comfortable temperature and humidity, and rooms that are large enough to be useful. Finishing the basement adds useful living space and may increase the resale value of the home.

High quality windows will contribute significantly to comfort and energy savings. If you would like to add bedrooms, the building code may require that each has a window. Basement windows typically serve as fire exits (egress) so minimum size, shape, and placement may be dictated by building codes.

Type of window wells

If windows are below ground level, your builder may offer standard window wells, which are enclosed with a sheet-metal product in a semi-circle, or stair-step window wells which are constructed on-site of wood in a rectangular shape. The wood-framed windows add cost but have two advantages: they are easier to climb out of if a quick exit becomes necessary and they are often larger, allowing in a little more light.

Location of rough-in plumbing

Whether or not you finish your basement, consider including "rough-in" plumbing. This is installation of the underground plumbing with pipes brought through the floor, ready for the future hook-up of plumbing fixtures. Easy to do now; much harder and more expensive to do later. If you sketch where rooms might go, remembering that any bedroom may need a window, you'll get an idea of where one or more bathrooms should be located.

Storm room

In tornado and hurricane regions, a storm room within the home can provide safety and peace of mind. As shown on the floor plan on page.110,.it can be located within the master closet or other location that is locally deemed appropriate.

The storm room may require framing connectors and strapping that tie the structure together. It is sometimes made of concrete block or structural panels. If storm rooms have windows, they must have laminated glass. Local builders are the experts on what would be the best design for you and your climate. Designs are available at all different price levels, so it is up to you whether and how much you would like to spend.

Wine cellar

If this possibility matches your lifestyle and budget, a basement room with a locked door can be made into a cool and secure wine cellar.

Media room

A windowless room that is well-ventilated is an excellent space for a media room if building code permits. Consider room dimensions for acoustics. You will want this room to be comfortable year-round, so heat and cooling "loads" for this room as living space should be factored in the HVAC plan.

Location of heating system

It is generally preferable to have a centrally-located heating and hot water system but if the design breaks up most of the usable living space, investigate the possibility of altering the plan with minimal compromise of its effectiveness.

Walkout/garden level

A walkout-level basement is above ground on at least one side, allowing for a full-height door to the exterior. A walkout requires either a natural or excavated slope to your land. Your main (upper) floor access to the backyard is likely to be to a deck with stairs, constructed one flight up. This can be a safety issue when stairs are wet or will be used by children, the handicapped or elderly.

For walkouts, consider what would be the best location for an exterior door. Who will use it and what landscaping is planned on or around this traffic path? Choose a door with convenience, attractiveness, insulation and security in mind.

A garden lower level is partially above ground, Its elevation allows the installation of standard size windows (and increased natural light) but not a door.

Excavating the Foundation

Site Preparation

Site preparation may involve clearing trees away from the building site. See page 102 for a description of how an arborist can be very helpful in site preparation. If you are building in a fire-prone area, be sure to clear an area wide enough to be fire-safe. Stumps should be completely removed rather than buried. The excavation crew will also grade the land to specifications. If you need a well or a septic tank, this will be dug, as will utility trenches. Ensure that any optional underground wiring (cable, Internet) is installed.

The Dig

A detailed discussion of excavation is beyond the scope of this workbook. The bibliography lists books in which these details are discussed thoroughly. Some buyers like to have the open hole inspected to check that it is dug to blueprint specifications, including its depth for correct house elevation.

Slab-on-grade

After the area is graded, all underground pipes must be laid before a concrete slab is poured. See page 126 for further details on slabs.

Basement and crawlspace

Footers are formed around the perimeter of the foundation and walls are formed. The foundation is then poured, creating the ground floor walls. Pipes and underdrains systems (if necessary) are installed, and the walls are waterproofed. For superior insulation, ask about having the outside of the foundation walls insulated.

Special construction for drainage/expansive soils

If you live in an area that has insufficient drainage or expansive soils, your builder is probably well aware of it. If this is the case, your foundation may need special construction. This could mean the addition of caissons, which are tubular cages of steel bars, designed to reinforce the concrete.

Backfill and Compaction

After the hole has been dug and the foundation walls formed, the space between the edge of the hole and the walls must be backfilled with soil. This replacement must be done carefully and usually in stages because soil settles.

If the backfill is replaced all at once, severe settling may occur sooner or later, leaving sunken spots near the home. A process called "full compaction" can be done at the time of filling to prevent this from happening. Ask your builder what the backfill procedure is and what measures are taken to facilitate proper settling. This is also a good question to ask of a builder's referral homeowners who have lived in their home for at least one year.

Topsoil should be stripped from the construction site and gathered away from construction debris. When construction is completed, your topsoil should be replaced before the sod or seed is laid. Non-porous (clay) soil should have organic material mixed in with a rototiller before replacing topsoil for maximum moisture absorption and watering efficiency.

Remember that keeping your foundation dry is important, so landscaping that requires moisture should be a minimum of six feet from your foundation.

Framing Exterior Walls and Openings

Exterior Wall Construction

$$$ Wall construction of 2 x 4 studs gives a 3½" wall thickness. An alternate method is to use 2 x 6 studs, which provides two extra inches of wall cavity to insulate.

The 3½" cavity can very satisfactorily insulated if the insulation is installed carefully. This includes filling all gaps created by wires, pipes and ducts, as well as foam air sealing around the perimeter of each cavity.

The 2 x 6 construction, in addition to creating additional insulating area is eco-friendly because less lumber is required. Insulation is important in cold and hot climates because superior insulation is need for both.

Insulated Concrete Forms

For superior insulation and structural stability, and additional cost, foundations can be made with insulated concrete forms. These walls can be made of two outer layers of styrofoam or concrete block that are filled with an insulating foam. This structure provides storm resistance and superior sound insulation. If this idea interests you, find a builder who has experience in installing "ICFs." Also check the Website Directory on page 234 to learn more about insulated concrete forms and structural insulated panels.

Structural Insulated Panels

Another newer technology is structural insulated panels (SIPS) which can be the home's walls, roof or both. They are made of two outer sheets of OSB (oriented strand board) which is the chipped wood product commonly installed as exterior walls, with styrofoam between. The concept is that this form of uninterrupted insulation improves its performance over other insulation that may be interrupted by wires, pipes and ducting. SIPS provides channels for the pipes, ducting and wires.

Sub-floors

A non-squeaking floor is made from prefabricated joists that are engineered to resist warping and shrinking. The sub-floor is glued, and then nailed to crossbeams. Sub-flooring can be ½", ⅝" or for greatest strength, ¾" plywood.

Holes are cut out of the sub-floor to accommodate pipes that go from one floor to another. Foaming or caulking in the space between pipe and wood helps to keep air and noise from infiltrating to the floor above. Floors that will include radiant heat need special preparation.

Front Entry/Balcony/Terrace/Porch

An attractive feature of your home's exterior is a front entry that is readily visible, has a distinctive form and offers some shelter.

Covered balconies and porches not only provide lovely outdoor living spaces, but also increase energy-efficiency. Their roofs serve as overhangs that provide natural shade to your home, most effectively within 30° of south on either side of due south.

Consider adding an enclosed or screened porch if you live in an area favored by mosquitoes. This addition will also provide protection from the sun's heat or from a cold wind. Keep in mind that an upper level balcony or terrace outside of children's bedrooms can be a dangerous place for them to play.

Garages

Garage location/style

Attached

If the garage is attached to the home, is the entrance from the garage to the home convenient to the kitchen, the staircase, or to another popular room? Does this attached garage dominate the front of the home and offer poor curb appeal? (See page 22.) How many steps must you climb between garage and house proper? The more garage steps, the more climbing, and the more garage space that is taken up by steps.

Detached

Detached garages, often accessed by back alleys, are making a reappearance in some communities. A separate garage is a greater expense but is one way to create a more attractive house front and better curb appeal. Access to the home needs to be sheltered. Other issues are maintenance of alleys and, in cold climates, snow removal.

Integral

Especially in hilly terrain, garages can be included as part of the ground level. This design requires less space, and if the garage is on the side or back, offers better curb appeal than a design that has an attached garage dominating the house front. Since it is on the lower level, you are likely to be climbing a flight of stairs to the main living area.

Garage size

Over-sizing

Consider over-sizing your garage to two and a half, three or four spaces. Increasing garage space generally increases value as well as making a statement of affluence. Extra garages are often used for additional cars as teenagers come of driving age. If you don't need this space for extra cars, you may have a camper, boat, motorcycle, snowmobile, ladder, or other household item that requires storage. If you can't foresee any possible need for this much space, your money may be better spent on other areas of your home.

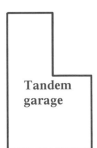

Tandem garage

Tandem

If you don't have the width to expand to the side, your homesite may accommodate a tandem garage that extends one or more of the garage spaces to twice its length. This allows for extra storage, a workshop, an extra room that can be finished, or space for a vehicle, especially one that doesn't come in and out daily.

Extra Height

Depending on how it affects any living space above the garage, you may want to raise garage height. The look of the exterior will also be affected but this option creates room for a full-size truck, camper, canoe, roof rack with skis, surfboard and more. The added height may also be useful for overhead storage of sporting equipment.

Garage doors

Single-width garage doors are lighter to operate and usually offer more space per car than double-width doors. Either style may be solid material or have plain or decorative glass inserts. New styles include "carriage house" and art deco glass inserts.

Automatic garage door openers

Automatic garage door openers are an enormous convenience in our automobile-oriented society. Because they are used so many times daily, pay attention to brand and quality. Springs tend to "get sprung" with frequent use. Whether you have openers installed or not, have each door's control button pre-wired. Include an electrical outlet on the ceiling near each potential opener

Keyless pad entry

Another popular option, especially for use by children, is a keyless pad entry. If they can keep the code a secret, your home will remain locked and secure without having to distribute keys that can be misplaced or forgotten. Codes can be changed when necessary, although this may not be an easy task on some models.

Circuit breaker

Being able to disengage the garage door openers by turning off a dedicated circuit breaker or a connection on the structured wiring is advantageous when leaving home for an extended period because codes are not completely burglar-proof. A low-cost alternative is to simply unplug the opener on these occasions.

Garage service door

Most garages are required to have either a door or window in the garage for safety, in case someone becomes trapped inside. Sketch each car, to scale, and all items to be stored, especially large items. This will help you to decide *where* this exterior door should be located.

GARAGE

Also consider how you'll use this door. Will people be using this entrance from the street? Will it be used to access the backyard? Should this door be included within a fenced area, or excluded from it? If the door is hinged, should it swing to the left or right and will it be able to open fully with cars in the garage?

Service door to back

Garage finishing

Garage finishing can include insulation behind the wallboard on ceilings and walls. Walls can be textured and painted. Concrete floors can be stained and sealed beautifully, if this has value for you. Another type of floor that may be available is a poured composite material, which comes in a variety of colors and finishes. A creative use of this space is to paint basketball court lines on the floor, and attach backboards on opposing walls. Back the cars out and play!

GARAGE

Service door to side

Since each idea has a cost, be clear on your budgeting priorities. Whether garages are finished or not, it is vital that insulation and foam sealing of walls between garage and living space are carefully and thoroughly done to avoid infiltration of toxic fumes to living spaces.

Driveway

Length/ slope/ width

The length and slope of your driveway may involve safety issues. Consider that someone may need a level area for wheelchair access; that those in cold climates should consider ice and snow shoveling; also the safety of children who might "zoom" their bikes down the driveway into the street.

For the snow removal issue, consider a southern or western orientation, so that the lingering afternoon sun can do some of this work. Do you need extra space for a camper or other vehicle? If your neighborhood is restricted by covenants, will the covenants (and your neighbors) allow you to park it in your driveway?

Basketball court

Might you want your driveway to also serve as an informal basketball court? This requires a relatively level driveway and a place to set up a backboard. If space permits, the backboard can be attached to the garage wall. Alternatively, a pole with backboard can be cemented into the ground, in front of the driveway, or a free-standing backboard can be portable. This is an item that is sometimes restricted by covenants.

Windows

Windows add beauty to our homes and allow us to enjoy the outdoors from the indoors. In addition to your home's walls, windows are part of the "thermal envelope" and therefore provide protection or lack of protection from the heat or cold of outdoors.

The idea of living in a glass house may have appeal, but the skyrocketing energy bills that often result from the home's systems attempts to effectively heat or cool that home aren't nearly as attractive.

Imagine living in each room to determine what shape and size of windows are desirable, and if any should be added or subtracted. Consider each window's orientation to views, light and wind or prevailing breezes. Windows on two walls give the best light, ventilation and feel of spaciousness. Where will furniture be placed in each room? Does a window eliminate necessary wall space?

Bathroom windows located high on a wall afford privacy and light but no view; lower windows may need textured glass for privacy. Is it important to you that these windows open? Efficient ventilation should be provided by the room's exhaust fan. Old-style inexpensive fans are noisy and ineffective, making newer models well worth the additional cost.

Window style

Double hung

This style allows some air to seep in and out along the tracks on each side. It can be raised from bottom or top, allowing ventilation through 50% of the window. It may also feature removable panes for ease of cleaning.

Double hung

Glider

Gliders or sliding doors allow some air infiltration along the seam where windows meet. The window can be opened slightly while maintaining security by utilizing breaks along the slide or by placing a block of wood along the runner. This style allows only half of the window to be open or screened for ventilation.

Glider

Casement

$$$ Casement-style windows are an excellent design for preventing air infiltration (escape of your warm or cooled air to the outside.)

They allow windows to be in a fixed open position, offering some security and also some protection from weather. Open casements can shake in the wind; protruding handles can interfere with curtains or blinds. Flatter handles are an available option. Casements allow full screen ventilation.

Casement

Awning

An awning window is often in combination with a large fixed window above it. This arrangement affords a large unobstructed view on top with ventilation below. The awning is a horizontally-placed casement window. Its handles allow the window to be open in a fixed position, providing some security and protection from rain.

$$$ Quality awning windows are excellent at preventing air infiltration, and allow full screen ventilation.

Awning

Picture or fixed

$$$ Fixed windows (the top part of the awning, illustrated) do not open and are used where windows are too high to be operated or in combination with other windows that do open. Fixed windows, if good quality and properly installed, are energy efficient.

Bay and bow window

Bay or bow windows, open or fixed, can be shaped to enlarge a room's area and add style. In some situations, a window seat can be built into the curved area created by the bay or bow.

Bay

$$$ When bay and bow windows are casement or fixed, and have proper insulation and air sealing around them, are good choices for energy efficiency.

Bow

Window frame material

Wood with vinyl or aluminum cladding

Vinyl- or aluminum-clad wood windows offer the rich look and superior insulation quality of wood on the inside and low maintenance on the outside. They are more expensive than single material windows, but this needs to be weighed against the cost of regular maintenance of the exterior wood.

Wood

Wood frames are attractive and can be stained or painted to match your woodwork. Wood is affected by both sun and moisture. All frames will expand and contract with weather conditions, and wood does this best. The outside of wood frames needs frequent painting. Interior stained wood can be protected by applying coats of sealing finish and by installing treated glass (see page 136) which can effectively reduce fading caused by ultraviolet rays.

If you are installing blinds, obtain window depth measurements from your blueprints, builder or architect and then consult with a window dressing expert to be sure they will fit. As long as you're doing this before framing, you may have the option of altering window dimensions or choosing alternate window coverings. The more you know in advance, the better you'll be able to plan and coordinate, getting what you really want.

Vinyl

Vinyl frames require little maintenance and come in colors that can match or complement your décor. They range in quality from unacceptable to excellent. There is difference of opinion about how their insulating capability compares to wood, but vinyl is clearly better than aluminum.

Fiberglass

Fiberglass frames are gaining in popularity as an attractive, low-maintenance alternative to wood and vinyl. Fiberglass window frames can be stained to look very much like wood.

Aluminum

Aluminum frames do the poorest job at blocking heat and cold from being transmitted. Some aluminum frames include a "thermal break" which improves this problem somewhat. Aluminum frames are maintenance-free except for caulking and are low-cost, at least initially.

Window pane dividers (colonial grid style)

In colonial days, windows were made of many small squares of glass. This look is achieved in modern one-piece windows by installing crossed strips of wood or vinyl that are inserted between the panes of glass, or on the outside of their interior surface.

Window jambs

Window jambs, the area between the window's interior and the main wall surface, are usually finished in wood or wallboard. Wood gives the home a richly-finished look and is often recommended as a good investment in your home's overall look.

$$$ Finishing windows in wallboard is a cost-saving measure. It does not have the "picture frame" look of wood trim,but can be decorated very attractively. If you plan to install draperies, window frames may not be visible.

Window quality

🌲 Windows are both functional and attractive. This is not the place to skimp on quality. Poor quality window frames and non-treated glass allow heat and cooling to pass through and around windows. This infiltration of heat in summer and cold air in winter creates discomfort and raises energy bills. Poor quality windows may also become difficult to operate as they begin to age.

Talk with a few window specialists. Get the names and addresses of homeowners who have a particular brand and style of window. If they have no complaints or never gave their windows a thought, they probably have good windows! If their windows are poor quality, this is often their biggest complaint.

In addition to checking on the performance of particular brands and styles of windows, you may want to check on the reputation of a particular window supplier. Do they have a good track record of providing quality windows and installation as well as servicing any window problems?

Window ratings

The National Fenestration Rating Council assigns ratings for windows, which measures heat transmission both from around the window frame and through the glass. This "U-factor" has a range of .01-.10 with LOW numbers the more desirable.

Although the window industry uses U-value, consider what the numbers would be in comparable R-value: walls typically have an R-value of 11 to 19; windows range from R-2 to R-4, with R-3 considered excellent! The NFRC's specifications are available on their website, listed on page 234.

Window glass

Double pane ("ig" for insulated glass)

Double-pane clear glass is least expensive and may be sufficient wherever intense heat from the sun is not a factor. Consider the value and cost savings of low-E windows that will allow the sun's warmth through in winter.

$$$ Low-E

🌲 Consider low-E (for *low emissivity*) glass, at least on south- and west-facing windows wherever solar heat needs to be controlled. The low-E coating(s) blocks the sun's higher-angled rays in summer, but allows the lower-angled winter rays to enter as solar gain. It is also one factor in reducing window condensation on the inside. "Low-E" glass, which continues to be improved (under various brand names) is today's popular choice, even in mild climates.

Argon-filled

🌲 Argon is a gas that can be included between two or three panes of glass. This measure is a superior insulator in a standard double pane window, and a successful combination with a low-E window. Check with local builders and window experts about the cost-effectiveness and advisability of this treatment in your climate.

$$$ *Tinted glass/Low SHGC*

Spectrally-selective window class has been tinted or otherwise specially treated to block the intense heat gain from the sun. SHGC stands for Solar Heat Gain Coefficient, which is the NFRC's standard for measuring the amount of heat that is transmitted through a particular piece of glass.

In predominately sunny climates, this treatment will be well worth the added expense on southern (unless protected by an overhang,) southwestern or western orientation windows. Your alternatives to this low-cost upgrade are covering the windows and view with expensive shades or cranking up the air-conditioning to counteract the heat from summer sun, and still losing the battle.

Laminated glass

For superior protection against very high winds, laminated glass is an expensive, but high-performing choice. Similar to automobile windows, two panes of glass are glued together, creating a "glass wall" that is very strong. Laminated windows also offer superior sound insulation.

Stained or cut glass

Stained (colored) or cut glass is an expensive but beautiful decorative statement. The fixed oblong window(s) on the side (sidelights) or over the top (transom) of the front door is highly visible. (See page 139.) A single cabinet door done in this glass can be a focal point of the kitchen. A stained or cut glass window on any exterior wall will be admired for its uniqueness and beauty.

$$$ Individual pieces of stained and textured glass can be purchased from an art glass store. See page 194 for details. Exterior windows should be professionally installed to prevent air infiltration in hot and cold climates.

Glass and acrylic block

Glass and acrylic block are wonderful alternatives to clear glass for security, privacy and a distinctive look. Their thickness provides an opaque view but allows light in. They are often used in a bathroom but can be used anywhere this look is desired. Today's glass block comes in translucent colors and can have a decorative object embedded in the glass.

Window size/shape

Large windows afford beautiful views of whatever is outside. Before choosing large and unusually shaped windows, consider the cost to cover and decorate them. If windows are at varying levels, will you cover them together, separately or not at all?

Also consider their heat loss and gain, and their potential to transmit glare.

With the orientation to the sun that this room will get and windows placed as planned, will you be inviting direct rays and glare on occupants or the television? If so, is the solution to be regularly shutting out the light and view, or to relocate the television or window?

The appearance and mood created by the combination of window shapes should look balanced from the interior and exterior. Sometimes window types and sizes are mixed within the same room.

Window orientation and overhangs

Consider each window's orientation and view (see page 105.) In sunny climates, consider the natural cooling benefit of a sufficiently deep overhang on the southern side of the home. Southwestern windows are the most difficult to shade because of the lingering low angle of the summer sun. An awning or porch will provide the most direct form of shade.

Northern windows in cold climates offer light without the sun's heat but must do a superior job of blocking wind in cold climates.

Solar Screens

Solar screens are popular in areas of the country that are very warm and sunny. Solar screens can be affixed to the exterior of the window, and as the sun beats down, the screen serves as a shade. Visibility is somewhat compromised but the improved comfort and energy savings make this an attractive option for some. An alternative might be tinted glass for selected windows.

Skylights

Skylights are a wonderful way to add natural light to an area without losing privacy or wall space. They are especially appreciated in darker, north-facing rooms. Skylights can be the only source of light in an interior room that requires no windows. A perfect seal at roof level is necessary to avoid leakage. In an exterior-vented attic, careful insulation of the skylight's vertical walls in the attic cavity should ensure good thermal protection to the home's interior.. Attics that are included in the conditioned space reduce or eliminate the need to insulate the knee walls.

"Viewing" skylight

Until recently, the only available skylight has been a cutout in the roof that allows natural light in. This skylight affords a view of the sky. Consider the sun's orientation. A southern or southwestern exposure will capture maximum light. Also consider the effects of both solar heat gain in the summer, and heat loss through the glass through the winter. Tempered or laminated glass is the popular option for durability and ability to handle expansion and contraction.

"Viewing skylights" can also come with an adjustable shade between two panes of glass. This more expensive window allows you to close the shade to avoid unwanted solar heat, and to save on air conditioning costs. Vents can release heat and be programmed to operate automatically when wired to the thermostat or included in the home's structured wiring.

Tubular skylight

Gaining in popularity is the tubular skylight. This type is much narrower than the viewing skylight and therefore can be installed in places where the larger skylight cannot. The round tube, which ranges from about 10 to 21 inches in diameter, is installed with an acrylic dome fastened on the roof.

The tube can be routed through a closet or other hidden area so that natural light can shine through from the roof and second floor onto the main level below. This type does not allow exterior viewing but does prevent the transference of a significant amount of heat or cold from outside air.

Exterior Doors

Exterior door style

Front door

Your front door can make an impressive statement about your home. Consider its style, privacy and security. In addition to wood, vinyl or metal, consider glass inserts, and one or two half, three-quarter or full sidelights, which should be double-paned and insulated in most climates. This may be a function of the available space on each side of the doorway. These windows can be plain glass, or as decorative and imaginative as budget permits.

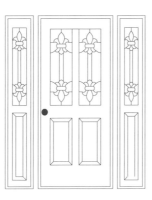

Door with two half sidelights   *Sidelight on side away from door opening for added security*

Windows located adjacent to doors offer light and visibility but may be a security issue for some homebuyers. An alternative is one window on the hinged side of the door, where the door handle is not within reach. A full sidelight affords you a view of your entryway, so that you'll be able to know at a glance if the newspaper or an expected package has arrived. If you choose to have no sidelights and no glass in the door, a peephole should be installed in the door.

If you have wall space over the door, an interestingly-shaped and decorated transom window can add style and light without compromising privacy. Many people like the elegant look of double front doors. Care must be taken that they fit very well to avoid air infiltration between them.

Other exterior doors

Exterior doors include left- or right-hinged, double doors and glider doors. Consider adding glass to hinged or double doors for light and style. Glider doors are most common near patios or terraces and offer the advantage of not requiring "swing" room. High quality gliders are less likely to develop difficulty gliding smoothly, and prevent the air infiltration that often comes with lower quality doors of this type.

Exterior door material

Exterior doors are made of metal, fiberglass or wood. All doors can be painted, but wood is often stained or left natural and sealed. Fiberglass doors are available with a stainable finish that when stained, look remarkably like wood.

Metal can be easily dented; fiberglass is much harder and more durable. Wood is its own beautiful statement but requires maintenance and may, depending on orientation, show the effects of weather with fading and warping.

Consider the strength of both door and frame for security. How deeply will deadbolts screw into the frame? Exterior doors from the home to the garage must meet fire code but don't have to be plain. Wood or a stainable wood substitute may be more attractive and also more practical than a white painted door full of fingerprints. Each upgrade must come out of your budget, so determine their relative value before spending.

Exterior door size

While front doors are typically 36" wide, back and side doors are usually 32" wide. Increasing their size four inches is a small additional expense. If there is any possibility that these doors would need to accommodate a wheelchair or large furniture or appliance, making doors wider is worthy of consideration. (See Universal Design on page 107.)

Exterior location

What will your daily traffic patterns be? Where will muddy or wet shoes and boots be stored? Where will people enter and exit? Consider what people will really do, rather than what you want them to do.

Pay attention to orientation. Doors, especially when painted green or any dark color, absorb heat in the summer. Doors with glass inserts let in solar heat, and are more challenging to cover than windows. From which direction does the wind blow? It might be preferable to hinge this door on the windward side to avoid a gust of wind and dirt each time you open the door.

What is the function of each door? Does the back door lead to the patio, and is it convenient to the kitchen for a cookout? Will this location afford maximum privacy if the neighbor's home is very close to yours?

Exterior door hardware

Locks

Locksets come in many styles. The functional difference is whether a deadbolt is the only lock or a secondary doorknob lock allows you to "lock and go." Deadbolts must be locked with a key from outside.

The advantage to having only a deadbolt is that no one can lock himself out from that door. This is less of an issue if you install a keyless pad entry at one entrance, as long as there are no locked doors beyond this entrance. Also, deadbolts are the most secure locks, and if this is the only lock, it will be used.

Style

While the standard doorknob is still widely used, remember that the front door is part of your curb appeal, as well as a statement to all guests, who generally enter through the front door. Handsome, decorative locksets are on display at design centers and home improvement stores.

Pet Door

$$$ If you have or expect to have pets that go outside, consider their traffic patterns. Pet doors from the home to the exterior allow animals to exit but also allow outside air in.

🌲 A more energy efficient pet door can be installed in a room that can be closed (and locked) from the rest of the home but will allow your pet to enter if you are away for the day or weekend. A safety feature of some doors is electronic entry. The collar that your pet wears is the only manner of entry, preventing other animals from entering. Planning for your pets' needs is part of matching "function to lifestyle," which is the creed of good design.

Interior Doors

Interior door style

Most commonly used is a single-hinged door. It can have a smooth or raised wood surface, real or faux slats. Double hinged doors, also known as French doors, provide a more formal look, are double width for ventilation and clearance through the doorway, which also makes them handicapped-accessible-width. Hinged swinging half or full "saloon doors" offer a distinctive style and some division while maintaining an openness between rooms.

Pocket door

Pocket doors work where space prohibits a hinged door. In small places such as a toilet room, the pocket door is opened by sliding it into the wall. This door is less convenient to operate but is often the best solution in a tight space. Quality hardware and installation are a must for this door to operate properly. Because it requires more construction, it is slightly more expensive than hinged.

Pocket door

Interior door materials

Wood

Will you be staining woodwork and cabinets? If so, you may want to match or contrast stained wood doors, either hollow or solid. Solid wood doors are the most elegant and expensive. You can multiply the number of doors by the additional cost of solid wood to see if this is worth fitting into your budget.

Composite

$$$ Highly compressed particleboard or other wood product, which is always painted offers the strength and contours of a solid door without the cost of wood.

Interior door width

If you'd like to have the ability to accommodate a wheelchair between rooms, having one or more interior doors 36" wide might be a good idea. Be sure the laundry room door is wide enough to accommodate your washer and dryer. Also consider furniture that you may want to transport through the basement or lower level door. (See Universal design on page 107.)

Interior door location

Which way does each door swing? Plan where furniture will be placed in each room and where light switches will be most conveniently located before you decide which way the door should swing.

Notice if any door will be in the way when left open. It is important to imagine all hinged doors in the open position. Do any doors that swing out block an entrance? Is someone likely to run into one? Will two opposing doors interfere with each other?

Corner doors bang into each other

Examine any room that has no door to be sure you won't later want privacy or quiet. See page 26.

My door story

I was standing in the unfinished master bedroom, on the spot where I had planned for months to put our bed. I had imagined just where all of the furniture would be. All of a sudden, as I was looking out the window, I realized that my view would be the baseball diamonds and fences around them in the part of the park that had been built. Not a bad view, but, if the bed were located on another wall, I would wake up to a spectacular mountain view.

The width of the double doors that were planned made the better wall too small for the bed and two nightstands. Panic! This was really important to me because I was planning to wake up in this bed, with this view, for many days and years to come. Was it too late to correct my mistake?

Since the door had not yet been framed, my builder was willing to reduce the door opening to 36" and order a hinged door. Phew! There would be enough wall space for our furniture, and the single door could swing the other way. I was so grateful to have realized my mistake in time, and grateful to my builder for his willingness to be flexible.

But that's not the end of this story. During one of my evening visits to the site, I discovered that the door had been installed, and that it swung the wrong way: right into the nightstand instead of against an empty wall. I don't know whose mistake that was; communication about all these details was a complicated thing. Anyway, the superintendent grinned, and assured me he'd fix that, which he did.

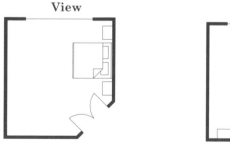

Original door plan   *New door plan*

Closet doors

Standard

Closet door openings of 36" or less may have a standard hinged door with a doorknob or handle. This door swings open and allows access to the entire closet area when open. Its simple design makes it easy to operate. If the closet is in the corner, the wall perpendicular to its door must be left vacant to allow the door to swing open.

Double-hinged

Having two hinged doors allows full access to a wider closet. The inside of one or both doors might be a good location for a full length mirror. This simple style of door also avoids the problem that too often occurs with bifold and bypass doors: falling off their track.

Bypass

Bypass doors are on a track that allows one door to glide in front of the other. Therefore, access to the closet is always only one door width. Bypass doors can be made with mirrored fronts that can be practical and attractive in the bedroom, as well as creating the appearance of a larger room.

Bypass doors

Bifold

Bifold doors fold at a hinge that divides each door in half or more. They hang from a track above and have the advantage of folding, accordion-style, when they are opened, creating greater access area to the closet. These doors can also be made with mirrored fronts.

Bifold doors

Interior door hardware

Hinges

Many of today's hinges have ball bearings, making them quieter and easier to operate. Two-hinged doors lack the structural support in the middle that is part of three-hinge design.

Coordinating hardware

Do you want all of your hardware to be coordinated? Brushed nickel door handles throughout the home may be your choice; what about the fixtures for each bathroom? Also remember the finish of the shower door, towel bars and toilet paper holders. Consider the cost of various finishes when determining what is the best choice for you and your budget.

Locks or no locks

Which doors should have locks and which should not? Should children have locks on their bedroom doors? Should any doors on a Jack and Jill bathroom *not* lock? (See drawing on page 120). Do you have a place to store valuables that should be locked? Check your floor plan to see where locks are a good idea and where they should be omitted.

Doorstops

The standard doorstop that screws into the wall and "bumps back" the door as it makes contact is not always satisfactory, especially in high traffic areas. A quality doorstop installed on the interior side of one of the door's hinges is very effective at stopping the door from creating any damage. Solid doors have strength at all hinges; hollow doors usually have support only in the middle. Another style of doorstop is round and rubber-covered, and is attached to the wall where the doorknob will hit it. This can be effective but unsightly and is subject to damage when hit too hard by the door.

Staircases

Staircases can be against an outside wall or centrally located. They can have two "stages" with a landing in between. A staircase against an outside wall allows for a decorative window, a shallow wall niche or a window seat. A curved staircase makes a dramatic entryway.

Consider the safety of staircase styles for the elderly or children. Curved staircases may not be appreciated by the less sure-footed. Are stairs enclosed by walls or open to the floor below? Is the rise of the steps wide and shallow enough? Is there a railing on both sides, from top to bottom? Is the staircase wide enough for two people to pass each other? Narrow staircases (less than 42") save square footage that can be used for living space but can feel too close. Footlights located on the wall next to several steps or imbedded above each step add to safety.

Railing end cap style, at the base of staircases, varies greatly. This is another item to notice as you tour model homes or magazines.

For homes with basements, notice the location of the doorway. Will the main level door to the basement stairs be in the way when left open? If the staircase has no door at the top, will there be a door at the bottom of the stairs to control traffic and noise into and out of the basement?

Fireplaces

Fireplace location

Is the fireplace located well for functionality and comfort? Where will the furniture be placed for conversation, for television viewing, for whatever function the room serves? You won't be moving the fireplace, so place it wisely. There may be architectural restrictions due to ventilation needs. If you are working from an existing plan, and choose to extend the length of the wall on which the fireplace will be located, be sure that it will be re-centered on that changed wall.

Also remember that fireplaces can generate a great deal of heat. Where would heat be advantageous and disadvantageous? Do you want a fireplace on the lower level? If there will be small children in the home, consider the safety aspects of fireplace styles and placement.

Fireplace style

Single or multi-faced

A single or multi-faced fireplace can be an elegant centerpiece in a corner or between the family room and dining room. A fireplace can be on the dividing wall between bedroom and bathroom or as a room divider for an open area, but be aware of the need for privacy and noise control. First-floor master bedrooms can have a double fireplace installed between bedroom and common living area if privacy isn't an issue.

Fireplace mantle/surround

The fireplace surround can go from floor to mantle (shelf) or continue to the ceiling. The surround can be stone, brick, natural of faux marble, tile or a combination of materials. The mantle can be a wood plank, a beautiful log that you've purchased and finished, stone or almost any material within your imagination and budget.

You may want your fireplace to have a six- or twelve-inch raised base of stone or brick, or be at floor level with a tile apron to protect carpet or wood floor. There may be fire code regulations that must be followed. Raised fireplaces can be a safety concern if "tumbling" children will be playing in this area.

Fireplace construction/fuel

Direct-vent sealed gas

A modern fireplace that is fueled by natural gas and is completely closed to the home interior is known as direct-vent. In place of a masonry chimney through the roof, a vent is directed out through the nearest exterior wall. Fresh air is also received through an external source.

$$$ The amount of heat that radiates through the tempered glass is surprisingly great. You may want to add a blower, which will force even more hot air into the living space, or install a switch for a future blower. Investigate the efficiency rating of fireplaces. If you plan to operate your fireplace frequently, spending a little more initially for a more efficient model may be a cost-effective choice.

Gas fireplaces have either a fixed or adjustable gas flow. Gas fireplaces, or wood fireplaces with gas logs may come with a floor or wall control, or have a wall switch which should be in a convenient location and safely out of children's reach.

How well the dancing fire through ceramic gas logs simulates a wood fire varies greatly. The arrangement of the logs must allow air to pass through them. Since the outside vent on the exterior wall is hot when being used, it must be high enough to be out of the reach of small hands and within code guidelines.

Chimneys/atmospheric or "B" vent

Fireplaces that provide open access to room air and are able to burn wood or may be plumbed for gas are called "atmospheric." They must have a chimney or chase to draw smoke and fumes out, and must also draw in air from somewhere. In the "good old days," the home was leaky enough to supply plenty of air. That's why the wing chair in the picture on page 144 was originally designed, hundreds of years ago, with those side pieces: to keep the awful draft off your head!

Wood-burning fireplaces, when local regulations don't prohibit them, provide the look, sound and smell of a real wood fire. However, unless the flue has a very tight-fitting seal when closed, this is a source of potential heat loss. When the fireplace is being used, some of the smoke will be entering the room and the air that you breathe. Is the location of the flue control convenient for you to operate? Can it be relocated?

$$$ A masonry chimney has traditionally been required for all atmospheric-vented fireplaces. Today's large fireplaces may be able to use a factory-built (Class A) chimney, eliminating the need for costly structural support, brick and masonry all the way to the roof. Any appliance that has been approved for emissions is probably safe to burn but check with your local municipality before purchasing.

Unvented

An unvented fireplace returns toxic fumes to the room, which may or may not be prohibited by your local building code but should be, because it is so unhealthy.

Free-standing stoves

See page 151 for information on free-standing stoves.

Fireplace insulation

$$$ Discuss the insulation procedure of every fireplace installation with your builder. If you live in a cold climate, incorrectly installed insulation and air sealing of the entire exterior wall won't be apparent until the dead of winter, when you're wondering where all the cold air is coming from. The air supply vents on atmospheric-vented fireplaces must have a tightly-fitting seal when closed.

Attic Expansion

Do you have an attic that will be constructed to allow for living or storage space? Will you want insulation appropriate for living space or for storage only? Will the attic rafters give enough depth for sufficient insulation (of living space below) and flooring over it? Do you want any dormer windows installed now or later? These questions relate to whether the attic will be part of the home's conditioned space or not.

If your entry to the attic is through a hatch in the ceiling, do you want fold-down stairs for convenience? Notice the location of the hatch on your blueprints. Is it accessible? Is it located in someone's bedroom directly over where the bed will be? The perimeter of the attic hatch is an important area to have air-sealed.

Interior Walls

Change/remove/add interior walls

Keeping in mind that some walls are load-bearing and cannot be compromised, others can be eliminated to make two small rooms into a larger area. Some walls can be half-height, so that furniture can be accommodated while openness is achieved. Walls can have arches, geometric cuts, plant shelves, or art niches. Anything that isn't made of straight lines is going to add to the cost because it will require more labor.

$$$ A cost-saving measure is to build your home with straight edges. Any angle that is created with flat walls is much faster and easier to construct than an arch, which requires labor-intensive cutting and finishing. Straight-edged cutouts have a cost, but generally less than curves.

Consider adding a wall where openness is going to create too much togetherness. If the doorway is properly framed, double doors (with or without glass) can be installed, which will afford privacy and reduce noise. Decorative columns can add an elegant architectural mood.

Wall architecture may include lighting options. An wall niche may need its own spotlighting. A twelve-inch deep enclosed soffit overhead lends itself to lighting that illuminates the sitting area below.

Window box/window seat

$$$ One way to enlarge the look of a room without the greater expense of expanding the entire room is to extend an exterior area that contains a window. With a seat added, this can create spaciousness and a focal point for the room. The window seat can also be handy for storage. Glass window boxes can be built in front of the kitchen sink or wherever desired. The nooks and crannies of this construction require special builder care to ensure that they are properly insulated and sealed.

Wallboard shelving

$$$ An entire entertainment area (for electronics) can be constructed out of wallboard instead of finished wood. This is also true of built-in shelving in bedrooms, the laundry room or any room. Wallboard is less rich-looking but can be beautifully painted in dramatic accent colors or a faux finish. Your imagination and budget are your only limits. Model homes are a great place to get ideas.

Ceilings

Raised height ceilings

Ceilings can be raised to nine, eleven twelve feet. This gives the home a wonderfully spacious feel, but adds significant cost. Windows can be placed high on the wall, giving light with privacy. For a two-story home, living space may be desirable above these raised ceilings.

Two-story ceilings

Sixteen feet high ceilings give a palatial feel to a room and can have windows placed at sky-viewing level. Because this design involves so much unbuffered wall space, voices may echo, working against a feeling of coziness. Ceilings this high also "waste" an upper level of living space, and provide the challenge of access for hanging decorations, removing cobwebs, painting, and reaching the ceiling fan or light fixture for maintenance.

Vaulted ceilings

Vaulted ceilings follow the roof line and leaves very little or no attic cavity above it. This can be an elegant addition to the master suite or any room and can make small rooms feel larger. It is necessary to ensure proper insulation above vaulted ceilings.

Coffered ceilings

An oblong ceiling inset bordered with molding, called a coffered or tray ceiling, provides an elegant look. The formal dining room, living room, study and any bedroom can benefit from a similar look, as budget permits. Add dramatic flair with indirect lighting.

Coffered or tray ceiling

HVAC
(Heating, Ventilation, Air Conditioning)
for
Health, Energy-Efficiency, Comfort and Safety

$$$ We are in the midst of a building evolution, with homes whose quality is **untested** to "high performance homes" that **have been tested** to prove that they "work." We expect the vehicles we buy to have been performance-tested to determined standards. Today's homebuyers deserve nothing less.

The price of the home may have nothing to do with how well its systems have been designed to work together for your health, safety, comfort and pocketbook. Quality builders are available for every size, type and price of home, but buyer beware.

Part of this evolution is builder participation in "green" certification programs. These programs may be national, state or local. Each should have a list of standards that must be met in order for your home to qualify at a specific level. Local builders need to apply the guidelines to adapt to best local building practices while adhering to program standards.

Because the "greening" of America is a work in progress, your most current information is available by determining what green certification programs are being used in your area. Every home will eventually be built to these standards. Why should you ensure that yours will be? The high performance home will pay you back, in your pocketbook and in other priceless ways.

High Performance Home

What is the high performance home? It's a home, in any price range, that has been designed as systems that must work together to create a home that is comfortable, healthy, safe and energy-efficient. Why aren't all homes designed and built this way? It's only a matter of time, but meanwhile, make sure your home makes the grade.

Lower operating costs

Much lower operating costs (some builders are offering guaranteed energy cost ceilings) put money back in your pocket. We know that paying a mortgage contributes to equity, while paying rent does not. Why pay high monthly energy bills? The cost of fuels for heating and cooling your high performance home should drop dramatically. Performance test results should provide some indication of expected costs to operate its systems.

Water usage should also drop. This includes elimination of all the *cold* water that was wasted as we waited for the *hot* water to arrive at our sink or shower. It may include less need for indoor air humidification and landscape irrigation. Explanations of each are located within its topic area on the following pages.

Health and safety

It's general knowledge that all of today's new homes are "tighter" than in previous decades. Along with this awareness is a concern about the home's ability to provide fresh, healthy air. It's a blessing, and good design that babies don't rely on their parents for respiration! Nor should our homes, which also need to "breathe."

In this wonderful age of technology, builders and HVAC specialists can determine the amount of fresh, filtered air that your home needs. They can also program the system to turn on and off at regular intervals. The homeowner need not worry about the quality of the air the family breathes. What is the "cost" savings of breathing air that is fresh, and preventing the introduction of pollutants and allergens into your home?

While most consumers don't typically worry about carbon monoxide poisoning from their mechanical systems, it does happen and is preventable. For an additional initial cost, a higher efficiency system has dedicated pipes for both fresh air introduction and toxic fume exhaust. This dedicated exhaust pipe prevents the possibility of deadly fumes entering the room due to "backdrafting," which occurs when the room is experiencing negative air pressure.

My comfort story

If my builder had realized how much my children's comfort would be affected by his workers' installation practices, I believe he would have insisted on higher standards. I didn't realize then that north-facing rooms that have unheated space below require carefully installed insulation and air sealing. Ducting that brings heated or cooled air to their rooms and draws old air out must be carefully sealed at each seam for proper air circulation and room comfort

For the past 11 years, their rooms have been horribly cold in winter, and insufferably hot in summer. What a shame! I share this story with builders nationwide, who "feel my pain," which I carry still, as I think of what my children experienced. They appreciate the reminder that real families live in the homes they build. My hope is that many homebuyers read it, too, and that it helps them to choose their builder wisely and spend their building dollars well "behind the walls."

Comfort

Comfort should be the birthright of every room of your home. As shown on page 40 the diagram of the circulatory system can be compared to the heating and cooling systems of the home. The heart represents the furnace, heat pump or air conditioner. The arteries correspond to the supply duct system, carrying conditioned air to every room. The veins correspond to the return duct system that brings old air back for re-conditioning mixed with fresh, filtered air.

Duct segments are pieced together on the construction site. A product called mastic should be applied to each duct connection to ensure that it doesn't leak. Imagine how cold fingers and toes would be if the body's arteries and veins were full of leaks!

The heating and cooling equipment needs to be properly sized. Factors that the HVAC expert should consider are square footage of the home, orientation to sun and wind, number, size and quality of windows and skylights, number and depth of strategically-placed overhangs that will provide natural shade, and any other factors that contribute to the home's "temperature reading."

Heating Systems

Hot air

A hot air system is the most popular type of system in most climates. It can include a standard, 80% efficient furnace or a 90-93% efficient sealed-combustion furnace that exhausts all toxic fumes through a dedicated pipe for safety.

Hot water

Radiant floor heat is quieter than hot air systems but is a significant added expense. If installing radiant floor installations, avoid having pipes installed under the refrigerator and food storage areas where heat is undesirable. *All* homes need a duct system or other way to ensure a supply of fresh air to every room year 'round. Throwing windows open may be one owner's choice but is not a satisfactory design solution.

Heat pump

Warm or cool air can be circulated around living spaces of the home with a heat pump. It is essentially a reversible air conditioner, which pumps interior heat out of the home in the summer, and exterior heat into the home in the winter. It can be fueled in a number of ways, and operated according to need. Heat pumps are appropriate for climates with milder winters.

Furnace fuel

Determine if your system will be fueled by natural or propane gas, electricity, oil, solar, wood or coal. Consider fuel cost and availability.

$$$ Know what energy efficiency rating goes with your mechanical system. The most commonly installed systems are minimum efficiency and may not be worth a small initial savings for higher energy costs for many years. See page 44 for a worksheet on which you can determine which option is less expensive when figured over a number of years, in addition to its impact on the environment.

Size of heating system

$$$ Oversized furnaces result in the equipment running for shorter periods at higher intensity. Similar to stopping and starting your automobile at every traffic light, the system's performance, efficiency and equipment lifetime are severely compromised. Properly-sized equipment will run for longer periods at a lower rate, providing evenness of heating and cooling and therefore greater comfort, performance and equipment lifetime.

Calculating heating and cooling loads

Part of a production home's design is that the number and size of supply and return vents in each room have been pre-determined by considering each room's dimensions, total home square footage, and number and size of windows. Not considered are the effects of hot western sun or cold northern wind hitting the "big window" side of this floor plan when placed with a particular orientation on its homesite.

Custom homes should have all contributing factors figured into calculations, so that every room in the home is comfortable in all seasons. For example, a master bedroom with a southern exposure and large windows will require more cooling registers than the same bedroom with a northern exposure, which will have a higher heat load. All of this is about your comfort, which will become very important to you *after* you've moved in.

Separate zone/separate system

Larger homes (over 2500 sq. ft.) *may* need more than one heating and cooling zone or system. As the building industry improves energy efficient designs, the average properly insulated and sealed house is less likely to need more than one system. If you have concerns about uniform comfort, find out if your home is a good candidate for a second zone or system, especially if individual room temperatures are desired, such as an elderly parent apartment. Radiant floor heat, which is operated with water or electricity, is a natural candidate for zoned comfort.

Another situation that may warrant the expense of a separate zone or system is when the main floor of the home receives daytime heat from the sun, therefore preventing the heating system from running, while the lower lever receives neither sun nor heat and therefore remains uncomfortably cool.

Location of heating system

Heating contractors are the experts, and they like to place the "mechanical systems" right smack in the center of the home. This allows the conditioned air to travel an equal distance to the furthest rooms.

The problem sometimes arises that the optimum location for the mechanicals is an inconvenient location for the homeowner's living space needs. For custom homes, this is something that can be discussed with the HVAC contractor. For production homes, no change is possible, so determine if the configuration is acceptable, or if another floor plan might be a better choice.

Free-standing Stoves

Some homebuyers want a wood-, gas- or pellet- burning stove as a heating zone or system. This may be on the lower level or in an area that is separate from the home, or it may serve as a rustic focal point for the main living area.

Stoves are chosen for their output of heat and their aesthetic value. Today's stoves can be beautiful! And where wood is plentiful, cheap or free, this can be a smart and attractive source of heat. Pellets are tightly-packed pine sawdust. Stoves can be front-, side- or back-loading.

Installation includes a direct-vent through an exterior wall or a stove pipe, either straight or with bends of 45 degrees or less (unlike the illustration!) extending through the exterior wall or ceiling. The area around this cutout should be carefully insulated to avoid heat loss through any gaps. Stoves will need a fireproof base that may be subject to material or dimension requirements. Local regulations should be checked to be sure you are in compliance.

Cooling Options

Whole-house approach to cooling

$$$ The most energy efficient plan is to design your home to be cooled
naturally, with no air conditioning necessary. This *is* being accomplished,
even in some southern states. Elements of such a design would include
utilization of shade trees, optimum plot placement for sun and wind
exposure, roof overhang, excellent windows, superb insulation and air sealing.

What orientation will each room of the home have at each time of day and
year? How large are windows and will they be able to deflect the intense heat
of summer sun? What shade will be provided by trees and extended overhangs
on your home? These questions can affect the land you buy, the placement of
your home on the land, your landscape design and your window budget.
Compare these costs and the immeasurable value of comfort to the cost and
benefits of air conditioning.

Reflective Roof Material

 Especially in southern climates, installing reflective roof materials can
be a highly effective way to cool the attic and home. Your builder will
know if this is a worthwhile expense in your region.

Air conditioning

Depending on climate, homeowners may want air conditioning, unless the
whole-house approach to cooling has been part of the planning process and can
sufficiently meet comfort needs. Central air conditioning cools the whole home
and leaves the noise and unsightliness of the unit outside. Window or wall
units are less expensive, but service one area only.

When to install air conditioning

$$$ Air conditioning can be added to a forced-air system at any time. An
advantage to having it installed by the builder is that its cost will be included
in your mortgage. Possible advantages to deferring this option are to see if it is
needed, to postpone additional cost, and to get a better deal on your own,
possibly off-season.

Correct Sizing and Efficiency of Heating/Cooling Equipment

$$$ Furnaces and air conditioners are too often over-sized for their load. See
page 150 for a description of the value of sizing equipment correctly. Air
conditioners are energy-rated by a SEER (Seasonal Energy Efficiency
Rating) quantification. The 2006 International Residential Code dictates
a minimum standard of SEER 13. The higher the number, the more efficient
the system.

Location of air conditioning equipment

An air conditioning unit is noisy. In some regions, it is roof-mounted. Often, it
is installed very near the home at ground level, along an exterior wall. But
which wall? Consider the noise and hot air that this unit will produce, and
locate it where it is least likely to cause disturbance.

Humidifier

In cold weather climates, it has been standard practice to include a central
humidifier to add moisture to very dry winter air. As homes are built with

better insulation and sealing practices, the moisture that is generated within the home from cooking and showers should provide a satisfactory level of moisture, eliminating the need for a humidifier. This is good discussion material for local builders, who know your climate best.

Dehumidifier

For humid climates, a dehumidifier may be needed, in addition to other equipment, such as an energy recovery ventilator. A floor drain or other plumbing installed nearby avoids the necessity of emptying water by hand.

Evaporative coolers

Evaporative coolers, also called "swamp coolers," can be effective in smaller one-story dwellings in mild climates. If a swamp cooler is right for your home and climate, you may enjoy the more comfortable air that it supplies, compared to the cold, dry air produced by air conditioners. Evaporative coolers do consume large amounts of water, and vary greatly in efficiency.

Whole-house fan

$$$ A low-cost energy-saving addition to a passively-vented attic is a whole-house fan, which should be sized according to the square footage of your home. Most common is 24" square. It is installed in a central location in the ceiling below the attic and pulls the hot air up into the attic, forcing cooler air from outside to enter the home as a breeze. It also pulls in allergens, dirt and pollution from the outside air and can be noisy, but this is a quick and inexpensive way to bring cooler evening breezes into and through your home. The whole house fan needs to have a sealed, insulated cover for winter months in cold climates.

Ventilation

Central ducting/venting of heated or cooled air

Ducting is an item that is often not discussed with the homeowner but should be, because it is so important to comfort and cannot be changed later without ripping out the walls.

For custom homes, the HVAC plan should be specified on blueprints. A major goal is optimum duct size and placement, ensuring strong, even air flow throughout the home. A whole-house approach to HVAC planning will result in a more compact, efficient system and afford more flexibility in location of ducts and vents.

As described in Superintendent's role on page 92, all vent openings should be covered during construction, to avoid wallboard dust and debris from entering the ventilation system. The heating system should not be turned on during construction.

Size /type of ducting

Is the ducting large enough to handle the volume of air the home requires? Is it rigid or flexible? Flexible is cheaper, but is much easier to kink. What is the longest distance the heated or cooled air must travel? Are there any turns or kinks in the ducting along its path?

Return registers (for the old air) must have good "draw," while supply registers must provide sufficient "flow." A cost-saving measure has traditionally been to use wall and floor cavities as the path for return air. For much less air leakage, dedicated ducts will improve comfort and energy savings.

Location of registers

Return registers should not be obstructed by
furniture or draperies. Floor registers aren't safe or
comfortable to step on and are better located when
not in high traffic areas. Pay particular attention to
this if you'll have a glider door. Typically, the door
should be ordered to accommodate the placement of
the floor vent, rather than the other way around.

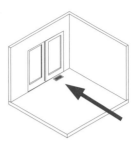

In cold climates, with the main focus on bringing heat
in near the floor and capturing cool air at the top,
return registers are often high while supply registers
are at baseboard level.

*Incorrectly installed
register in front of glider
door*

In warm climates, return registers may be low, to
capture warm air, and supply registers are high or on the ceiling, to bring in
fresh, cool air. The location of registers isn't nearly as important as their ability
to deliver conditioned air or draw old air out of the room. When both work well,
air circulation should be assured.

Basement ducting/vents

If your home will have a basement, request that its ducting be installed flush
(even) with the ceiling so that the basement can later be finished at maximum
ceiling height. Trades can usually at least improve this problem if specifically
directed to do so by the builder. Ideally, the ducting system is properly planned
before installation occurs.

Transfer grilles

Transfer grilles are an effective alternative to individual room registers for
closable rooms such as bedrooms. These grilles are simply holes in the wall,
usually over the door, that allow old room air to be drawn out of the room and
into the central return. They are covered with a vent and should be baffled for
noise and light. Alternately, a gap can be placed over the door top (that serves
as a transfer grille) with the door molding hiding the gap.

Using the space under bedroom doors does *not* allow sufficient draw of old air.
Because the room's air pressure will remain even, the amount of fresh air
entering the room is equal to the amount that is drawn out.

Questionable locations

Ducting should not be
located in
unconditioned space,
including against
exterior walls where
outside air can
adversely affect its
warm or cool contents.
If registers are located
on cabinet toe kicks, is
there a vent right
where you'll be
standing? Will you
want this hot or cold
air blowing on your feet?

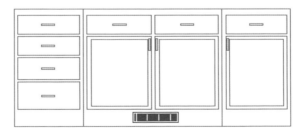

Floor vent in toe kick directly under sink

Hidden vents

More often than you might imagine, holes are not cut in the sub-floor to allow for ventilation through every duct opening. This doomed vent will never be seen or used, but it will leak. Sometimes the hole is cut in the floor, but the carpet installer accidentally covers it.

Quantity/size of ducting/vents

See "Factoring Heating and Cooling Loads" on page 150.

$$$ Your builder should be confident enough of his installation quality to have the duct system inspected or tested (see page 160) for leaks *before* wallboard is installed, for a tight system and long-term comfort and energy savings. You may think that a thorough inspection will be done by the municipal authority, but this is too important an item to leave to chance.

Air filtration

The quality of air filtration has increased greatly, as has the cost of high performance filters. HEPA (high efficiency participate air) filters can theoretically remove at least 99.97% of dust, pollen, mold, bacteria and any airborne particles.

MERV (minimum efficiency reporting value) ratings range from 1-12. A MERV rating of 6 is tested to remove 35-50% of measured particles; a MERV rating of 11 is tested to remove 85-95% of measured particles.

Energy recovery ventilator/heat recovery ventilator

Introducing fresh air into the home also brings in air that needs to be conditioned to room temperature. Air that is exhausted takes with it the conditioning that has been done (and paid for.) The idea of the heat and energy recovery ventilators is to capture the energy before it is released. It also provides some humidification control, although not to a sufficient level for high humidity regions. While the ERV or HRV is an added expense, this is another item that will pay you back in recovered energy and improved air quality. Check with local builders about which system is best in your climate.

Kitchen stove venting

As a cost-saving measure, buyers often choose a recirculating fan in a hood or stove. This makes noise when turned on but does little to eliminate odors or fumes. Strongly consider the extra expense of venting to the outside. For adequate air pull, the ducting must be free of sharp turns or kinks and must be securely taped and sealed to the fan.

Bathroom venting

Bath fans must be vented to the exterior to remove excess moisture. Most bathroom fans in new homes are noisy and not very effective.

Newer models are much better quality and are quieter but are an additional expense. For an item that is used so many times on a daily basis, this expense will be worth it.

Bathroom fans can be switched separately, in combination with a light (so the fan is guaranteed to be turned both on and off whenever the light is) or attached to a timer so that the fan continues to operate for an additional ten minutes or so to remove the excess moisture from a hot shower.

A much pricier option is to have a dual system that blows fresh air into the bathroom while another vent draws air out. This will keep bathroom air especially fresh.

Carbon Monoxide Detectors

Even if your local building code doesn't dictate the installation of carbon monoxide detectors, you may want to have one installed on each floor. This can provide peace of mind if your mechanicals are anything other than electric.

Radon Venting

Radon is a noxious gas that is a decay product of naturally-occurring uranium. Passive venting includes the installation of pipes under the foundation and along the inside of a wall, with the end of the common pipe open to the outdoors, so that gas may escape.

When pipes are installed on an interior wall, the warm pipe will encourage some passive venting as the cooler foundation air heads toward the warmth. In existing homes, active venting includes a powered fan that is attached to the end of the pipe to draw the gas up and out of the home to an exterior wall or the roof. In new construction, power exhausting can be driven by the home's ventilation system.

Other Noxious Gases

Other noxious gases may exist underground in various regions of the country. Your "perc" (percolation) tests should indicate any problems of which you should be made aware. See page 125 for more information.

Central Flue

Your blueprint should show the location of the central flue. This is the main pipe for the release of a hot air system's exhaust fumes to the outside. This is useful to know if you want to build into the wall where the flue is located, such as installing a cabinet or a wall niche.

Thermostat

Modern thermostats are digital and programmable and may be included in your home's structured wiring. They can be set to provide optimum comfort when occupants are home, and a more energy-efficient setting for when occupants are not home. You might want to try operating some of these digital thermostats in a showroom to determine which model is best for you.

The thermostat reads the temperature of the air in its vicinity, so should be located where it can get the truest general temperature reading. If your home is built properly, temperatures throughout should be relatively even.

Also check that the thermostat is installed at general eye level and is in a location that will not be obstructed. It should not be subjected to either sunlight or other source of significant heat, such as a fireplace. The thermostat should always be located on an interior wall.

Insulation

Insulation works when a "dead air space" is created. Insulation by itself cannot do the job; an air barrier such as wallboard or plastic must inhibit air from reaching the insulation on both sides. When this is achieved, along with proper air sealing, very little outside air travels through or "infiltrates."

Tight thermal envelope

The high performance home ensures near-total control over the interior air temperature and quality by providing as tight a thermal envelope on the outside as is possible. Intentional leakiness is NOT the way to introduce fresh air,. Properly-designed ventilation should be part of every new home's birthright. So how do we achieve a tight thermal or building envelope? By paying attention to all of its parts: roof, exterior walls, windows, skylights and doors.

Types of insulation

Growing in popularity is blown-in or sprayed-on forms. Fiberglass and cellulose are blown into a wall or attic cavity, between the sheathing on the outside and whatever air barrier is used on the inside. Foam, usually in open-cell form, is sprayed into walls, on roof interiors, anywhere a cavity exists.

Insulating the attic

Conditioned attic

Including the attic cavity as part of the home's conditioned space contributes to the solution to two common problems: circulating air removes excess humidity, and normalizing the temperature of the otherwise stiflingly hot summer attic and frigid cold winter attic. This helps the home to remain comfortable and reduces its energy need in heating or cooling. Talk with local builders about the advisability of this practice in your region.

Gable vent   *Ridge vent*

Unconditioned attic

If the attic is to remain outside of the conditioned space, it must be properly vented to allow the living space's rising moisture to be released. This includes the proper type, quantity and location of passive vents.

$$$ The minimum R-value (resistance value) for attic insulation may be determined by building code but you should also research optimum R-value for your climate. The Department of Energy (DOE) has a website (see page 234) that lists R-values by zip code.

Insulating Exterior Walls

Housewrap

$$$ Housewrap effectively protects the home's sheathing from wind and sheeting rain. This product is similar to the material used in those indestructible white mailing envelopes. It provides a continuous barrier but is permeable to allow moisture to escape from the home's interior.

Rigid board

Many high performance home builders install sheets of an extruded polystyrene product such as Styrofoam™, sometimes referred to as rigid board, to the exterior of the sheathing. Its job is to contribute to a tight thermal envelope.

Insulating behind exterior wall fireplaces

$$$ In cold climates, the area behind and around fireplaces (which is often a cantilevered or "bumped out" wall) must be well-insulated. This includes sufficient insulation against every exterior wall surface and an air barrier and air sealing to prevent outside air from "sneaking in" around or through the insulation.

Insulating special care -- exterior walls

Bathtubs

Exterior walls with bathtubs and showers against them should have an air barrier, insulation, moisture-resistant "backer board" and caulking behind the tile wall or the fiberglass bath/shower enclosure. This needs to be done prior to tub installation.

If you plan to inspect work on your home, do so before the tub is enclosed and walls are up. Plumbers have been known to leave big holes around small pipes, sometimes allowing bathroom air to get into insulated exterior walls, which can cause heat loss and condensation. Detecting heat loss, either by level of discomfort or by use of an infrared camera is the more expensive way to correct this problem.

$$$ A sweet little tip for comfort and energy-efficiency is to have the outsides of the bathtub wrapped in fiberglass batting before the tub is enclosed. Along with proper wall insulation, this measure will keep the water in the tub warm for a longer time and will muffle noise. Free-standing tubs may have some level of built-in insulation.

Walls behind cabinets

In cold climates, the exterior wall behind cabinets in the kitchen and elsewhere should have the same insulation, air barrier and air sealing as all other walls, to prevent pipes from freezing and heat from escaping. When these walls are inadequately sealed, the cabinets can be very cold.

Washer/dryer and dishwasher

Your builder should ensure that areas behind washer, dryer and dishwasher are properly insulated and foamed or caulked if they are exterior walls, to prevent pipes in cold climates from freezing and to keep the whole home warmer and more energy-efficient.

Attached or integral garage

It is crucial that air sealing between garage and home is carefully done to prevent any carbon monoxide from entering the home. This includes walls and doors and can be achieved with blown-in or sprayed-on product and foam caulking.

Attic

In unconditioned attics, all meeting points between the attic and the interior of the home should be carefully foamed or caulked to keep conditioned air in and unconditioned air out.

Insulating rooms over the garage

Any room in a cold climate that is located over an unheated space is a greater challenge to keep comfortable. Unless insulation (preferably blown-in) and air sealing are done properly, this room will be affected by the outdoor temperature. A completely filled cavity is less likely to succumb to gravity, which encourages air gaps.

Ask questions about how this area will be made comfortable. The heating and cooling systems must provide sufficient air return and supply. Factoring heat and cooling loads, which includes consideration of the size of the area, number, size, quality of windows and their orientation to sun and wind, and effectiveness of insulation, will significantly affect the area's comfort.

Insulating vaulted ceilings

Vaulted ceilings follow the shape of the roof. They add spaciousness to a room, and extend the height of the walls, allowing for more window area. Because vaulted ceilings are not horizontal, gravity doesn't help insulation to stay in place. Unless insulation is properly installed, with all gaps foamed or caulked, heat or cooling will be lost and comfort compromised.

Whole-envelope foaming/caulking

Where walls have been drilled or cut for electrical outlets, wall switch plates, windows or anything else, the area around the cutout should be foamed or caulked. This includes cutouts around pipes in the kitchen and bathroom and in exterior walls for water, air conditioning and sprinkler stub pipes. The perimeter of each window and where exterior walls meet the foundation should be thoroughly foamed or caulked.

Interior Wall Insulation

$$$ A low-cost measure that can improve the quality of the living space is to add insulation between interior walls. This adds sound as well as thermal insulation. Consider rooms listed on page 45.

Resilient channel

$$$ Another effective, low-cost measure is resilient channel. This is a specially-formed strip of metal which is fastened to studs before wallboard is applied to reduce sound transmission between floors. It does a surprisingly good job for a modest charge.

Whole-house Testing

A "tight" house allows you to control the flow of air and is therefore a good interview subject before choosing a builder. Many builders are on the learning curve with this concept while others are downright passionate about energy efficiency and quality insulation. Remember that, while quality building is likely to add to the initial cost, the smart homebuyer will reap the benefits of reduced energy costs and improved comfort for many years.

Sight check

One quick and useful method of helping to have your new home function as designed is to visually check all insulation and air sealing before wallboard is installed. This will be even more effective if an educated eye is available.

Blower door

$$$ After the home is completed, air leakage throughout the home can be detected with a blower door test. This "door," which is made of cloth and has a large, built-in fan, completely fills a doorway. All windows and doors are closed, the fan is turned on and the house becomes pressurized or de-pressurized. A technician checks all areas with a special chalk dust device. If heat is escaping through a crack, chalk dust will be sucked into (or blown away from) the crack which can then be caulked.

Duct blaster

$$$ A test that is similar to the blower door test can be performed on the entire duct system to determine its level of leakage. A maximum of 10% leakage is the goal for the high performance home. This test can be performed before the wallboard is installed, allowing for tightening of the duct system during construction.

Infrared photography/thermography

$$$ An infrared camera, used on a cold winter day, will show areas of heat loss. With a color camera, cold will appear blue. If black and white, cold areas will be dark. The challenge is to access the area that needs attention, which is likely to be behind the wallboard.

Roof

Shape/Overhang

Drive around neighborhoods, observing
different roof shapes and combinations
of shapes, materials and colors as they
look on existing homes.

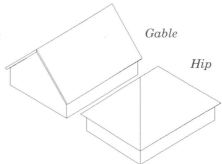

Gable

Hip

If you are working with an architect on
a unique design, you may want
unusually shaped roof lines to make
an architectural statement.
Combinations of shapes can create
interesting forms but add significant
cost.

A metal strip installed across the lowest edge of the roof is called a drip edge.
This allows water to flow into gutters without soaking the edge and underside
(eave.) In cold climates, many roofing experts strongly recommend installation
of an ice and water shield if a drip edge is installed to prevent build-up. Talk
with your builder about either of these options.

An extended overhang on southern, eastern and western exposures
provides excellent natural shade. Overhangs, at a depth of 1 foot for
every 8 feet of wall, are most effective within 30° degrees of due south.

Roof Material

Asphalt and tile shingles come in a variety of colors. Concrete tile is made in
barrel, shake and slate shapes. Tile is best at reflecting heat, as are light
colors, so both are preferable in warm climates. Reflective tile is popular in
southern climates.

Other options include sheet metal and metal shingle, shake shingle and
natural slate. Each of these materials gives the home a specific look and can be
part of a coordinated architectural design. There are roofing materials made
with recycled vinyl plastics that are made to resemble slate, tile, or other
traditional materials. They are extremely durable, but carry a cost premium.

Advanced solar technology features the incorporation of solar energy
collectors directly in the roofing materials. These are available for both
thermal solar and photovoltaic systems, and are virtually indistinguishable
from a "normal" roof.

Check covenants for any requirements or restrictions on roof material or color.
Also consider fire resistance rating, local fire history and fire insurance cost.

Roof Color

Before deciding on a roof color, preview both the color and style on an existing
home. Colored tiles or shingles tend to look much brighter in quantity than on
a single sample piece. Roofs last a long time and their color will be a bold or
neutral feature of the home. Be certain that you want to live with this roof
color for the next twenty years and are not concerned about how this might
affect resale value.

Dormers/Cupola/Attic

Dormers may be added for function or style or both. Functioning dormers add light and the feeling of spaciousness to the room. They require special attention for proper insulation and air sealing.

Decorative, non-functional dormers are "outside of the envelope." Both styles offer an interesting roof design and added cost. Decorative cupolas, such as weather vanes, add a distinctive touch to the overall style of the home. This can be part of your plan for ultimate curb appeal.

If you want the capability to expand your living space upwards at a future time, or use this space for storage, special construction and insulation may be necessary to allow for flooring and standing height. Stairs would be necessary for living space rather than an attic hatch.

Gutters

The purpose of gutters is to keep water away from the home's foundation, so that it remains dry. Gutters should drain water at least five feet away from the home, depending on climate. They are usually galvanized steel and can be painted to match exterior trim.

Exterior Wall Siding

Siding Material

Drive around neighborhoods noticing various exterior treatments, including clapboard or lap siding (either wood or composite material,) brick, stone, stucco, stained wood and anything else you discover.

Solid brick or brick veneer adds significant cost to your home but then requires almost no maintenance, while wood must be painted or stained periodically. Stucco or synthetic stucco is also more expensive but creates a special look, requires less maintenance. Brick or stone accent on a home adds some cost but may improve both the presentation of the home and its eventual resale value. Log homes (or logs of composite material) are usually a specialty of particular builders and should be carefully researched.

Address Plaque

With a brick or stone front wall, consider including an engraved concrete block or glazed tile insert which can be built into the brick or stone for a lovely and permanent finish. If your front wall is already completed, the address plaque can be fastened to the brick or stone but won't be recessed. A lighted address plaque is the most visible at night.

My address plaque story

I admired engraved concrete address plaques on several houses. They looked much classier to me than nailed-on brass numbers and were a permanent part of the house. One evening, while checking with the superintendent in charge of my home, I mentioned that I wanted to have a plaque installed in the brick. He informed me that the masons would be arriving the next morning!

I learned the address of the nearby manufacturer and visited them the next day. I chose a style and wrote down the plaque's exact dimensions. I headed back to the construction site and left the information with the masons. They were happy to leave a space for the plaque, bricking around it. Several weeks later, I picked up the plaque, which the masons eventually cemented in. My builder and the masons were very nice to accommodate my late request. If circumstances (including scheduling issues) had been different, they might not have been able to help me. My address plaque is beautiful!

Exterior Paint

A good quality exterior paint job will be a cost savings because re-painting in a few years is expensive. Will the builder provide one color only, a second color for trim, a third color for accent? If possible, get addresses of houses displaying your color choices.

Exterior paint colors look much *lighter* on walls than they do on a paint sample. Interior paint colors look much *darker* on walls than on a paint sample. This is due to the effect of light on each.

If there are areas that shouldn't be painted, such as a fiberglass front door that is to be stained, be sure that the superintendent is clear on what gets painted and what does not, since attempting to remove paint is not an attractive chore.

Plumbing

Water Heaters

Tank

Hot water tanks are heated by electricity, natural gas, propane or oil. Determine the efficiency rating of whatever brand and model your builder provides in the specifications and materials list. If you expect to have water demand that include a large bathtub, family or frequent guests who shower at the same time, or you plan to run the dishwasher or washing machine at shower time, consider installing two standard-size water heaters. Oversized water heaters are generally less efficient.

Two tanks

One method of operating two heaters is for the secondary heater, which is kept at a lower temperature, to feed its warm water, as needed, into the primary heater, which is kept at the desired temperature. The other method is to operate the heaters in parallel, keeping both at the desired temperature. The "series method" offers some energy savings while the "parallel method" provides the largest amount of hot water at a given time. Plumbers are the experts on what configuration is best for your home.

$$$ Energy-efficient, safer water heaters feature sealed combustion. They have a higher efficiency rating and avoid the danger of carbon monoxide escaping into breathing air with the installation of a dedicated pipe that is vented to the outside.

Tankless

Tankless water heaters heat water on demand, avoiding the expense of keeping water hot 24 hours a day. This is clearly a good choice for vacation homes that aren't occupied year 'round. It is also the choice of many high performance home builders for all of the homes they build.

Tankless heaters vary in how quickly they provide water, ranging from 1 to 13 gallons per minute. Determine your water needs (see Website directory on page 234) and consider any high demand situations such as an 80-gallon soaking tub.

The tankless heater's small size is easily mounted on a wall. It comes in gas and electric models, interior and exterior. Gas models are much more efficient than electric but must be vented to exhaust toxic fumes. Its life expectancy is about 20 years but has a higher initial cost. Larger homes may require multiple units.

Circulating

A loop plumbing system can have pumps installed at each end point (sinks, tubs) delivering hot water on demand. The pump can operate by motion sensor or a push button. The pump is activated, supplying hot water within a few seconds. The pump then automatically stops.

Solar

Solar or thermal systems are growing in popularity as homebuyers choose to lower their energy usage and utilize the sun's powerful "free" rays. Solar systems can be supplementary or stand alone for hot water; they can operate for multiple energy needs in concert with a photovoltaic system. See the Website directory on page 234 for the most current information on solar technology.

$$$ Wrapping water heaters in fiberglass blankets and pipes in foam saves energy and money.

Location of Water Heater(s)

Homerun plumbing

A solution to standing at the sink in the morning, wasting cold water as you wait for the hot water to arrive, is homerun plumbing.

Instead of having one loop that carries water all through the home, a separate connection is made between the hot water source and each destination, minimizing its travel distance.

For tankless systems, the number of tanks needed will help your builder determine best locations.

Water heaters should not be located near windows because small cracks in the window openings can adversely affect draft patterns. If your water heaters are in the basement, does the location break up an otherwise large, usable room?

Pipe Size and Material

If you build in the same area as the model homes you've visited, test the water pressure. You may want to ask your future neighbors about their water pressure. If it is too low, you can ask your plumber or builder about the advisability of installing larger diameter pipes.

The homerun plumbing configuration described and illustrated above requires PEX vinyl pipe material. The noise level from rushing water may be higher with the PVC or vinyl pipes, but its cost may be lower. Ask local builders about the advisability of using PEX or copper piping.

If you know that you will be shopping for specific or unusual faucets, check that the valves installed will accommodate your chosen faucets.

Surge Protection

Building code should require surge protection in the water pipes. This feature can also be added to an existing system by installing pressure balance faucets. This prevents a scalding shower at the moment someone else flushes the toilet.

Shut-Off Valves

If water should suddenly pour from a faulty or broken toilet, faucet or washing machine, you may want a shut-off valve at that site will be appreciated. The cost-cutting measure of centralizing shut-offs won't be appreciated in a plumbing emergency.

Kitchen Plumbing

Kitchen sink installation

Under-mount

Today's kitchens often feature countertops that have no "lip" or raised edge around the sink, so that food scraps and liquids can be more easily pushed from the countertop into the sink. The countertop material must be non-porous in order to have a separate under-mount sink, which is attached to the underside of the countertop.

Drop-in

Laminate countertops, which are made of a thin layer of plastic that is glued to a permeable wood product usually require drop-in (self-rimming) sinks. There is currently a sink available made of a composite plastic material that is integrated with a laminate countertop seamlessly.

Tile countertops often have self-rimming sinks but can have a grouted-in sink that achieves the same benefit as under-mount sinks. The choice of mounts affects the type of sink that must be ordered.

Kitchen sink material

Porcelain

Porcelain (porcelain-enameled-cast iron) sinks come in many colors and have an attractive glossy finish that should last for decades. Their hard nonporous surface makes them easy to clean but they can be chipped, and are unforgiving when a glass or dish is dropped.

Stainless steel

Stainless steel can be coordinated with other appliances. This surface requires frequent removal of fingerprints, and is subject to dulling with frequent use, but stainless steel sinks offer some cushioning when breakables are dropped. Sinks can be dropped into any countertop or be under-mounted with composite, marble, granite or concrete for a smooth edge.

Composite

Composite material is a polymer (some form of plastic) that has no seams, is heat resistant and can be made into a single-piece sink and countertop, affording easier cleanup of debris. The issue of stain resistance should be investigated before purchase.

In-sink hot water

Many homebuyers appreciate a tap at the sink that dispenses instant hot water from a heater that is located under the sink. It is an additional cost, but can be a worthwhile convenience.

Garbage disposal

See page 198 in the Appliances section for a description of garbage disposal options.

Kitchen faucets

Style

Visit a plumbing showroom to see the latest among many designs. Some faucets have built-in sprays. Options include single handle or two handles for hot and cold water. Also useful are separate pump dispensers located next to the faucet for liquid soap, liquid detergent and hand lotion. Most sinks have a number of pre-drilled holes that will easily accommodate one or more of these pump dispensers, which can be included now or after construction.

Color

You may want your faucets to be a color that will match or complement your décor. Dispensers or other accessories can match or be in different colors that will remind everyone of the contents of each.

Filtration systems

Built-in water filtration systems can provide purified water through faucets and the refrigerator's ice and water dispensers. For areas with hard water, built-in water softeners are available.

Bathroom Plumbing

Bathtubs

Soaking

Standard bathtubs are five feet long, measured from one edge of the entire enclosure to the other, meaning that the tub isn't five feet long. Many master bathrooms now have triangular or six foot (total length) long bathtubs which allow average-height bathers to stretch out in the tub. With its greater width, this is also a friendlier arrangement for two. Filling this tub requires about 40 gallons of water.

A hot tub for a small or large group is a luxury to consider as budget permits. This can be located in a generous master bathroom, outdoors on the patio, on or under the deck or in a gazebo or other outbuilding.

Jetted

Tubs that include a water-moving motor, in jets or a fine stream of tiny air bubbles is much-appreciated by anyone seeking the therapeutic value of moving water. Notice the location of jets, which varies by manufacturer. Do you want them to hit the small of your back or be located along the sides of the tub?

The electric motor that moves the water may require maintenance at a future time. A panel should be constructed that provides sufficient access for repair. Too often there is no access panel or one that is too small to be useful.

A luxurious "tub within a tub" allows the bather to be fully immersed in warm water as excess water spills over into the outer tub. Some models feature colored lights so that you can have a green-, blue- or violet-colored bath!

Material

Tubs are usually porcelain-enameled-cast iron, enameled-steel, acrylic or fiberglass but can also be natural or cultured marble. Porcelain offers a much more durable, rich finish for very little more than enameled-steel. Acrylic or fiberglass requires very careful maintenance in order to remain clean and attractive. Marble is the most costly but will retain its beauty for many years.

Since bathtubs are rarely replaced, make this choice wisely. All bathtubs, except free-standing "footed" tubs, can be wrapped under and around their outside with fiberglass batting. This small extra detail will help to keep the water warm and reduce noise.

Bathtub/shower combination

The combination bathtub/shower can include a bypass glass shower door, in two or three sections. Less expensive are a shower rod and curtain, which can be part of the room's décor and allow openness. Glass enclosures avoid the annoying "hugging shower curtain" that occurs when air currents so direct.

Shower stall and niches

The 36" by 36" shower is too small for many homeowners, including larger people and all women who need enough "elbow room" for shaving legs. One or more shower seats may be desirable.

Cultured marble or tile shelves or niches for shampoo and soap can be inset in the shower wall for a modest charge. Be sure that their depth and height will accommodate your largest, tallest bottles.

Multiple jets/steam enclosure

Multiple jets in the shower offer a "vertical" massage. One or more jets spray water at various parts of the body.

A steam shower is completely enclosed, including a tile ceiling and a bottom-to-top shower door for a luxurious experience with steam. Some models allow you to add your favorite aromatherapy oil to this experience.

Shower door

Bypass doors (one door slides in front of the other on a track.) offer the advantage of not dripping water outside of the shower, but require a double-wide opening. A hinged shower that swings *out* deposits water along its path. If your shower is large enough, you may be able to have a hinged door that swings *in*.

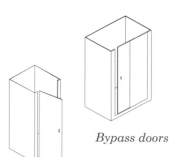

Bypass doors

Hinged door swinging out

Shower doors are tempered glass or Plexiglas® for safety, so that if someone falls against the glass, it will not shatter. It can be ordered in clear, tinted or textured glass. Translucent glass gives a spacious feel to the room. Tinted glass comes in several shades including bronze and smoke. Textured glass comes in a variety of patterns and prices but is usually more expensive than clear or tinted glass.

My shower story

I had priced some shower enclosures in a home improvement store, so when I arrived for my appointment at the glass specialty store to choose the colors of metal frame and glass for shower and tub enclosures, I was surprised at how much more expensive they were than those I had seen in the home improvement store. I asked the clerk about it, who seemed to be insulted and didn't have much to say.

But I later discovered that there was an answer; after having used my new shower, I appreciated that the quality of the custom-built shower and bath doors was much higher than that of the ready-made enclosures I had been pricing, and I realized that the clerk could have spoken with pride.

Toilets

Quality-built toilets are well worth their cost, so a little research in this area is advisable. Asking your builder's references about the functionality of their toilets may be a little embarrassing but daily use of plungers is worse.

Today's toilets are made more efficiently and use less water for flushing, usually 1.6 gallons or less, which is sufficient if well-designed. In addition to standard and low height tanks, toilet base heights come in 15" standard and 18" chair height. Also available are two-stage flushers, a concept that requires no explanation.

Toilet seat shapes

Toilet seats come in two basic shapes: round and elongated. Many people choose elongated for greater comfort. The only consideration here, besides the possibility of a slight additional charge, is that elongated toilet lids may require elongated lid covers. "Try on" various shaped toilet seats when away from home, as you realize that this building adventure is making you think of things that you never before noticed!

Bathroom sinks

See page 50 for a list of sink materials. Many buyers spend handsomely on the master bathroom, but choose the cheapest fixtures in other bathrooms. This often means enameled-steel, a finish that is challenging to keep clean and shiny, and chips easily. Powder rooms are often called the "jewel of the home" and may merit a distinctive sink.

Bathroom faucets

Bathtub faucets can be basic or ornate. Plumbing showrooms are a candy store of possibilities but watch your budget. The faucet should be (and is not always) located within a comfortable reach when standing outside of the tub. Its placement should not make entering and exiting the tub difficult or dangerous.

Shower faucets come in styles that allow you to adjust the water flow or to have only one rate of flow. The shower control(s) should be within a comfortable reach while standing outside of the shower. Some showers have a separate hand-held shower spray which can be used for personal spraying and also for rinsing walls after showering or wall cleaning.

Sink faucets come with a single or two handles, and in polished, antique or brushed finishes that include nickel, chrome, copper, brass, pewter and enamel in a variety of colors. Single-handle faucets can be push/pull or lift-handle style. Try them out in a showroom to determine your preference. Pump dispensers for soap or lotion can be added to bathroom sinks but holes will have to be drilled by the plumber in the sink or countertop.

A special drain can be installed in some sinks that is designed to catch contact lens that are headed down the drain. Inquire about this feature if you want your sink to be capable of housing this type of drain.

Laundry Room

Laundry sink

If you have pets, small children, muddy boots or clothes that need to be soaked or hand-washed, this option will be worth the extra charge. Laundry sinks can be low-cost fiberglass, stainless steel, porcelain-enameled-cast iron or enameled-steel and are usually larger and deeper than other sinks. A laundry sink installed in the garage (heated in cold climates) can also be a great convenience for outside clean-up.

Consider the extra expense of a cabinet enclosing the sink. This provides very handy counter space around the sink for a soap dish, bottles and work area as well as storage space beneath.

Laundry sink faucet

You may want an inexpensive faucet in this area, but decide on single or two handles. Will your hands be free to operate two handles while you wash the dog or wrestle with a stubborn stain? You may want a faucet with spray. Do you need any pump dispensers in this sink?

Special use sink

An extra-wide sink can be used for pet and plant washing. Pay attention to the height and access (from a standing position) to this sink to avoid back strain.

Plumb for Washer

Plumbing in the laundry area should include a washer box, which is inset in the wall with hot and cold shut-offs. It must be installed at a higher level than the entry point of the water to allow for correct water flow downward.

Plumb for Dryer

In addition to a 240-volt electrical outlet to accommodate an electric dryer, notice where the exhaust is located on the back of your dryer. It may be on the left, right, center or side. An exhaust hole will be cut in the outside wall of the home. If it doesn't match up with your dryer's exhaust, you'll have to add an elbow duct, requiring the dryer to stick out further than the washer.

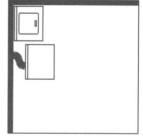

Using flexible ducting can significantly affect dryer efficiency. Some builders install a recessed box to help alleviate this problem, but the flexible ducting issues remain unsolved. This problem gets worse if the protruding dryer then blocks an entryway. See page 120 for diagram.

Dryer vent doesn't align with wall cutout

Where to Plumb for Gas

There is a cost to have gas plumbing installed for appliances, so you'll want to decide if this is necessary. Gas dryers may be considerably cheaper to operate because gas has historically been cheaper than electricity. Decide on the type of kitchen range you'll be installing to know if you'll need gas in the kitchen. Consider a gas rotisserie or a stub-out for a gas barbeque on the patio and an outdoor gas fireplace.

Plumb the Basement

Sketch a floor plan to find a good location for a basement bathroom. Determine if a shower or tub combination will be needed and used.

Plumb House Drains

The mechanical system and dehumidifier need a drain for water runoff. This drain should be slightly lower in the floor for downward water flow. Basements should have a sump pump which is used to empty a flooded basement. In drier climates, a rough-in for a sump pump is installed. The mud room, or wherever wet boots and coats will be stored, may be a good place for an additional drain.

Plumb Garage Floor Drain

A drain in the garage floor is a nice touch. Garages should be built with a floor that slopes away from the house, but a drain helps to ensure that there will be no standing water in the garage that can seep through seams to the foundation below or remain on the floor for days.

Plumb for Fire Sprinklers

If code dictates or you desire fire sprinklers throughout your home, this needs to be part of your plumbing design and installed by an experienced contractor. Adding sprinklers may quality the home for lower insurance rates.

Plumb for Irrigation Sprinkler Stubs

If you live in an area where a landscape irrigation sprinkler system is desired, consider having a sprinkler stub (the connection through the exterior wall to the water supply) installed even if you don't want to install the system yet. You may want to consult with a sprinkler expert to determine the best location for the stub as part of a sprinkler system design.

Plumb for Hose Bibbs

This is a builder's term for outside water spigots. Think about where you'll need access to water outside. Consider where might you want to store garden hoses. What might be a partially hidden location? Where might you wash cars?

Plan any fence so that a gate is installed if the fence would otherwise block access to hose bibbs. In cold climates, ask if the hose bibbs should be designed to prevent freeze-up.

Plumb for Pool/Spa/Fountain

Consider any landscape features that may require plumbing. Some of these projects may be completed after construction, but if plumbing would be difficult to install later, the necessary rough-ins will be worth including in your plumbing plan.

Electrical

The electrical plan is extremely important because it is so difficult and unsightly to alter after construction is completed. Make a sketch of each room, including furniture and cabinets, to see where outlets, switches, telephone, cable, computer wiring and lighting should be placed.

After blueprints are drawn, pay attention to when the electrical work will be completed. Your builder should schedule an electrical walkthrough with you to make sure you're happy with the placement of switches, outlets, light fixtures and appliances. Use your workbook checklists and notes to guide you during the walkthrough.

Bring your camera (print, digital or video) and take pictures of all of your walls before the wallboard goes up. Label each room and wall (e.g. south wall, northeast corner) so that you can refer back to them when you want to know where studs and wires are.

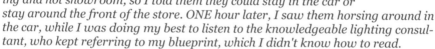

My lighting story

My builder's assistant sent me over to the designated lighting store to choose light fixtures. My children were 10 and 8 years old. I knew they would not appreciate another boring and hot showroom, so I told them they could stay in the car or stay around the front of the store. ONE hour later, I saw them horsing around in the car, while I was doing my best to listen to the knowledgeable lighting consultant, who kept referring to my blueprint, which I didn't know how to read.

This place was dizzying; lots of brilliant lights, BIG price tags and a wide variety in types of lighting. TWO hours later, I noticed that my kids were climbing up through the sunroof and out the car. Poor kids, I thought; I'm making them wait so long. The consultant and I were deciding whether this and that spot needed a light or two or six.

THREE hours later, I realized that the lights I needed totaled much more than the lighting allowance, so I decided to undo some of the decisions I had made. My kids were wrestling on the cement at the store's entrance.

I had embarked on this task completely unprepared, unaware of how important each of these decisions was. I did realize that this consultant, as capable as she was, couldn't visualize my house as she was making her suggestions, which made me nervous. Because my builder was unwilling to install fixtures from other stores, we ended up purchasing some of the lighting store's fixtures, and having bare bulbs installed (to pass electrical inspection) elsewhere. Additional fixtures would be purchased and installed after closing.

Your Lighting Shopping

Shopping for lighting involves many decisions. Don't try to do it all at once. Visit lighting stores several times, checking styles you like and their prices. Because this process takes hours, find a babysitter for the children if at all possible. You may find fixtures you like and not mind the price. If this isn't the case, you may want to explore your options.

Some builders are happy for you to shop wherever you like for fixtures. Other builders prefer or insist that you shop only at a lighting store with whom they have a relationship.

Lighting specialty stores usually guarantee the fixtures and installation. Builders lose time and money on fixtures that have been purchased from here, there and everywhere, that when delivered, are discovered to be defective or missing parts.

The problem with this policy for the homebuyer is that the lighting store builds its service policy into the price of the fixtures and you'll probably find that your lighting allowance of $1000 or $2000 or $5000 doesn't go very far. Ask what your builder's procedure is for adjusting the allowance either up or down.

$$$ One compromise is to agree with your builder that you will shop where you please but that if parts are missing or a fixture needs to be replaced, the extra labor charge will go on your bill. You'll have to decide who is responsible if the fixture fails. Whatever agreement you make with your builder should be spelled out clearly in the contract.

One advantage to using a lighting store is that experienced lighting designers will sit down with you to discuss where lighting should go and what fixtures might be best in a particular spot. If they don't visit your site, many details that can affect the lighting plan will be unknown to them. Bring your blueprints to the store if you aren't sure that the builder has provided them. If you choose to buy from this store, ask if a consultant will visit the construction site before making recommendations.

$$$ Another solution for the handy homebuyer is to have plain ceramic fixtures or the lowest cost fixtures installed at selected locations. After closing, you can buy fixtures of your choice and have them installed. Understand that if anything goes wrong with these fixtures, no builder warranty is likely to apply. This can get sticky if the problem turns out to be in the wiring rather than in the fixture.

Interior Lighting

Architects often suggest that you light the walls, and not the floor.

Interior lighting types

$$$ A revolution in lighting is on the horizon, just in time for your new home. Compact fluorescent bulbs are gaining in popularity as the cool, energy-efficient choice. The exciting news is *dimmable* fluorescents are becoming available. These lights can be extremely bright or dimmed to a romantic hue. They includes recessed cans in the kitchen, in chandeliers, almost everywhere. Remember that heat = energy and every HOT halogen light in your home not only adds significant heat to the area but adds to your energy costs. Also coming are LED (light emitting diode) bulbs, which will be brighter and probably more costly.

Old-fashioned lighting includes halogen, xenon (for under-cabinet lighting) and incandescent. They are still widely available and are the integral bulb for most fashion lighting.

Family room lighting

Do you want any built-in lighting in the family room? If you have a fireplace or objects d'art on your walls, you may want them spotlighted. You may want a ceiling fan with a light fixture or indirect lighting around the room. You'll want switches that operate the fan and light separately. Switches should be conveniently located, usually at each entrance to the room. Some ceiling fans now come with a remote control, but if wiring should ever be necessary, now is the time to install it.

Kitchen lighting

Wherever the sink, stove and other major work areas are located, consider placing overhead lighting so that your body won't block the light. Inexpensive recessed "cans," shine light directly down. They are often placed every few feet over cabinets but be aware that, if halogen, they'll give off considerable heat. "Eyeballs" are cans that have an adjustable metal covering to direct the light.

Built-in microwaves or hoods over the stove or stovetop often have an integral light. Under-cabinet lighting casts light directly on your workspace and can serve as indirect soft night lighting.

Cable or monorail light systems are another popular option. These lights have a modern look and can be pointed in any direction. They also gather dust. Do you want lighting over cabinets to accent decorative items?

If your kitchen has an eating area, do you want a hanging chandelier in this informal eating area or something flush with the ceiling or recessed cans? With any of these, consider if the light will be centered over the table or over people's heads. Do you want dimmers installed on any lights?

Dining room lighting

If you don't plan the furniture to see where your chandelier should be centered, you may end up having to "swag it." Should it be over the table or in the middle of the room? These may not be the same place. You may also want accent lighting. Dimmers are popular in dining rooms for ambiance. If you have a coffered ceiling, does this require any special lighting?

Wiring not centered

Living room lighting

You may want wall sconces that provide soft indirect mood lighting. This is a good place to have switched outlets for floor or table lamps that are away from any wall. With floor outlets, lamps can be operated from a switch located at each entrance to the room. Recessed lighting is appropriate in any room and can be dimmable.

Study lighting

If you will have built-in cabinets and bookcases, you may want lighting that can be operated by switch. This can be overhead, track lighting or switched floor outlets for table lamps.

Hallway lighting

Hallways can serve as a lighted family picture or art gallery while they light the passage, and should be switched at each end.

Foyer/staircase lighting

If you have an entrance or living area that would show off a chandelier, decide where it should be centered. All staircases should be lighted and switched at the top and bottom. Footlights, which are the size of electrical outlets but contain a small light with a vented cover for "downlighting" may be installed at intervals on the staircase walls, close to steps. Alternately, lights can be embedded under each step to light the step below.

Bedroom lighting

Consider wall lighting in place of or in addition to lamps. Overhead lights and ceiling fans, switched separately, provide useful light and air circulation. Consider having them switched near the bed for handy operation and at the room's entrance. Indirect or recessed lighting can be dimmable and can help to create a quiet or intimate mood. If your bedroom includes a sitting area, how will it be lighted?

If you will have bunk beds in a child's room, be sure that a ceiling fan won't be near this bed.

Bathrooms/toilet area lighting

This is a place to be generous with light, especially around the sinks. You may want a heat lamp over or near the shower entrance. If you like to read in the bathtub or in the toilet area, have your lighting placed so that your body won't block the light, preferably on the wall.

Closet lighting

Lighting will be necessary in the master closet and in any other large or deep closet. You pay for this, so be sure a particular closet warrants the expense.

Attic lighting

Building code may require at least a bare ceramic fixture in an unfinished attic. You may want additional wiring and an outlet for current or future needs, such as power venting, cable, telephone or other modern convenience, unless the attic is already included in your structured wiring.

Outlets and Switches

Notice if switch locations are convenient. In some places, there is *no* good place for a switch. Doors may block the only wall that can accommodate a switch. Nothing can go on a wall that houses a pocket door because the door must be able to slide into the wall.

Switches can be standard, rocker, lighted, touch sensitive, and even sound activated. At entrances to central rooms, there may be up to four switches, which are most attractive when grouped in one plate rather than having single switches strewn across the wall.

Part of a structured wiring package can be a programmable multi-scene preset control which will allow you to control lights by zone. This type of control allows you to combine many switches in a single box.

Outlets can be single (2-gang) or double (4-gang.) Building codes specify the minimum number of outlets per room but there may be areas of your home where you'll want additional outlets.

Kitchen outlets and switches

The outlets and switches checklists in the Electrical section on page 58 can serve as a guide through this important room. Have a switch for each light next to each entrance. A switch for the kitchen eating area is handy to have within reach while sitting at the table.

Take a mental or written inventory of all of your countertop appliances to determine your outlet needs. Planning this carefully now will avoid the need for unsightly adapters later. Outlets can be mounted horizontally and at a lower height, although by code, safely away from water.

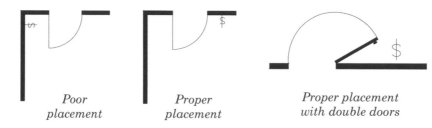

Poor placement   *Proper placement*   *Proper placement with double doors*

Great room/family room/study outlets and switches

Each entrance should have a wall switch. The best design is to group switches wherever possible, creating a central control for all nearby rooms. If the fireplace has a switch, choose a safe and unobstructed location for it. Switches should be convenient to operate when doors open against a wall. Consider the top and bottom of staircases as entrances.

Do you want cable and telephone outlets or do you use satellite and cell phones exclusively? Some satellite services require connection to a dialup line for remote updates to their service. Including this wiring makes sense because it is so inexpensive to do now and so ugly to do later, either for you or at resale time. Will there be a computer connection needed in this room? Wherever your television and electronic equipment are located, count the number of items that will require an outlet.

The checklists for Interior Lighting on page 55 will guide your search for any outlets that should be switched. An outlet is wired to a wall switch so that a lamp plugged into this outlet can be operated either by the wall switch or the lamp switch.

If you will have niches in which pictures or other items will be displayed, consider lighting and switches for them. If you plan to have a sitting area in the center of the room, do you need a floor outlet? If you plan to put a freezer or other large appliance anywhere, be sure to have an outlet installed with the adequate amperage in that location.

Bedroom outlets and switches

Decide where the bed(s) and other furniture will be placed in order to determine the quantity and location of outlets. You may want switches near your bed so that the ceiling fan and light can be conveniently operated.

Bathroom outlets and switches

Make a list of your favorite bathroom electric appliances to help determine how many outlets you'll require. Because it is very important to keep the humidity level of bathrooms low, talk with your builder about wiring the exhaust fan to do its job well.

Laundry room outlets and switches

You may want to have a 240-volt outlet installed to accommodate an electric dryer even if yours is gas. When you sell your house, this can help with a sale to a gas dryer owner. If your laundry room is spacious, you may want to add a full-size freezer. Be sure to have an appropriate dedicated outlet if necessary.

Garage outlets and switches

If interior space is tight, or access to drinks for active children would be handy outside, the garage may be a desirable location for a second refrigerator or freezer. If you plan to organize the garage with shelving, where will you want outlets? Is there a workshop area that needs additional outlets or 240-volt service? "Walk" through every exterior doorway, including side or back garage doors. Every entrance to the garage should have a light switch so you aren't walking into a dark room.

GFI outlets

Building codes require GFI (ground fault interrupt) outlets wherever moisture could cause a short circuit. This includes bathroom, kitchen and laundry sink areas, any anticipated high-power need areas, and exterior outlets. GFI outlets come in two styles: one has a little button on the outlet so that if it is tripped, you can push the reset button on the outlet. The other type has the GFI in the circuit breaker so that if it trips, you'll have to reset it at the breaker box or wiring center.

Do you want electrical outlets on exterior walls for appliances, tools, a grass trimmer or electric lawn mower? Since many of these items demand a large surge of electricity when they are turned on, check with the builder or electrician about maximum capacity of these outlets. If it is insufficient for the initial surge of an appliance's start-up, the GFI circuit will shut off every time.

Exterior Lighting

Travel around neighborhoods at night to view various types of outdoor lighting. You'll see coach lights attached to walls and lights hanging from porch ceilings. You may also see spotlights, garden lights and post lights along pathways.

Spotlights can be adjusted to point in many directions. Some people like motion-controlled lighting for security. Some of the light fixtures can be purchased at a later time, but planning now will allow the necessary pre-wiring to be done.

Recessed "can" lighting can be installed in the porch roof or roof soffit (overhang.) Cans direct the light *down* instead of *out* for a distinctive look. A dimmer may be installed with either type.

Where would switches be most convenient? Do you like to string holiday or other decorative lights outside? Would it be convenient to have soffit (under-eave) outlets with an interior switch?

Quality Installation

Outlets and switches should line up with each other, should not be loose, and no space should show between wall and outlet cover. Check for the first two items at the electrical walkthrough and don't accept shoddy workmanship.

If you have questions about electrical, request a meeting with your builder and electrician. This is very important to have done to your liking because it's all behind the walls: easy to adjust now, forget about it later.

Structured Whole-House Wiring

Taking advantage of the convenience and comfort of well-planned systems is one of the wonderful benefits of new construction. Now is the time to do it right! Installing low-voltage wiring can be inexpensive and easy to do before the walls go up, so consider these options well.

Communications

This category includes wiring for telephones and computer networking. Currently, satellite systems may require connection to a dialup line for remote updates. Another fun part of structured wiring is its ability to offer you central control of all communications. The correct type of wiring and proper installation are essential to the system's success.

Video and home theater

Included here are satellite and cable systems, including distribution of programming from a centralized server.

Audio systems

Consider all rooms that should have speakers, and if these speakers should operate independently, so that occupants can use them individually. Rooms can be wired for monitors to rooms for baby and for teens (who may otherwise be difficult to reach in their sanctum.) Take into account which rooms require higher fidelity speakers than standard built-in flush mounted speakers.

Speakers in outdoor living space

If you plan to spend considerable time or entertain in your yard you may want a sound system that is independent or connected to the interior sound system and controllable from both locations.

Home automation

Becoming common in homes with fully structured wiring is a central touch control panel, with remote access to all systems. This can include "smart appliances" that respond to a remote command, such as turning on the oven at a specific time.

Central vacuum

A central vacuum system offers the important advantage of ensuring that targeted dust and debris are successfully drawn out of the home. This is the way to escort dust, pollutants and allergens outside!!

Daily food debris can be swept toward a special "broom" outlet, located at floor level in the kitchen. it. When this small, covered outlet is lifted with the tip of the foot, *whoosh!* The crumbs are sucked away.

The base unit, containing the motor, is ideally placed outside the home (and safely away from indoor air) in a sheltered area, such as the garage. It is sometimes installed in the basement or in a storage closet, although these locations invite some dust to remain in the breathing space.

If the vacuum hose seems too long, adding additional vacuum outlets allows for a shorter hose. The power hose for carpets should have electricity built into it and therefore not require a separate outlet. This requires accurate communication between electrician and system installer, but their effort will result in the best system for your home.

$$$ If the cost of a central vacuum system is prohibitive, consider having the inexpensive plastic pipes "roughed-in" to the walls. The system can then be completed by adding the expensive part, the motor, at any time. If you never install it, the rough-in may add to the value of the home at resale time.

Additional remote functions

A luxury item that will be easy to get used to is motorized operation of window shades. Maintenance of a swimming pool or water feature can be built into your home automation wiring. Security systems can be controlled remotely, including audio and video.

Lighting control

Lighting can be controlled for any immediate need, as well as having lights go on just before your expected arrival home. Vacation lighting is another benefit of being able to control lights remotely.

Climate control

In place of a standard thermostat, temperature can be controlled through your structured wiring, for any area of your home. This includes the control of smoke and carbon monoxide detectors.

Wireless

This is a subject unto itself, best researched at the time of purchase to learn of the latest trends and features.

Home security systems

This includes intrusion detection, remote cameras that monitor entrances, fire/smoke and carbon monoxide detectors, and intercoms.

Finishing Interior Walls

Wallboard

Wallboard quality/thickness

Wallboard (often known as drywall, gypsum board and the branded Sheetrock®) comes in ½" and ⅝" thickness. While ½" is slightly less expensive, ⅝" is stronger (less chance of gapping) and offers better sound insulation. When the finish work is done correctly, no wallboard seams will show. This is difficult to verify until the walls are painted.

Backer board

Backer board is the new standard of the 2006 International Residential Code's requirement for walls that are against showers and tubs.

Paperless wallboard

A product known in the industry as "glassmat" is paperless wallboard. It has a fiberglass front and back over a gypsum core. Its advantage is that it offers no "food" on which mold needs to thrive. This is a higher priced product that may be a good choice in some climates and locations within the home.

Wallboard style

$$$ Do you want rounded corners (bullnose) throughout the home? Do you want decorative niches? These touches are labor-intensive and have a cost but much less than wood paneling or molding. Visit model homes to experience creative wallboard shaping. Many homes feature one-inch or half-inch recessed areas that can be decorated with an accent color of paint; others have niches in which objects can be displayed and showcased with the addition of low-cost recessed lighting.

Wallboard texturing/stomping

In some areas of the country, wall texturing is a popular way to finish walls. The texture is applied before the walls are painted. One style is called "orange peel," which looks like little bumps on the surface. "Knockdown" is achieved by applying texturing and then wiping it down with a flat implement so that the texture is recessed rather than protruding. Stomping is applied with a brush. For a look of elegance, a special design, such as a distressed wheat pattern, can be textured on the walls or ceiling.

Plaster

A more costly but elegant alternative to wallboard is plaster. Color can be mixed into the plaster before application. This creates a wall that will require little maintenance but also locks the plaster into this color.

In addition to the increased strength of plaster, texturing possibilities are endless. Color can be uniform or varied in interesting tints. Shapes can be imprinted into plaster and then gone over with a darker shade of color. Visit high-end model homes for ideas.

Interior Paint

Paint type/quality

$$$ The brand and style number of your paint should be included in your specifications and materials list. It is worth paying extra for a superior quality interior paint that is truly washable. You'll want this big paint job to last a long time, because the next one will not be in a vacant space, and will therefore be more costly and much more trouble. Satin or eggshell, with a slight sheen, is often recommended as the most durable choice.

Low VOC paints

That new-car or new-house smell may connote excitement, but what you're smelling is off-gassing of toxic chemicals. Paints are available that have low- or no-VOC (volatile organic compounds.)

Paint color

Many people choose a soft, neutral color because they prefer to either have their furniture and décor as the focal point or have neutral colors as their decorating statement. You may prefer brighter or more unusual colors, but having rooms painted in different colors will be more costly. Weigh this expense against the value of having just what you want before moving in. Note that, when perusing paint samples, exterior colors look *lighter* on walls than on the sample; interior colors look *darker* on walls than on the sample.

Wall preparation for painting

Your materials and specifications list should include one coat of primer and one coat of paint or two coats of paint, which is usually applied with sprayer. If woodwork will be painted, you may want a high-quality washable finish that can withstand fingerprints and cleaning.

Wallpaper

Wallpaper is more expensive than paint but is a fashion statement and is usually durable enough to last for many years. The advantages of having wallpaper applied during construction are avoiding the inconvenience of moving furniture, the mess of wallpaper wetness and glue, and the opportunity to include the cost of the wallpaper and its application in the mortgage.

Other Wall Treatments

Specialized texture/stenciling

Do you want fabric glued to wall, faux finish (antiquing, sponging) or stenciling on the walls? Wainscoting is the practice of decorating the lower portion of walls. The reason to consider this now is to avoid mess after moving in and to have this expense included in your mortgage. Otherwise, leave these possibilities for the future, after you've had time to decide what you want.

Stained wood/stucco/brick

Consider wood finish in the study, family room, dining room or bedroom. See page 201 for information on this finish carpentry item. Stucco finish can give a southwest or mission look and requires little or no maintenance unless you tire of the color and re-paint. Brick or faux brick can be applied to all walls or used as an accent. Real brick will be maintenance-free but its roughness and sharp edges can be a hazard.

Mirrors

Would one or more full-length mirrors be desirable in the master closet or other bedroom? Should mirrors be installed behind decorative niches or elsewhere to give a room the look of added spaciousness?

Wall Tile

Tile is wonderful because of its beauty and resistance to moisture. It allows for unlimited creativity (budget permitting) in shape, texture and color and is easy to keep clean. Some tile showrooms are better than others at displaying tile patterns and in carrying several sizes of the same style of tile.

If a particular tile comes in different sizes and in matching border or accent tiles, creating tile arrangements becomes easier. In addition to stock tiles, you may want custom-painted or decaled tiles. You can also accent tile with beautiful borders.

It is important to understand what your tile layout will be. Tile must be lined up in a certain way so that it fits wall dimensions. Make an explicit diagram of your tile plan and discuss it with the tile installer to avoid miscommunication and mistakes.

Grout color

Grout, the material that fills in the gaps between tiles, comes in a variety of colors and your choice will affect the look of the tile. Keep a supply of each style and color of tile for replacements. Also keep either some grout powder or the brand and color number of the grout so that it can be replaced.

Tile cost saving measures

$$$ Mixing and matching colors and patterns of basic stock tiles probably adds no cost, so this is a wonderful way to be creative.

$$$ Tile showrooms have a selection of decals that can be applied to tiles and glazed to be permanent and waterproof. Instead of paying an extra labor charge for the necessary cutting and fitting of a different size of decaled tile, ask to have the decal split and applied to several of the size of tile that you are using. This should not be an expensive proposition.

Shopping for tile can bring out your creativity. Because this is one of the long-lasting items in your home, choose styles and colors that you will want to live with over time and be proud to pass on at resale time.

$$$ It may be possible for you to hand-paint standard tiles, which come pre-glazed. Estimate the number of tiles to paint and add a few extras in case they're needed. After painting the tile, either stenciled or free-hand, repaint this area only with glazing and have tiles re-fired at your local ceramics shop. Try this with a sample tile first to be sure you are pleased with the look. If not, investigate the possibility of hand-painting unglazed tiles.

My tile story

After entering the tile store that my builder used, I quickly realized that the beautifully painted tiles that I was admiring cost $25 each. I knew that was out; I suddenly had an idea. I estimated how many tiles I would need (for accent) in the master bathroom and on the kitchen backsplash. I revisited the tile showroom to pick up that number of tiles in the style and color I had chosen for each room. There was no additional charge for them since they were the builder's standard tiles.

I carried the box of tiles on the airplane trip back to Pittsburgh (the home we were leaving.) One afternoon, I sat in a ceramics store with a helpful clerk assisting me. We worked for several hours; I painted, and she re-glazed only the areas that I had painted. She fired the tiles over the weekend, and I later returned to Fort Collins with my box. The tile installer placed them according to my drawing and they have since been admired by friends who did not know who painted them. The extra cost for my beautiful, hand-painted tiles (about 48 total) for paint and firing was $32.

$$$ One of tile's few maintenance issues is deteriorating grout between tiles, and the caulking that is necessary in corners and wherever tile meets another type of surface. A high quality silicone caulk will maintain this professional look much longer and provide extra years of wear, delaying the need to re-grout and re-caulk.

Bathroom wall tile

Shower/tub walls

Will you want ceramic, marble or granite tile or slab in the shower? If you have a separate bathtub, you'll probably want matching or complementary tile or slab around the base of tub (called the apron) and on the wall area surrounding the top of the tub. Tile in the shower/tub combination allows you to design the space.

Grab bars

For the safety of all occupants, young and old, grab bars that are accessible for tub entry and exit should be installed. They cannot rely on tile for strength; they must be secured by wood "blocking" behind the tile.

Storage for bath/shower items

Consider your supply needs: shampoo, conditioner, liquid soap, bar soap and a place to store your sponge, washcloths and razor. Cultured marble manufacturers make inexpensive stock and custom insets in a variety of shapes and colors that can be installed in a tile wall or corners. An advantage to these one-piece units over a tile inset is that there is less chance of moisture leakage through grouted areas.

Shower/tub walls – with fiberglass

Fiberglass shower walls can be smooth or can come with texturing that looks remarkably like one-color tile. This doesn't have the richer look of real tile but is less expensive, and avoids the aging grout issue. Fiberglass must be very gently maintained in order to keep its finish.

Sink tile backsplash

A partial tile backsplash behind sinks protects the walls from moisture and adds decorative value. This tile usually matches other tile in the bathroom but you can be as creative as you like.

Kitchen wall tile

A tile backsplash on the wall above the countertop and stove is much easier to de-grease and keep clean than a painted wall. Your backsplash can be just a tile or two high or full to the wall cabinet. This is another opportunity to be creative with color, style and pattern of tiles.

Laundry room wall tile

If you have a laundry sink installed, a tile backsplash, even one-tile high, is a practical addition to a wall area that will be subjected to water.

Fireplace wall and floor tile

Tile is a practical and beautiful part of some fireplaces. It can be placed above and around the fireplace inset as well as on the floor in front. Choose size, style and color that will be versatile, since this tile is not likely to be replaced. Grouting comes in a variety of colors and your choice will affect the overall look of your tile.

Carpet

Types of Carpet Construction

- **Cut pile** - won't unravel
- **Textured saxony** - won't unravel, luxurious feel, shows footprints
- **Berber** - loop pile that can unravel, durable
- **Cut and loop** - can have interesting patterns

Types of Carpet Material

The material used and method of construction are important to know when shopping. Push your fingers into the carpet to see how easily they touch bottom. Feel the harshness or softness of the carpet. If you or other family members (including crawling babies) walk barefoot on this carpet, its softness will matter to you.

- **Nylon** - bounces back, has stain and soil resistance
- **Corn-based polymer**- organic, environmentally-friendly
- **Olefin** - good for indoor/outdoor, stain resistant, rough to the touch
- **Polyester** - less resilient than nylon, vivid colors, stain resistant
- **Wool** – organic, soft, stain resistant, durable, expensive
- **PET** – soft, bright, inexpensive, made from recycled pop bottles

Low VOC carpet and adhesives

Natural, untreated fibers, such as wool and corn are considered to offer the least chance of toxic off-gassing. The adhesives used to manufacture carpets are also worth asking about.

Types of Padding

- Rebond – firm, durable, retains shape
- Urethane foam
- Fiber
- Rubber

Thickness of Padding

Carpet experts will often suggest a high quality pad even if you're installing inexpensive carpet because the better pad will not only feel more comfortable underfoot but will also increase the life of your carpet. Also consider a better pad on staircases because of the heavy use they get.

Cushion should not exceed ½". Cushion density is the single most important factor when evaluating performance. Rebond urethane cushion offers quality density for its price range. Rubber offers exceptional performance and is usually the better option over radiant heat floors that will be carpeted.

Where to Carpet

Carpet is a color statement and a noise suppressor and has a soft and warm look. It is also subject to permanent stains, shows wear and holds dirt. Consider where carpet will be a good choice and where it will be impractical. Avoid carpet in entry ways and along any high traffic area, such as hallways.

Kitchen Carpet

The kitchen floor is the natural landing place for grease and food. Keeping kitchen carpet clean is nearly impossible.

Bathroom Carpet

Carpet in the bathroom feels wonderful to bare feet and may be desirable, but installed carpet cannot be removed for cleaning. Keep this in mind when considering carpeting the toilet area.

In the shower/tub area, any flooring or carpet will be subjected to contact with water. Non-skid tile is most resistant. Carpet is subject to stains and moisture damage but isn't slippery. Vinyl will resist moisture except at its edges.

Carpet Installation

You may want to research the carpet installer's reputation or references. Carpet must be properly stretched and attached to tacking around all edges. If not done correctly, the carpet will loosen and buckle over time. We too often assume that professionals know this and will automatically do what is right

One measure of quality is CFI certification of installers (see Website address on page 234.) As always, a referral from a trusted professional and references from satisfied customers are golden.

Attention to details will result in seams that are hardly visible. Lighting and traffic patterns should be considered when determining seam direction and location. Carpet must be installed in the same direction throughout the home. Seams must be sealed before joining sections to prevent sprouting and raveling. Some carpets come in 15-foot widths, which can avoid the need for seaming, if your room doesn't exceed this dimension.

Your Flooring Budget

$$$ Your contract, if for a fixed price, should state what dollar amount per square foot or total dollar amount you have as an allowance, as well as where you may shop. If you have the freedom and time to shop anywhere, you may have increased opportunity to get better value for your money.

My carpet story

We wanted to finish the basement but had a tight budget for that luxury. While visiting a showroom, I asked to speak with the owner, and told him the price I had received elsewhere for builder-grade carpet and the quantity I needed. I asked if he had any bargains for someone who wasn't fussy about the color or pattern.

He did; a beautiful blue two-tone carpet that someone had ordered and then not accepted. He had about 100 square yards; I was looking for 94. We bargained a little on the price, and I got a much higher quality for less than the cost of the builder-grade carpet!

Flooring

Vinyl and Natural Linoleum Flooring

Vinyl and natural linoleum come in a wide range of prices, based on thickness and quality. They come in many colors and styles and can be an important part of a room's color and style statement.

🌲 Natural linoleum is made of linseed oil, cork, limestone, tree resin and natural minerals, and is considered a "green" product.

$$$ Many stores offer books or wall samples of all vinyl and linoleum that is available. They may also have rolls of vinyl in stock. Advantages to purchasing in-stock vinyl and natural linoleum are that you may get a better quality vinyl for a lower price, and you are able to see the vinyl in a much larger piece. Be aware that vinyl can and probably will suffer cuts and other abrasions through normal wear. You may want to consider this when choosing quality, color and pattern, especially in heavily used areas.

$$$ Laminate floors have a wood look at moderate price points. They are easy to install and are suitable for active areas of the home, offering some scratch and dent resistance. They are available in a wide variety of design options.

Vinyl, natural linoleum and wood, unlike tile, become much less slippery once they've been walked on for a while. Consider vinyl or natural linoleum in the foyer, kitchen, powder room, laundry room, shower entry, toilet area, bathroom, bedroom, exercise area, playroom and basement.

Wood Flooring

Wood flooring is a higher-priced option but may be a good investment. It gives a warm and rich look to the home. When protected with a high quality finish, it is quite durable. It is warmer on the feet than tile (unless radiant heat is installed) and is more forgiving when something breakable is dropped. It may suffer dings and marks from use, which can be repaired with wood filler, but won't look damaged since wood is expected to have imperfections. Radiant heat is being installed under wood, for even warmer floors.

Flooring materials

Some of the woods used in flooring include oak, birch, cherry, mahogany and pine. Harder woods include maple and hickory. All wood floors will show dust and debris and may require frequent care, but dark floors offer the greatest contrast. Children, pets or dirty work boots will keep you challenged on a daily basis.

Bamboo flooring

🌲 The appeal of bamboo flooring is the environmentally-friendly abundance of the fast-growing bamboo tree. The cost of bamboo varies with its level of hardness.

Cork flooring

🌲 Natural cork flooring comes from the bark of cork trees. This sustainable product makes sense while providing a beautiful decorative statement. It comes in a variety of colors and is stain-resistant when properly sealed.

Engineered wood floor

Engineered wood floors have a deep layer of beautiful wood over a very strong base of less-expensive high-density fiberboard. The engineered floor offers the beauty and durability of solid hardwood along with better resistance to shrinkage, making it a smart choice that is destined to grow in popularity. The engineered floor is also environmentally-friendly since it requires less wood.

Flooring styles

Styles include narrow or wide strips of wood, wood in patterns and wood mixed with tile insets. Be careful that, in fixing materials, a small but dangerous height difference isn't created. It is this type of subtle difference that goes unnoticed and has stumbling potential.

Wood floors can be tongue-in-groove, nailed or glued. Wood comes pre-finished or to be finished after installation. Three coats of polyurethane or other sealing finish may be needed to adequately protect the floor, since the first coat soaks into the wood completely. Sealants come in matte (flat), semi-gloss and high-gloss finish.

Tile Flooring

Tile flooring comes in a variety of materials, styles and colors, which are best viewed in a tile showroom. Tile is wonderfully washable and resistant to moisture and dirt, although the grout around each tile is a porous product.

Tile makes a decorating statement. Generally, larger tiles are showier. When considering tile over any structural floor, be sure to factor in the cost of installing an anti-fracture system, such as schluter ditra. Your tile expert will be glad to offer more information.

Possible locations for tile are the foyer, kitchen, powder room, laundry room, shower entry, toilet area, bathroom, bedroom, exercise area, playroom, exterior patio or any area of your home where you like the look of tile or want its durability, water resistance and washability.

Tile is a wonderful alternative for anyone with allergies because its hard surface repels everything. Tile can be part of a whole-house approach to healthy air for your family to breathe.

Tile maintenance

Some tile experts recommend that a protective sealant be applied to some kinds of tile. Tile can be cracked or broken but individual tiles can be replaced. It is important to replace broken tiles promptly because moisture can seep through the cracks and cause further damage. This is a good reason to retain a supply of original tiles and grout.

One maintenance issue is difficulty in cleaning the grout between tiles where dirt tends to remain. Installing grout as flush with the tile as possible helps to reduce this problem, as does sealing the grout. There will always be some valley because grout shrinks when drying. Grout color affects the overall look, so shop for light and dark shades. An epoxy grout system will add to initial costs, but will resist stains well.

Stone Flooring

For a distinctive look, visit model homes or showrooms that display natural or cultured stone flooring. It can be stained to match your décor and will be very durable. It will also be cold and hard. If the stone has a rough surface, find out if it needs to be sealed and what maintenance is required. Also determine the cost of labor, based on the stone and arrangement you choose. Stone should be installed by someone experienced in the craft.

Concrete Flooring

Concrete is no longer just for driveways. Concrete can be stained, swirled, textured and sealed to a beautiful finish. This can be an option on any slab floor or the patio and walkways. As with most of these choices, it has its cost, but this is a good time to check possibilities so that you make choices you'll be pleased with for years to come.

Cabinets

Choose cabinets as you would choose furniture. Visit one or more showrooms to get a good idea of the wide variety of styles, colors, materials and prices that are available.

If your builder usually installs a particular brand and style of cabinet, seeing those cabinets on an existing house or in a showroom is the best way to know what you'll be getting. Brand, style and dimensions of cabinets should be on your specifications list and/or your blueprint.

Cabinet Materials

Wood can be stained or painted. Solid wood has a rich look and sturdier shelving. Laminate offers color options and ease of cleaning.

$$$ Less expensive and very popular are wood doors on a particle board "box." The construction will not be as solid as wood (depending on thickness,) which is a consideration if the shelves must support heavy items. The cabinet walls and shelves are hidden behind closed doors most of the time and the cost savings is significant. The overall look will not let anyone know how much you've saved.

Cabinet Style

Some of the least expensive styles are single-piece wood or laminated doors. Raised panel wood cabinet doors are popular and attractive.

Box-style cabinets have traditionally had a bar between two cabinet doors, called a mullion. Framed or frameless doors that have no center mullion allow greater access to the shelving. Country-style cabinets have doors that close flush with cabinets. Craftsman-style cabinets have beautiful wood trim across the top, and no mitered (seamed on the diagonal) corners. Many styles may be seen at kitchen design centers.

Stock wall cabinets are usually available in 3" increments, e.g. 24", 27", 30", but some manufacturers offer 1½" increments. Most costly are custom-built cabinets built on-site by a cabinetmaker. Cabinets can be made to fit any unusual size or space, if you are willing to pay for this level of customization.

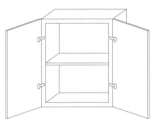

*No center mullion and
European hidden hinges*

Craftsman style doors

Open space/soffits

Cabinets can be "stair-stepped" at varying heights for an interesting look. "Open" gives the room a more spacious look and creates a place for plants and decorations. For cabinets that don't extend to the ceiling, personal preference will dictate whether to have open space between the top of the cabinets and the ceiling or to enclose the space.

Enclosing the space with wallboard eliminates dust collection over your food preparation and provides space for decoration. The wall created is a highly visible location for wallpaper or stenciling.

Cabinet Hardware

Cabinet hinges

Hinges are hidden in the popular "European" style hardware. They are attractive but doors can't swing open fully. Consider this, especially with base cabinets that children may run into or push against. Whether you choose hidden, or outside-mounted hinges that are visible, try them out in a showroom. Some hinges are designed to stay open at a certain point, but then "self-close" with a little assistance.

Cabinet handles/knobs

Do you want or need handles on the doors and drawers? Handles and knobs provide something to grab, but many popular cabinet doors and drawers have beveled edges, which make handles or knobs unnecessary.

One reason to omit handles or knobs is to achieve a more formal, less busy look to your kitchen, especially if it is part of a great room. This choice will also result in cabinets having lots of finger contact, which will need regular maintenance. If the cabinets are wood, they can be effectively cleaned with lemon oil. Laminates are easily cleaned with polish, your favorite cleaner or water.

Handles and knobs can't eliminate the grime that is generated from daily use, but do reduce contact. They also provide an opportunity to decorate with your favorite style and color. Handle and knob hardware and installation add a small additional cost.

$$$ Unless the cabinet price is increased for beveled edges, using edges instead of knobs or handles is a cost savings in hardware and hole-drilling.

Cabinet Height

Wall and base cabinets are usually hung at a standard height but if you are unusually short or tall or have special needs, consider having cabinets installed at a height that will be more comfortable for you. This is an item that can affect resale value but if this is important to you, it may be worth doing.

Wall cabinets can extend to the ceiling, affording extra storage space but less accessibility.

Cabinet Measuring

It is the cabinet specialist's job to determine the correct measurements for all cabinets. When cabinets are mis-measured, when stock sizes don't fit, or when cabinets are installed at an angle, extra matching wood or laminate, called filler, is used to hide any gaps between cabinets or between a cabinet and a wall. When filler is properly matched and installed, it is hardly noticeable, but if a cabinet is ordered smaller than it should have been, you get narrower drawers or doors and therefore less storage space.

Cabinet Toe Kicks

A toe kick or kickplate will be glued to the outside of the cabinet where it meets the floor. This can be wood, wood laminate or vinyl. Wood or wood laminate looks richer.

Cabinet Drawers

Visiting a showroom will be the best way to learn about drawers. Pay attention to how they are constructed and the ease with which they slide. Take one out and examine it for quality and durability.

Drawer quantity and size

Notice the depth and width of drawers. Drawers vary greatly in size, depending on the style and manufacturer. The type of drawer mounting affects the amount of usable drawer space you'll have. Because drawers are expensive to manufacture, three deeper drawers take up the same space as four shallower size drawers. This cuts down on the total cost but gives you one less drawer.

Examine your current drawers to see if the quantity of each size of drawer is sufficient for all that you want to store. Do you have a flatware tray that will fit or would you like built-in dividers? It takes some time and effort, but consider taking inventory of your kitchen storage items. This will give you a better idea of what configuration of drawers will best meet your needs.

Drawer construction

The sturdiest and most expensive drawers are dove-tailed at corners. This craftsmanship involves intertwining perpendicular edges in a similar way to crossing the fingers on your left and right hands. Doweled drawers are also solidly constructed using dowels (shaped like chopsticks.) "Dado" is a reasonably sturdy (depending on usage) notch-and-glue procedure, while staple-and-glue is the poorest construction.

Drawer style

You may want swing-out or roll-out pantry drawers. Both have a significant added cost but may be worth the convenience they offer. Roll-out drawers work most effectively with short items such as cans, rather than tall items like bottles, that can fall over when moved. There are pull-out or roll-out drawers constructed especially for spices. Large drawers for pots and all shapes of pans are an alternative to shelving.

Kitchen Cabinets

Island/peninsula cabinets

Islands and peninsulas are popular additions to today's larger kitchens. As with geography, the island stands alone while the peninsula is attached at one end to other counter space. Either can be designed in whatever shape fits your needs and space. The surface can include a double or triple sink, a stovetop, a wet bar, a countertop with eating bar overhang or can be dedicated as a large, uninterrupted workspace.

If your island or peninsula has an overhang that serves as an eating counter, consider that the covering on the outside walls of the island or peninsula will be kicked. Will it be solid wood, a wood " skin" (plywood covered with a finish that looks like wood) to match cabinets, or will it be wallboard? Wallboard is soft and easily dented.

The island or peninsula can have base cabinets with doors or drawers. Evaluate all of your kitchen counter space to see if it is sufficient and which areas will be most useful to you. If there is no living space over the kitchen, consider adding a skylight over the island for more natural light and a feeling of openness.

Pantry closet

Pantry closets are an old concept that has regained in popularity. Today's pantry closets are configured in many shapes and offer a wonderful opportunity to finally have sufficient storage. Shelving should be shallow and well-supported for the weight of its contents. Since this room is likely to always need light, many pantries are wired for the light to go on automatically when the door is opened. The pantry closet door can be designed to look like cabinet fronts or contain a decorative glass insert.

Pantry cabinet

An alternative to a pantry room is a large cabinet. If this cabinet has adjustable shelves, it can be optimized by adding extra shelves, since many items, such as canned goods, require less height than cereal boxes and bottles.

Shelves are much less likely to bow under the weight of pantry contents if supported every 18" or less. Short plastic inserts offer little real support. The wider the shelves are, the more weight they may hold, requiring extra support.

A few kitchen cabinet options

Corner lazy Susan wall cabinet

If you'll have corner cabinets, consider a built-in "lazy Susan." A solid-piece angled door comes with one adjustable tray that rotates 360 degrees. A hinged door can have a pull-out shelf. Both styles may have room for a second tray at a small additional charge, giving you three shelves (including the bottom of the cabinet.)

This is a great place to store spices, baby food or any items that would benefit from a circular tray. Corner wall cabinets can also be useful in the bathroom and the laundry room.

Corner lazy Susan base cabinet

For one or more corners in the kitchen, you may want a base cabinet with either of the styles mentioned. These rotating shelves lend themselves nicely to tall items such as cereal boxes, which will be within the reach of wheelchair-bound adults or smaller children.

Lazy Susans offer less storage space than fixed cabinets and cost more, but do offer more accessible storage. If you have items that are used rarely, a standard fixed cabinet will provide full-corner storage space without incurring the additional cost of a lazy Susan cabinet.

Desk

Do you want a desk in the kitchen? People often end up paying bills at the kitchen table because the desk is too small or faces the wall, away from the center of the room. If you plan to sit at this desk, what is your view?

Today's desks can have built-in computer keyboards. A practical desk needs to be deep enough for a computer and/or space to work. A drawer that will accommodate hanging folders can be a helpful household management feature.

$$$ Do you want a desk only for bill storage or your cookbooks? Would a bookcase or built-in cubbies serve your lifestyle needs better and at less cost than a desk?

$$$ An alternative to a built-in desk is a separately purchased desk that has a finish that is similar or complementary to the cabinets. The desktop can be left alone or finished to match the kitchen countertops, with matching edge finish. This can be significantly less expensive than a custom-made desk and gives you the flexibility to move or remove the desk. A matching wall cabinet over the desk provides handy storage and a place for under-cabinet desk lighting.

Wine rack /charging station/appliance garage

Wall cabinets can have a built-in wine rack or a garage-type closeable door for countertop appliances. "Charging stations" are a convenient place to unobtrusively store recharging units for all cell phones, PDAs, cameras, and iPods. Built-in cubbies can have multiple purposes. The possibilities are almost endless, and are on display in home improvement and kitchen specialty stores.

Recycle bins

A 21st century kitchen should have some provision for recycling, so now is an excellent time to build in one or more recycle bins for maximum convenience. If your recycle bin is made with dividers, be sure that each area is large enough to be of practical use for cans, milk containers, newspapers and other recyclables. Also consider if removal of its contents will be convenient.

Glass door inserts

Whether you have wood or laminate cabinets, doors can be made to accommodate inserts. These doors look like empty picture frames. Spaces can be filled with clear glass, stained or textured glass in a whole piece, or with a custom-made insert of cut or stained glass or other decorative panels.

Custom-made panels will be the most expensive but can be a focal point of the kitchen. Clear glass panels will show the cabinet's contents, as will any transparent decorative glass. Where do you want cabinet contents visible and where would solid doors or opaque glass be better?

$$$ A whole piece of stained or textured glass is relatively inexpensive and can be a wonderful decorative touch. Art glass specialty stores spend their days creating custom windows, which creates many pieces of leftover glass. Visit this type of store and ask to see spare pieces of glass. Many colors and textures will be available in the range of $20 to $40, depending on size. This glass can be caulked into your cabinet door frame, and *voila!* You have beautiful cabinet fronts for very little money. In fact, the cost of the glass may be offset by a savings in ordering cabinet door frames in place of solid doors.

Interior lighting

You may want lighting installed inside of all, several, or one special cabinet for decorative value or for night lighting, possibly installed with a dimmer. You may also want "uplighting" on open space above cabinets. Either of these types of lighting can be conveniently switched.

Bathroom Cabinets

Bathroom base cabinets can be ordered taller than standard height base cabinets. This allows the countertop to also be raised, requiring less bending. Cabinets are practical storage areas, so evaluate how well your current cabinets meet your storage needs. Bath cabinets can match those in other rooms or be unique to this room. They can be ordered with or without handles or knobs, as long as the edges are beveled.

Bathroom cabinet drawers and doors

Storage of bathroom items has cried out for better organization for years. Consider what configuration of doors and drawers will best utilize this space in storing all of the items that belong under the sink.

Drawers are one way to keep items organized. Remember that the sink bowl utilizes space under the cabinet, so drawers need to go on one or both sides of it. Within doors, you may want pullout trays or multi-level shelving.

Medicine cabinets

If you choose to have one or more medicine cabinets, notice (before wallboard is installed) if the framing in this area has been built to accommodate them. This is sometimes overlooked in the framing orders. If medicine cabinets are mirrored, how will edges be finished?

Bathroom mirrors

Bathroom mirrors usually provide only a two-dimensional view but when installed on an angled wall can offer the advantage of an angled view. This effect can also be achieved by installing hinged mirrors on one or both sides, which allows for a multitude of views. How will edges be finished? Beveled edges are more elegant but also more expensive.

Laundry Room Cabinets

Do you need a built-in ironing board with a storage place and outlet for your iron, and an *accessible* hanging pole for freshly dried or ironed items? If you have a stackable washer/dryer, consider where to place any cabinets. How much storage do you need in the laundry room? Use the checklists on page 69 to help meet your needs while staying within your budget.

Appliances

Although located after Electrical and Cabinets, your appliance decisions involve wiring and dimension requirements that may affect the electrical and cabinet plans. It is therefore a good idea to plan appliance decisions before the electrical plan is completed and cabinets are ordered.

Stove Unit

The cost of stove units varies from least inexpensive to the top-end "professional series." While it is a good idea to invest in the kitchen, the stove need not break your budget. A lower-end model should be self-cleaning and have a large enough oven to accommodate the proverbial Thanksgiving turkey.

While self-cleaning models are more expensive to purchase, they are recommended because of their superior insulation which will help to reduce energy costs and improve comfort. The stove unit may have side-by-side double ovens, six or eight over-sized burners and/or a grill and a downdraft ventilation system (see page 197.)

A visit to your local appliance store will reward you with a demonstration of the latest appliances. Some of them include gas/electric combinations, with gas burners and an electric oven for more even heating and slide-in models that prevent food from slipping between range and countertop.

Stovetop/Wall Oven(s)

Stovetops that have a tempered glass surface for easy cleaning are electric. Also pay attention to the number and quality of coils. If you don't like the slower heat-up and cool-down or the higher cost of electric stoves, another option is a gas stovetop with standard or oversized burners. Modern gas stoves have sealed burners and one-piece pans that are easier to keep clean. For those at high altitudes, gas burns less efficiently, translating into longer cooking times and higher energy costs.

With either of these stovetops, add a single or double wall oven, standard or convection, or a wall oven and microwave combination. Two ovens can be very convenient if you are baking foods that require different temperatures.

Convection ovens, which have a small fan inside to circulate the heat for more even baking, heat food more quickly and efficiently.

Microwave Oven(s)

Built-in microwaves make room for more counter space. They can be built into a wall over a conventional wall oven or a microwave/convection combination. Two microwave ovens will double your zapping power when a quick meal is being prepared.

A microwave oven that is located near the other cooking appliances is convenient for meal preparation, but having an additional microwave within reaching distance of the eating table may also be appreciated.

Kitchen Exhaust Options

Exhaust built into microwave

Microwaves over the stove or stovetop usually have a built-in exhaust fan and light that serve as a stove hood. This exhaust fan probably does not, however, cover the front exhaust burners and therefore is much less effective in drawing out its toxic fumes and odors.

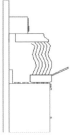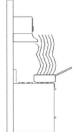

*Exhaust fan vents
all burners*

*Exhaust fan misses
front burners*

Exhaust built into hood

An exhaust fan can be located in the stove hood or at roof level (called a remote fan) to draw odors and toxic fumes (if gas) up and out.

While fans have traditionally been noisy, quieter and higher quality models are now available. Stove hoods are traditionally as large or larger than the stovetop and should therefore effectively draw fumes from all of the burners.

Exhaust built into stove (downdraft)

A downdraft exhaust system is featured on many stovetops or stove units. This system effectively eliminates odors and fumes by pulling them into the vent located either on the stovetop, or on the stove back, which is often retractable.

Closed exhaust system in kitchen

Unless the exhaust system is ducted to the outside, it will do little more than stir the foul air around and back into the room.

Downdraft fan

Dishwasher

Features

Compare brand reliability and features. Higher end models have a timer that allows you to program the dishwasher to run during the night.

Rack configuration

Examine the loading capacity. Does the shape and spacing of racks accommodate your plates and glassware? Dishwashers vary greatly in their rack configuration. How much room is there for all of the cereal bowls your family uses? Is there a wide enough space for your favorite casserole dish?

If the flatware tray is against the dishwasher door, will food become trapped behind the tray? Does the amount of water used vary with brands? It will add up over time.

Soundproofing

Soundproofing is an important feature, especially if the kitchen is open to other rooms. Ask your appliance expert not only which models are the quietest, but which ones will remain the quietest after several years of use.

Energy-efficiency

 New dishwasher design includes double-drawer style that lets homeowners operate one drawer at a time for small loads. Also available is a small in-sink dishwasher that occupies one side of a double sink.

Location

Dishwashers can be raised above floor level to reduce bending. With this choice, an overhead microwave and a drawer below the dishwasher provide maximum use of valuable space.

If the dishwasher is located on an exterior wall and you live in a cold climate, be sure that the area behind the dishwasher is carefully insulated to maintain a tight thermal envelope and protect plumbing.

Garbage Disposal

Most popular is a basic 1/4, 1/3, or 1/2 horsepower garbage disposal. It is often the case that none of these basic models is powerful enough, nor has high enough quality blades to sufficiently grind food. Eventually, the sink pipe can become clogged with partially ground food. Consider buying the most powerful garbage disposal available. If this is not affordable, a better disposal may be installed at a later time, if and when needed.

Trash Compactor

Many communities now require trash companies to charge by volume, which may make a trash compactor a wise investment over time. Keep in mind that the trash compactor's job is to store garbage, which will accumulate and only get riper with age. Locate it accordingly.

The eco-friendly alternative to a garbage disposal and trash compactor is to create a "compost farm" in a specially-designed barrel.

Under-counter Appliances

Counter-height refrigerators, freezers and wine coolers may be added as budget permits. They may have a glass, enamel or stainless steel door and add convenience in the kitchen, butler pantry, master suite, entertainment and outdoor living areas.

Refrigerator

See floor plan considerations beginning on page 109 to be sure that there is sufficient clearance when refrigerator doors are opened fully. Manufacturers continue to improve the energy efficiency of refrigerators which makes newer models much less costly to operate. Visit your local appliance store for the latest models and their features.

Countertops

Kitchen/Bathrooms /Laundry Room

Engineered quartz

A wonderful new product that is competing with granite is engineered quartz. A number of manufacturers are working hard to match the beauty of natural granite, while providing a surface that offers antimicrobial protection, is seamless, burn- and scratch-proof, and never needs sealing. It will maintain its beauty indefinitely, regardless of use or care. It is comparably priced with granite.

Granite countertops

Granite is a very popular choice with today's homebuyers. It is elegant and durable. It is seamless and is unlikely to burn or chip. Granite is, however, a natural product that is porous, and therefore requires regular sealing to prevent introduction of bacteria and staining. Granite is expensive, but often has an attractive payback since kitchen upgrades usually have a positive effect on resale value. The porosity of granite varies, as does its price.

Granite tile countertops

Granite squares or tiles can be somewhat less expensive than slab (one continuous piece) if the additional labor cost for cutting, setting and grouting is less than the savings on materials. The grout between tiles makes clean up more of a challenge, on a daily basis and in maintaining the grout.

Composite countertops

This countertop is a composite made of engineered plastics that comes in a variety of colors and patterns.

This surface may be more expensive than tile and laminates, but has a high quality look. It is installed with no seams and because it is so hard, if ever chipped, can be repaired to flawless condition. It is subject to fine scratching, similar to stainless steel, but can be gently buffed to restore its luster.

A wonderful, clean feature that is available with this surface is a one-piece sink and countertop. The sink can be in one color while the countertop can be in another color or pattern. The great advantage to this design is its ease of cleaning, since no caulking or cleaning between seams is necessary, and there is no sink lip to climb over.

Laminate countertops

Laminates have fallen out of favor in recent years as granite has taken center stage. As you learn in this workbook about the importance of quality behind the walls in your high performance home, countertops may be a good place to economize. Today's laminate countertops are beautiful! Among the newest selections are finishes that are textured to look like granite and slate.

Laminate countertops are an affordable surface that comes in hundreds of colors and styles, in matte and glossy finish. A plastic material is glued to the countertop, which is made of particle board or plywood.

One disadvantage to laminate is that it will show wear over time. Even with the greatest of care, scratches and chips are likely to occur. A hot item placed on this surface is likely to cause it to burn or stain. If there is a bend in the counter, seams may be necessary and they will be visible.

The edge of the countertop can be finished with matching laminate or with wood that matches your cabinets. Either edge may be beveled with wood, or in matching or contrasting laminate, which adds a stylish accent.

While having countertops laminated, consider including matching laminate on a kitchen desktop, a vanity table or a hamper.

Ceramic tile countertops

Ceramic tile serves as an "everywhere hot plate" that comes in many colors, styles, finishes and patterns. It is more expensive than laminate but is very durable and creates a distinctive look. Tile countertops can be edged in tile or accent material. Cleaning the grout between the tiles is a chore that tile lovers accept. Tiles can be chipped or broken but can be replaced individually.

Concrete countertops

Concrete can be colored and marbled into beautiful designs. Concrete is strong and durable, but as a natural product, is porous and must be sealed periodically. Soapstone is a blue-gray natural stone countertop that is highly durable but also requires regular maintenance. Both are in the same price range as granite and engineered quartz.

Multiple level counters

Counter designs can include multiple levels, especially at a kitchen island that includes an eating bar overhang. The levels can be all of one material, or a combination of several. Many attractive combinations may be seen at kitchen design centers.

Extended overhang over base cabinets

If your base cabinet doors and drawers have knobs or handles, extending the overhang slightly will prevent constant bumping into them as you work at the island.

Protruding knobs

Pet counter

If you have a small pet, consider having a pet counter installed. If it is standard height, you may want to place something next to it that serves as a step-up. This is especially handy if you want to keep the cat or dog food away from other pets or small children. This counter also defines the pet counter from the people food counters.

Bathroom banjo counter

See Bathroom floor plans on page 119.

Finish Carpentry

Model homes display many varieties of elegant (and expensive) finish carpentry. Take notes when you see a good idea. Built-in bookcases and desks are relatively permanent and limit rearrangement possibilities.

Molding

Do you want stained or painted baseboards and trim? For stained woodwork, builders often choose a wood veneer because it is much easier for carpenters to cut, and the veneer looks like solid wood after it is installed. A visit to your home improvement store or lumberyard will let you see various widths, styles and prices.

Staircases

Staircase railings and spindles can be stained to match woodwork, can be a combination of painted and stained wood, contrasting stains or stain and decorative iron. Stairs can be wood, marble or a combination. The outside walls of the staircase can be beautifully finished in wood.

$$$ Smoothly stacked and glued wood planks can become a beautiful wood skirt along the outside of an open staircase without the higher cost of a solid piece of wood.

Chair Rails

For a touch of elegance, consider chair rails in the dining room or elsewhere. They can also be practical wherever chairs may repeatedly hit a wall. This is a nice wood accent without the greater expense of wood shelving or paneling.

Crown Molding

This molding at ceiling level is often used in the dining room but can add elegance to any room, as your budget permits. Coffered ceilings are a handsome statement when outlined with a rich wood or attractively painted molding.

Wall Paneling

Stained wood or raised wood paneling gives a warm but usually darker look. This rich-looking and expensive wood can be put on the lower third, half or more of the wall. Natural wood is subject to small and large dings and has the maintenance needs of all wood.

Built-in Cabinets

Many model homes feature built-in cabinets throughout the home. This gives the home a coordinated look and can make use of unusually shaped spaces, but adds cost. Compare the furniture that you would otherwise use with the option of new custom furniture that is designed to fit in a particular space.

Built-in Shelving

Built-in shelving can be added to the study, the entertainment area of the family room, the laundry room, bedrooms or anywhere your lifestyle dictates the need. Beware of shelving that is built into a movable door because its contents will be subject to shifting each time the door is operated.

Shelving is much easier to install now than later, especially if you want particular walls to accommodate shelving in a certain way. Valuable floor space can be saved but shelving will be permanently located. Individual shelves can be designed to be adjustable.

$$$ For less expensive shelving, use painted plywood or particle board instead of more expensive stained wood. Look for nooks and crannies in rooms where a single shelf can serve as a desk, a place for collectibles or a space to drop things when you walk in the door.

Welcoming areas

Welcoming areas will be appreciated at popular entrances to the home. They should feel like your butler, offering a bench on which to sit and that can open for storage, built-in shelving, cubbies and hooks for jackets, caps, backpacks and boots. Mud rooms may be tight on space, but a small seat or corner location might fit.

Other areas for built-in seating

Window seats are often built in a family room or on a staircase landing over a beautiful glass window. In children's bedrooms, they offer a place to actually sit, as well as serving as storage space for toys. Be sure that they are built at a convenient height for children. The attractive shape of a bow window makes it a natural setting for a functional and beautiful window bench or seat.

My desk story

My kitchen floor plan did not include a desk, but the shape of the eating area would accommodate one. When I asked the builder for a price, he came back with a prohibitively high number so I quickly decided against it.

I found just what I wanted in a discount furniture store: an attractive desk with a file drawer and a storage drawer, for a fraction of the builder's price. Its stained finish was almost identical to my cabinets.

My kitchen countertops were laminate in a pattern that I really liked. The idea hit me one day during construction to find out when the countertops would be finished. The night before they were laminated, with my builder's okay, I took my desk over to the home. The workman not only laminated the top of the desk to match, but also added the same attractive beveled wood edge that the other countertops had.

I saved a considerable amount of money and achieved the desired result of having a desk that looks like part of the kitchen, and can be temporarily removed if necessary. I added a matching wall cabinet above it, with a small fluorescent fixture from the home improvement store, to light the desk. It looks and works great!

Exterior Design

Design Planning

Your home's exterior is very visible and is as important to many homeowners as the inside. Some planning will be well worth the time and money. Checklists that begin on page 76 will give you a good idea of all the parts that need to fit together aesthetically and practically, and in what order the planning should be done. You need to decide if you are able and willing to do your own plan, or if a landscape designer would be a good investment.

Hose Bibbs

What are commonly called water spigots are often known in the construction industry as hose bibbs. You'll want them spaced no further than double hose length apart. Also consider where hoses will be stored. A hose bibb should be convenient for car washing and gardening. Your planning should include gates for any fences that could block your access to hose bibbs.

Access to hose bibbs blocked

Lot Pins

$$$ Early in the building process, you pay for your lot to be surveyed. Metal pins are pounded into the ground, marking your property lines. Unfortunately, these pins can quickly disappear under dirt and grass. You'll want to know exactly where your property ends, especially before the installation of fencing or underground sprinklers. Be sure that these pins are visible at the time of closing so that you won't have to pay for another survey.

My fence and sprinkler story

Shortly after closing on our home and moving in, we had a wonderful young man ready to build a custom fence that was to enclose our dog's "powder room." It was located on the side, abutting our neighbor's property. At the same time, the sprinkler system crew arrived. Both wanted to know where to dig. Oh, my! Where was my property line? I didn't want to be digging on my neighbor's property, nor did I want to exclude land that was mine.

I hurriedly called my builder and was told that lot pins had been placed in the corners when the survey was done, before construction. I searched extensively but couldn't find them. There was nothing to do but err on the side of caution, and have them dig on what I was sure was our land.

I later paid another $75 for the same survey company to return, locate the buried pins, and replace them at surface level. Sure enough, both the fence and sprinklers were within our lot, but a good six to twelve inches inside our property line. Another example of something important that I never thought to even ask about.

Easements

An easement is the right of someone else to use part of your property for a limited purpose, such as a right-of-way for underground utility lines. Easements may be part of the original deed or may be obtained after you own the property. Be sure you understand what easements exist on your property because you are not allowed to obstruct the use or exercise of the easements for their intended purpose.

Grading and Drainage

Your builder is responsible for having the grading and drainage done properly. This may or may not be checked by the local municipal authority. Drainage needs to be "positive," meaning that the ground should slope downward from the home's foundation. If you do your own landscaping, exercise great care to not disturb the drainage plan, lest you or your neighbor discover water or mold issues have developed, often undetected for too long.

A professional landscape designer should be knowledgeable about this and incorporate proper grading and drainage in an overall design. This is an especially good idea if you have hilly terrain, which presents additional challenges.

Driveway(s)

Driveways can make a fashion statement when finished in concrete, stone, brick or crushed rock in a multitude of shapes. Circular and oval driveways require a large area and will be a focal point. All shapes of driveway can be landscaped. Even basic single or double straight paths can have a narrow strip of Xeriscaped® landscaping down their center. Be creative!

Concrete is a long-lasting option and can be finished in various colors and textures. Do you want a smooth or brushed finish, and will the driveway serve an additional purpose such as a sports floor?

The slope of the driveway is important for proper drainage and should be carefully constructed according to blueprints.

Expanded Driveway

If you have an extra car without an additional garage, do you have room for an extra width of driveway for it? Will you be allowed by neighborhood covenants to park it outside?

Pathways

Builders often plan for a straight path that is the shortest distance between two destinations. You may want to incorporate curves and angles that add to the style of your home and yard.

Although paths will be laid before landscaping is done, plan where you'll want shrubbery so that paths will accommodate them. A path against the home is "hard against hard" and may look much better with some "soft" ground cover between it and the home. Dry landscaping is advisable to avoid having moisture seep into the foundation.

You can also be creative with the material used for pathways. In addition to concrete, stone, brick, crushed rock or other decorative material, you might want a combination of materials for a unique and interesting pattern.

Patio

A patio is usually the area for outdoor dining. Is there sufficient room for your table and chairs? If you are planning to install a gas barbeque, it will need to be plumbed. A GFI outlet will be handy to have near the barbeque.

Consider patio dimensions and shape. Might you want to enclose this area with glass or screens, either now or later? If mosquitoes come out in the evening you won't, unless you have screening. Does this area lend itself to a future addition? Consider this patio your foundation for any future enclosure.

Deck

Engineered deck material

 You may want one or more decks around the home or need one if your land is sloped. Also available is an engineered wood product that is strong and maintenance-free, as well as splinter-proof.

Natural wood

Wood can be left natural or stained. Pressure-treated wood is resistant to moisture and insects but includes some concern about the safety of the chemicals that are used in its manufacture.

If the deck is at least one story high, the wood beams used must be large enough for sturdy support and solidly imbedded in cement. A deck should have a staircase, also firmly supported in cement, so that you have access to your yard from the deck. Decks of natural wood will need periodic resealing with a good wood preservative.

Play Areas

What will go in the backyard? Do you need a flat, safe area for a swing set or sandbox? Is there room for a trampoline? Are you planning to have an in-ground pool or spa? Consider having foundations installed for any of these. Do you have the space for basketball, volleyball or tennis?

Plan your yard space as part of your landscape design. For a well-planned yard, consider talking with a landscape designer who will have helpful suggestions and past work to show you that can give you some new ideas.

Separate living area

A separate guest house is sometimes called a *casita* or granny flat. A finished space over a detached garage is called a carriage house. Determine the purpose of this space to plan its design. Be aware that including some items, such as a stove, oven or sink may qualify this area as "rental property" even though you may have no intention of renting it. If it is so qualified, your property taxes would, of course, be increased. Check local zoning regulations.

The carriage house, which is typically above the garage, may have exterior or interior stairs. The advantage to interior stairs is that they are not subjected to the weather and possible slippery conditions.

Pool/Spa/Sauna

If your climate, budget and lifestyle are a good match for an in-ground pool, determine its location even if it won't be built immediately, so that you can plan the rest of the yard accordingly. For the ultimate in elegance, ask a landscape designer or pool specialist about installing a connected pool and spa, with the spa overflowing, waterfall fashion, into the pool.

Another luxury item is a sauna. If this interests you, determine if plumbing or electricity is needed. Its location should be part of a well-planned landscape design. Saunas can also be part of an indoor exercise area.

Garden Area

For those who plan to garden, consider the orientation to sun and wind of each potential area. If you would like to have a raised garden area to allow for greater depth of rich soil, include this in your landscape design, remembering to keep the grading and drainage positive.

Dog Run

If you plan to have a dog run, plan a practical and if possible, aesthetic location. Don't locate it where the dog will bake in the sun at any time of day, nor do you want it as the focal point of your or your neighbor's yard. Consider the feasibility of having a pet door that connects the dog run to another area so that the pet will have two forms of shelter, and possibly convenient and appropriate access to the house. Also consider the protection possibilities for your pet in case another animal intrudes.

Exterior Storage

Based on your lifestyle preferences and the storage capacity of your garage, will you need or want to store items outside in a separate storage building? Consider trash cans, tools and yard equipment. Give some thought to a convenient and attractive location, checking that outbuildings aren't prohibited by neighborhood covenants.

Turf and Bedding Areas

Planning

Do you know where you want grass and what area will be shrubs or flowers? You can see how all of these decisions are inter-related and best made in concert with each other.

$$$ A cost saving measure is to buy small, less expensive shrubs and get them planted right away. Landscaping often gets put off for years. If you plant during the first year, you'll have a beautiful garden in just a few years. By the time you make a thorough landscaping plan, you'll have decently-sized shrubs that are located where you want them or that will be ready to transplant.

Assistance is available at the local nursery. Do you want trees that provide the best shade or that flower? Do you want trees that grow narrow and tall or short and wide? Will the trees provide desirable shade or will they block your favorite view? Do you want sod laid or would you rather seed and spend that money on more trees or shrubs? How much sod do you really need and want to have to maintain? Do you need a privacy hedge anywhere? What grows quickly and densely, and how far apart should shrubs be planted?

The popular term Xeriscaping® refers to the increasing trend of planting native varieties that survive well in their climate with a minimum of watering and maintenance. An understanding of this concept may be helpful in creating your overall landscaping plan.

Soil preparation

Seek the advice of your local nursery about how to prepare the type of soil in your area. Both clay and sandy soil types benefit from having organic material mixed in to a depth of at least 8" below the surface before adding topsoil.

Homebuyers sometimes arrange with their builder to have sprinklers and sod installed before closing so that they don't have mud to deal with during their first few weeks in the new home. If you have animals or children who will be running in and out of a dirty or muddy yard onto your new flooring and carpets, talk with your builder about the possibility of a formal agreement that would allow for this arrangement.

Sprinkler System

If you live in an area where rainfall will not be sufficient to maintain your landscaping, strongly consider installing a sprinkler system before laying sod or seed. It is an expensive item but is enormously convenient and should increase property value.

Popular types of systems include sub-surface, pressurized and self-draining.

Sub-surface, the newest type of sprinkler, has a grid system of buried tubes that "drip" below ground and gently soak the area without losing water to mis-directed spray and evaporation. A visit with your landscape or sprinkler system expert will help you to decide which type is best for you.

Create a good sprinkler plan for your watering needs. Ideally, group plants together that have similar watering requirements. This allows the builder to install a sprinkler stub in the correct location. If you plan to eventually finish the garage, have an interior-mounted sprinkler controller installed at finished-wall depth so it won't have to be disconnected and re-mounted. With whatever system you have installed, obtain a blueprint of the entire system for future reference.

Sprinkler controllers can now have humidity sensors, enabling them to water only when the humidity of the soil demands it. As part of your structured wiring, your controller can be directed from information received from a weather satellite! This saves on unnecessary watering, as well as improving the health of the lawn.

Water Feature

Does your landscaping budget allow for a decorative water fountain at the entrance to your home or in the backyard near the patio? A koi lagoon (koi look like large goldfish) can be swimming year round in many climates. Now is the time to do the planning so that pre-wiring and rough-in plumbing can be done underground, even if you won't be installing these items now.

Outdoor Lighting

See page 56.

Fencing

If you live in an area that is governed by covenants or building zoning restrictions, read them carefully. Fence construction is often restricted to a certain height, material or location, or prohibited altogether. If you fence an area, consider installing gates on each side of fencing so that you won't need to take a long walk around. Plan the locations for hose bibbs and fencing so that the hose bibbs can be accessed conveniently.

If you have or plan to have children or pets, fencing may be necessary or desirable. A well-designed plan will show where doorways should be included or excluded from fenced areas. Fences also afford privacy and protection from wind. Wood fences are attractive but will require periodic maintenance.

Consider engineered wood or composite material for a strong, much lower maintenance fence.

Contract

DO THIS RIGHT!

Your sales contract is an important legal document. Strongly consider hiring an attorney with experience in real estate transactions to examine it before you sign. The more clear and thorough this document is, the less likely you are to become mired in conflict over misunderstandings. This contract is your blueprint for success.

Choose your builder with care

After you have reviewed this workbook, consult with an architect, if desired. Create a preliminary budget and a list of questions for builders. Shop for land and visit model homes as you prepare to interview builders and their references. You will learn as you go and become ready to choose a builder and a blueprint or floor plan. The builder you choose may or may not have a contract form with which he or she is familiar but you are not.

Soliciting bids

In order to get the lowest bid, some buyers have a schematic (simple drawing) or a blueprint created, which they then submit to several builders. If the bids come back with similar bottom lines, you may be comparing "apples to apples" and are therefore helping to get fair bids.

On the other hand, because the building process is so complex, essential items may have intentionally or unintentionally been omitted from the bid, items that will eventually end up in the bottom line. Other builders will include these items, consequently submitting a higher but more accurate bid. This is a game in which you can be the loser. How are you to know how thorough each bid is? Many good builders refuse to do business this way.

Examine a real contract

Included in this section is a sample contract and addendum from a semi-custom builder. You may notice that most of the language seems to be directed at protecting builder rights. Builders do, indeed, accept a great deal of risk, and do need protection. However, anything that is important to you as the homebuyer that is not in writing will not be "guaranteed" to you because it not part of the contract.

All essential information needs to be included. If your attorney draws up the contract, your builder needs to read it carefully and agree to it, or identify any areas that need to be changed or discussed. All parties must sign the contract and shake hands in a genuine spirit of cooperation and mutual respect. Without this, trouble lies ahead. With this, important ground work for success has been created.

Do your part to make this project a success

This relationship need not and should not be adversarial. The builder is in business to make a profit but wants you to be happy with your home. This can only enhance his or her good name and probably bring referral business. If you've done your shopping and can make confident and timely decisions, he should welcome your involvement. Sitting down before contract signing may give you a better sense of his willingness to work with you. Read more about preventing and resolving problems, beginning on page 93.

Payment Policy

You need to be in agreement with your builder about payments you will be required to make before closing. Payment is often done through a bank escrow account (that is kept for this purpose only) or directly by the owner upon receipt of invoice, although when trades are paid by the builder, they are much more likely to respond to his direction. As change orders or allowance overages occur, immediate payment to the supplier may be expected. You need to plan for all payments in your cash flow or budget.

Basic Information Contained in Contract

A general list of items is located on page 86.

Specifications and Materials List

A general checklist is located on page 86.

Allowances

In order for the builder to determine a total contract price, an allowance is usually assigned for items such as lighting and flooring. The more realistic this number is, the more easily you will be able to stay within your budget. A visit to a few stores will give you a clearer idea of how much the allowance will actually buy. If the allowance remains at a standard amount ($1000) but you know you will spend more like $3000 or $5000, add the extra to your upgrade budget as early as possible.

Change Order Policy

The builder's change order policy should be stated in your contract and all change orders should in writing, for his protection as well as yours. Builders get burned much too often by late change orders that are expensive and disruptive. The policy should include when, what, how and who. *When* is it too late to request a change order? If you are completely unhappy with something that has already been done, can you have it changed if you're willing to pay for all costs incurred because of the change? The answer may still be no because the change would disrupt the construction schedule (yours and the jobs following yours) so much that no price is worth it.

After going through the customizing checklists that begin on page 32, ask **what** kind of change orders your builder is willing to do. Remember that change orders are alterations to your contract. You will **save a significant amount of money,** as well as experience much lower stress by having a thorough plan that fits within your budget *before* construction begins. **How** does this process work? Is there a separate charge for the administrative time required and for materials and labor? **Who** should you contact and how will you get the information you need including availability, features and cost?

Construction Timeline and Schedule

A sample timeline is located on page 18. The best laid plans will face challenges and actual construction rarely follows the schedule exactly.

Your builder should provide you with a schedule that outlines the phases of construction and approximate dates of completion. This information is crucial to your planning. Coordinate the closing date with your lender, keeping in mind that there may be factors beyond everyone's control that may affect it.

When the home isn't completed by contracted date

What will happen if your home isn't completed by the expected date? You may have a firm closing date on your old home and need to vacate. Where will you live and who will pay for this temporary housing? Sometimes contracts have explicit penalty clauses for late completion. Under what conditions does the builder accept this responsibility? This should be included in your contract. How about having a bonus built into the contract for early or on-time completion? How would delays outside of the builder's control affect it? What if you ask for changes that cause delays?

When workmanship or products are not satisfactory

If you are watching the construction of your home carefully, you will probably be able to have mistakes and problems addressed and remedied promptly. Consider having language included in your contract that addresses what will happen if there are any significant problems that haven't been or can't be resolved.

Approval authority

Who is the final word on whether something is acceptable or not? Remember that this builder was hand-chosen and deemed trustworthy, but you also trust your own judgment. Come to agreement about this with your builder before contract signing.

Termination procedure

This is about as much fun as talking about your own funeral, but do you and your builder want to spell out what the procedure will be if either of you wants out? It's not likely to happen but having it all spelled out can bring a subconscious peace of mind to both parties.

Contingency Clauses

What could go wrong? Too many things to list. They probably won't, but the more specific your contract, the smoother the path to solution, should any arise. Some contracts include an arbitration clause that gives decision power to a third party. This is an expense and forfeiture of your legal right to dispute, so be certain that you understand this policy thoroughly before agreeing to it.

Site Visit Policy

How much access will you have to your new home as it is being constructed? This is important to discuss with your builder. You need to mutually agree on this policy and then adhere to it. Your builder's point of view may be that you'll be in the way, that you could get hurt on the site, that you could cause damage on the site, and that you are constantly looking over his shoulder.

Consumer quality control

Seeing a work in progress can be frightening to us "amateurs." We don't know what is normal and what is wrong. Instead of jumping to conclusions, take note of any concerns and bring them to your next meeting with the builder. If you feel that it is an urgent matter, call with your concern. It is often the case, though, that the mistake you see has already been noted by the builder and the correction ordered.

What, who, when, how

Your attention to detail is important and if guidelines can be agreed upon, your visits can be productive without being disruptive. Use common sense; don't visit during the day if it means interfering with workers. Don't give instructions to workers if they are being directed by the builder. This is especially tempting if you are nervous about something they are doing, but confusion and mis-communication are almost guaranteed. If you visit only at night, this temptation is removed.

If you have children, it will be well worth the trouble and expense to hire a babysitter. This is a construction site with nails, nail guns, all kinds of sharp objects, holes, and missing railings. You will be much more welcome on the site on a regular basis, you'll be able to focus on all of the details that you're trying to take in and your children will be much safer and happier elsewhere.

My visiting story

We were able to rent a house very near our building site, so were able to visit frequently. It was fun to watch the house take shape, to be able to dream of what was going to be. It also became a major source of stress and worry because we were finding mistakes regularly.

I had received no preparation for visiting a construction site. I only later learned that much of what I saw was pretty normal for a project as complex as a whole house. Projects may remain idle for a few days because of scheduling of materials or workers. I was reporting errors before the builder had a chance to correct them. The superintendent told me that he felt like I was always looking over his shoulder. On one hand, I felt compelled to do so because I didn't want irreparable mistakes made. I did, however, appreciate his viewpoint and wished the communication could have been better.

Communication Policy

There probably is no written communication policy but that might be a good idea for everyone concerned. Much of the stress homebuyers experience builds up because of lack of good communication. If there is a clear understanding of how important information is to reach the buyer, and a way for the buyer to reach the builder when necessary, miscommunication will disappear and the buyer will be able to enjoy his day and sleep at night.

The wonderful world of the Web

Builders are to be encouraged to communicate as much as possible on the Internet, for their sake and yours. It's fast, easy, and lets you obsess over your "baby" at all hours of the day and night! Ideally, a website or section is set up for your building project, especially for custom homes. This website can have updated photos, and allow you to shop online for product features and details. This isn't a substitute for face-to-face meetings but it can serve as an efficient way for you to follow your home's progress, ask questions and get helpful product information.

Inspection Policy/Walkthroughs

The contract should state exactly when in the construction schedule inspections will take place. Even the biggest production builders should allow you a walkthrough after framing and electrical. Bring your workbook and check EVERYTHING; now is the last chance for some items to be corrected.

Notice if switches and outlets are installed evenly with each other and square with the wall. There are million dollar homes with obviously crooked switchplates. Some people will never notice while others will see that switch every time they pass by it.

Private inspection

Another option worth consideration is having a private inspection done at one or more points in the construction process. Multiple inspections can be at "jurisdictional inspection points" (i.e. foundation, framing, electrical, etc.) *Inspection just before wallboard is installed lets the inspector see many important elements at a time when the builder is able to make any additions or corrections.*

Remember that while an inspector is looking for code violations and construction irregularities, you will want to check that change orders have been properly executed and that the light fixture is centered under the staircase. Many of these details are beyond the scope of an inspector and squarely on your shoulders.

Builders are beginning to welcome private inspection, as long as it is done by someone who is qualified and experienced with new construction. In addition to standard construction, the inspector should have received training on what to look for in the high performance home. You'll also want to be sure that your money is well-spent by choosing this professional carefully.

Builder's Warranty Policy

Builders will usually correct any items during your first year of ownership, and structural defects for 8 to 10 years. Some builders warranty for a longer period of time, especially if a problem is clearly faulty products or workmanship. Ask your builder, and if necessary, your attorney, about implied and express warranties, which vary from builder to builder and state to state. This is a good item to discuss when interviewing builders.

Many homeowners would love to have their "bumper-to-bumper" first-year warranty continue past the first year. Your builder may offer an extended warranty, often provided by a completely separate company.

Product Warranty Policy

Is all work being done by local workers? Written warranties are important but subcontractors who must travel a long distance for a callback may want to charge you for their time, even though they contracted for this work in the first place. Check the written warranties of each product but if at all possible, use local companies.

Contract Inspection

If your real estate attorney has not written the contract, it is worth the cost of having him or her check it before you sign. Consider how much money you are spending on this project and give it the care it deserves.

Sample Fixed Price Semi-Custom Contract

ABC Construction Company, Inc.
123 Rosemont Lane
Anytown, USA 12345
555-555-0000

ABC Construction Co., Inc, (known as "Contractor",) acknowledge having received from Purchaser the sum of $_____ in the form of a personal check to be held by Contractor as earnest money and part payment for the following described real estate (known as "Property) at Lot __, Block __, of _____Subdivision in the Town of _____ , County of _____, State of _____. Also known as _____ .

The undersigned person(s)_____, as joint tenants, (known as "Purchaser",) hereby agrees to buy the Property, and the undersigned owner (Contractor) hereby agrees to sell the Property upon the terms and conditions stated herein.

The purchase price shall be U.S. $ _____ payable as follows: Contractor, hereby receipted for as earnest money and part payment. Purchaser to supply Contractor with a copy of loan approval before Contractor will begin construction. Final payment is due upon substantial completion of home. Substantial completion has been met at such time as Contractor receives a Certificate of Occupancy.

If a new loan is to be obtained by Purchaser from a third party, Purchaser agrees to promptly and diligently (A) apply for such a loan (B) execute all documents and furnish all information and documents required by the lender, and (C) pay the customary costs of obtaining such a loan. Then, if such loan is not approved on or before _____, this contract shall be null and void and all payments and things of value received hereunder shall be returned to Purchaser, excluding monies spent for blueprint and bidding which are non-refundable, regardless $1,000.00 is non-refundable. Purchaser to apply for said loan within 5 (five) working days from signing of this contract. Failure to make such timely loan application shall constitute a default hereunder, entitling Contractor liquidated damages, being said earnest money deposit.

Purchaser shall pay cost of any appraisal for loan purposes.

TITLE COMMITMENT: A current commitment for title insurance policy in an amount equal to the purchase price shall be furnished on or before the date of closing. Contractor shall deliver the title insurance policy to Purchaser after closing and pay the premium thereon. Contractor shall choose title insurance agent and/or company. The title insurance commitment shall commit to delete or insure over the standard exceptions which relate to parties in possession; unrecorded easements; survey matters; any unrecorded mechanics' liens; gap period (effective date of commitment to date deed is recorded); and unpaid taxes, assessments and unredeemed tax sales prior to the year of Closing. Any additional premium expense to obtain this additional coverage shall be paid by Purchaser.

DELIVERY OF DEED/EXCEPTIONS TO TITLE: Contractor shall execute and deliver a good and sufficient general warranty deed to Purchaser on the date of conveying the Property free and clear of all taxes, except general taxes for the year of closing and free and clear of all liens and encumbrances except those that are created by Purchaser.

PRORATIONS: General taxes for the year of closing shall be prorated to the date of closing based upon the most recent levy and most recent assessment. All adjustments and prorating at the time of closing shall be final. Purchaser understands that Purchaser will need to change all separately metered utilities to the property from Contractors name no later than one day after conveyance occurs. Purchaser does hereby agree to be obligated to pay the costs of such utilities.

COLORS AND OPTIONS: Selections. Purchaser shall have ready color selections upon the request of Contractor.

CHANGE ORDERS: Purchaser may request changes in the plans or specifications, but shall do so through a written change order. If the request for change is feasible, in Contractor's opinion, then Contractor shall give Purchaser an estimate describing the change and estimating the cost. All change orders in excess of $1,000.00 shall require a written response from Contractor. Purchaser may accept such estimate for the change by signing said change order within three (3) days after presentation. All said agreed upon change orders shall become part of the Contract. A builders fee of at least 15% shall apply to all cost increases arising from change orders.

If Contractor has given Purchaser five written estimates in response to Purchasers' request for change orders, Contractor may charge a $100 processing fee for each written estimate given by Contractor thereafter, in response to Purchasers' request for changes. Such processing fee shall apply whether or not a final change order results from such written estimates.

DIRECTION OF WORKING FORCES: Purchaser agrees that direction and supervision of the working forces, including, but not limited to all subcontractors, rests exclusively with Contractor, and Purchaser agrees not to issue any instruction, or otherwise interfere with the working forces.

ADDITIONAL WORK: Purchaser agrees not to contract for additional work with ABC Construction's contractors or subcontractors and not to engage other contractors or subcontractors to perform work on the Property until the residence is complete and title is transferred to Purchaser. Purchaser doing any work on home will be done at their own risk, as builder is not responsible for same. Purchaser shall have his or her own insurance.

CHANGES: Any changes which alter or deviate from the work and specifications provided herein must be requested by Purchaser in writing and paid for at time of ordering.

SPECIFICATIONS: See Exhibit A.

OCCUPANCY: Purchaser shall not occupy the residence, nor shall any property of Purchaser be stored therein, until the residence is fully completed and title is transferred to Purchaser. There will be a daily rental fee of $50.00 if Purchaser moves in before closing. If Purchaser moves in, Purchaser accepts home as is.

WALK-THROUGH INSPECTION: Purchaser shall inspect the residence with Contractor prior to the closing and, at such time, shall specify, by notice in writing to Contractor, all matters which Purchaser claims do not conform to the requirements of this Agreement, and which matters may be repaired or remedied by Contractor after the date of closing. Contractor shall designate the date and hour of such inspection, acceptance by Purchaser of the deed to the Property shall be deemed to be full performance by Contractor of each and every obligation of the Contractor hereunder, including any oral statements. The Certificate of Occupancy shall be deemed conclusive evidence of completion.

In addition, ABC Construction Co., Inc. will pay all contractors and subcontractors which it employs upon the real property and agrees to indemnify Purchaser and hold Purchaser harmless for any and all mechanic liens placed upon the property if said subcontractor actually worked upon the property at the request and behalf of Contractor.

DATE OF CLOSING: Within 5 (five) days from the date Contractor gives Purchaser notice that the residence is substantially completed, Purchaser and Contractor shall close the transaction contemplated by this Agreement. The date, hour, and place of closing shall be as designated by Contractor and shall deliver possession of the Property to Purchaser on the date of closing.

LIMITED WARRANTY FOR CONTRACTOR WORK AND MATERIALS:

A.   A1.   Purchaser is also fully aware that due to various climatic conditions, including weather and moisture, molds may form during the construction process, and may have a negative, adverse effect on the purchaser or their guests. Purchaser understands that Contractor will use all reasonable construction methods in an attempt to prevent any such mold growth. Notwithstanding these construction practices, Purchaser hereby agrees to waive and release Contractor from any and all claims concerning molds, or the presence of mold, in and around the finished Property.

    A2.   The level, if any, of radon gas that may be present in the Property after its construction is not predictable. Contractor shall have no liability or obligation if radon gas is present in the Property. If radon is present in the Property at such a level that Purchaser desires to mitigate it, Contractor shall cooperate in the correction of the problem with such work to be billed at cost plus a 15% builders fee. Purchaser agrees that Contractor shall not be responsible for the presence of any radon gas in the Property. Purchaser waives any and all claims for negligence, failure to mitigate, or other legal theories upon which such issues could be raised as it relates to radon gas.

B. Contractor EXPRESSLY WARRANTS for a period of ONE YEAR from closing that all work performed by Contractor shall be completed in a workmanlike manner according to the standards of care and competence of the construction industry in _(town)__, __(state)__. Contractor also EXPRESSLY WARRANTS that all materials supplied by Contractor are guaranteed to be as specified in this proposal for a period of ONE YEAR from supplying of same, EXCEPT IN THOSE INSTANCES WHERE A MANUFACTURER OF AN ITEM SUPPLIED PROVIDES ITS OWN EXPRESS WARRANTIES. In such cases, all manufacturers for items installed shall be delivered directly to Purchaser and Contractor shall not be responsible in any way for warranting same, nor shall any claim for warranty of merchantability of fitness for a particular purpose be maintained against Contractor by Purchaser regarding the same. Rather, Purchaser agrees that s/he shall look directly and exclusively to the manufacturer in any claims regarding the quality of performance of items, which have been warranted by the manufacturer. Purchaser agrees to accept the EXPRESS WARRANTIES provided for above IN LIEU OF ANY AND ALL IMPLIED WARRANTIES REGARDING THE WORK AND MATERIALS supplied by Contractor including, but not limited to, warranties or fitness for particular purposed, merchantability, habitability or workmanlike construction.

C. If any work or materials supplied by Contractor are found not to be in conformance with the warranties provided for herein, PURCHASER SHALL GIVE WRITTEN NOTICE OF SAME WITHIN 3 (THREE) DAYS OF DISCOVERY, OR SAID NONCONFORMITIES SHALL BE DEEMED TO BE WAIVED by Purchaser. Upon receipt of proper written notice, Contractor shall provide such labor and material as are necessary to correct the non-conformities.

D. Under the terms of this limited warranty, CONTRACTOR SHALL BE RESPONSIBLE ONLY FOR THE COST OF LABOR AND MATERIAL necessary to correct the non-conformity and SHALL NOT UNDER ANY CIRCUMSTANCES BE LIABLE FOR ANY CONSEQUENTIAL or INCIDENTAL DAMAGES of whatever nature.

E. Purchaser recognizes and understands the limited nature of Contractor's responsibility and warranties and expressly agrees to the terms outlined herein regarding same, waiving any other rights, remedies and potential damages s/he may have regarding the work and materials to be supplied under this contract.

F. The contractor will do what it can to mitigate the cracking of the concrete, but cracks that form in the different slabs that make up the residence are not covered by this warranty. Only excessive cracking due to improper compaction or settlement shall be covered by the one-year warranty.

G. The Contractor shall not warrant any work performed by Purchaser or their agents.

H. **Soils Conditions.**   Contractor has required that a soils report be
obtained for the benefit of Purchaser. If such report reveals that
engineering designs will be required for the foundations or subfloors, such
designs shall be prepared by XYZ Engineering and XYZ Engineering shall
be requested to review such plans with Purchaser and Contractor.
Contractor agrees to oversee the installation of the foundation according to
any such design requirements, but Purchaser hereby agrees to waive and
indemnify Contractor from any and all claims that may be brought
pursuant to soils conditions of the property, except for those claims
specifically identified in Paragraph 13. Purchaser, being fully advised,
understand that they are waiving all possible claims, including, but not
limited to negligence, breach of warranty, and claims brought under the
State Consumer Protection Act against Contractor for any issues involving
the soils contained on the property. Both Purchaser and Contractor
understand that XYZ Engineering shall be responsible for the engineering
and designs necessary to prevent adverse conditions identified by the
testing. Purchaser acknowledges that soils testing may not accurately
predict the adverse effects of any soil condition.
**Contractor shall provide final grading, per the requirements of XYZ
Engineering. PURCHASER ACKNOWLEDGES THAT PROPER
DRAINAGE MUST BE MAINTAINED, AFTER THE RESIDENCE IS
CONSTRUCTED, AND THAT LANDSCAPING CAN ADVERSELY
AFFECT DRAINAGE. CONTRACTOR SHALL HAVE NO LIABILITY
FOR DRAINAGE/LANDSCAPING PROBLEMS OF ANY KIND.**

**Any modifications to structural or basement design that become
necessary after closing, due to soil conditions, shall be performed by
Contractor on a cost plus 15% basis.**

The Developer and/or Builder shall have the first right of refusal to repair any
and all items relating to the construction and development of said dwelling
and/or subdivision. Any disapproval as to how or as to the extent of the repairs
shall be specified in writing. The Developer and/or Builder within forty-five
(45) days shall advise party in writing, matters regarding the disapproval.
Both parties at this time shall decide on a resolution for said disapproval.

ARBITRATION: In the event the parties herein deem the other to be in default
of any terms contained herein, all such controversies shall be resolved by
arbitration. Said arbitration to be controlled exclusively by the Uniform
Arbitration Act of the State of __(state)__ as that Act is now in force and
amended from time to time. In the event arbitration is had, each party
expressly agrees to be bound by said arbitration except there shall be only one
arbitrator who shall first be mutually agreed to by the parties in accordance
with the statutory provisions provided from same, and said arbitration shall be
a condition precedent to pursuing any claim. The prevailing party shall be
awarded its costs and reasonable attorneys fees by the Arbitrator.

Each party shall be responsible for its share of the arbitration fees in
accordance with the applicable Rules of Arbitration. In the event a party fails
to proceed with arbitration, unsuccessfully challenges the arbitrator's award, or
fails to comply with the arbitrator's award, the other party is entitled to costs

of suit, including a reasonable attorney's fee for having to compel arbitration or defend or enforce the award.

TERMINATION BY CONTRACTOR: If Contractor does not receive payment when due hereunder or if Purchaser otherwise breaches this Contract and fails to correct such breach within ten (10) days after written notice specifying such breach has been given to them, Contractor shall have the right to cease work on the Property and to recover from Purchaser payment for all work performed to such date, together with all other items of loss resulting from such default, including reasonable overhead, profit, and other consequential damages. Such remedy shall not be exclusive, and Contractor, may pursue any and all other legal or equitable remedies available to them in such event.

TERMINATION BY PURCHASER: If Contractor commits a breach of this Contract and fails to correct such breach within ten (10) days after written notice specifying such breach has been given to Contractor, Purchaser may elect to terminate this Contract. In that event, Purchaser may finish the property by whatever method they deem expedient, after which a final accounting shall be made between the parties. In such accounting, Contractor shall be entitled to a pro-rata portion of Contractor's overhead and profit based upon the work properly completed by Contractor, less any additional costs above the price due hereunder, incurred by Purchaser in completing the Property. Such remedy shall not be exclusive, and the Purchaser may pursue any and all other legal and equitable remedies available to them in such event.

NON-ASSIGNMENT: Neither party may assign this Contract, or delegate their duties and obligations under it, to any third party, without the prior, written consent of the other party.

BINDING EFFECT: This Contract shall inure to the benefit of, and shall bind, the parties hereto and their respective heirs, grantees, personal representatives, administrators, conservators, successors, and assigns.

NOTICE: Any notice or tender required or permitted by this Contract shall be in writing and shall be delivered in person, sent by Certified Mail, or sent by overnight courier. If such notice is hand delivered, personally served, or delivered by overnight courier, it shall be effective immediately upon such delivery or service. If sent by mail it shall be sent by Certified Mail, return receipt requested, and shall be effective three (3) days after deposit of the same into a United States Mail Depository with sufficient postage attached for delivery to the parties at their following addresses.

PURCHASER:	CONTRACTOR:
_____	ABC Construction Company, Inc.,
_____	Attn: John Smith. ABC, Vice
	President
_____	123 Rosemont Lane
_____	Anytown, USA 12345

Change of address shall be treated as any other notice.

CONTROLLING LAW: This Contract shall be interpreted and enforced in accordance with the laws of the State of _____ .

EXCLUDED WORK: Contractor shall not be responsible for landscaping, fencing or topsoil, nor for performing the following work on the Property, which shall be separately arranged and paid for by Purchaser and shall not be warranted by Contractor:

_____

_____

INTEREST AND LATE CHARGES: If Purchaser fails to make payments as agreed all such payments shall be subject to 18% late interest, as well as $50.00 late charges per day.

ORAL STATEMENTS: In the event Contractor, its employees, servants, officers, owners or agents make any ORAL STATEMENTS about the quality of the repairs, modifications, building or supplying of work, but not limited to, all materials and labor, it is recognized by Purchasers that such ORAL STATEMENTS DO NOT CONSTITUTE WARRANTIES, same were not relied upon by Purchaser and are not part of this contract for services. The entire contract is embodied in this writing and same constitutes the final expression of the parties' agreements, being a complete and exclusive statement of the terms of that agreement and is binding upon all heirs, successors and assigns of the parties herein. Same may not be modified unless in writing and signed by both parties.

TIME IS OF THE ESSENCE/ REMEDIES: Time is of the essence hereof. If any check received as payment hereunder or any other payment due hereunder is not paid, honored or tendered when due, or in any other obligation hereunder is not performed or waived as herein provided, there shall be the following remedies.
If Purchaser is in default, Contractor may elect to treat this contract as cancelled, in which case all payments and things of value received hereunder shall be forfeited and retained on behalf of Contractor and Contractor may recover such damages as may be proper. If Contractor is in default, Purchaser may elect to treat this agreement as cancelled, in which case payment shall be returned, excluding monies spent for blueprints and bidding. Purchaser agrees not to do anything that would alter their financial and employment status before closing.

LEGAL COUNSEL: Purchaser acknowledges that Contractor advised them to consult with their own, independent legal counsel for information and advice concerning this Contract, prior to signing it.

ACCEPTANCE: By setting forth my signature below, I hereby acknowledge that I have thoroughly read and agree to all conditions, terms, specifications, exhibits and particularly the provisions for the LIMITED WARRANTY for Contractor's work and WARRANTY DISCLAIMER PROVISIONS for Subcontractor work and materials. I have had an opportunity to discuss or negotiate said terms with ABC Construction Co., Inc. as well as with legal counsel of my choosing.

Fixed Price Semi-Custom Contract: EXHIBIT A

Attached to, and made a part of that certain contract dated   , 2007
between ABC Construction Co., Inc. (Contractor) and
(Purchaser), regarding the property located at   County of   ,
State of

To build a two story home, plan # _____Victorian Model, Craftsman Style
Elevation A), with approximately 1800 square feet finished on upper 2 floors
with approximately 595 square feet of finished basement and unfinished
basement mechanical room. The finished areas of the basement are to include
the stairway, family room with a bar, bathroom and a bedroom. Builder to
furnish all labor and materials according to plans and specifications in
contract. Changes different than plans will be an extra charge or credited
accordingly.

The purchase price includes the following:

1. Design, Permits & Fees: Building permit, water & sewer taps, inspection
   fees, design review fees, drafting and engineering fees.
2. Foundations & Flatwork: 8 foot tall concrete foundation walls with a 1'
   framed pony wall for 9' walls in basement, white steel window wells, damp
   proofing, interior and exterior flatwork all with a broom finish, excavation,
   backfill, water settling or compaction, and interior drain system with a pit.
3. Utilities: Electric, gas, water, sewer services lateral installed on property.
4. Framing: Framing lumber, framing labor, engineered roof trusses with
   vaults.
5. Windows & Doors: Amsco Legacy white single hung windows with standard
   grids in all. Front Door (See "Front Door Allowances" below), Garage man
   door to be steel ½ light with internal grids, Great room patio door to be a 6'
   Thermatru smooth star in-swing door with grids.
6. Plumbing: Bathtub-one piece fiberglass tile stamped in main bath, standard
   fixtures (white), round sinks, Delta 2530 double lever control faucets and
   hardware chrome, Americast 10" deep kitchen sink with 1/3 hp disposal and
   white faucet with sprayer, round front stools, Master bath to have a Jetta J-
   11 whirlpool tub and an acrylic shower base. 1 water line to fridge, 2-40
   gallon water heaters, 2 frost proof sillcocks, gas lines to 1 furnace, 1 water
   heater, 1 fireplace, & 1 BBQ. Water piping is to be Aquapex.
7. Heating: Lennox 80% furnace, 3 ½ ton air conditioning system, humidifier,
   programmable thermostat and furnace filter.
8. Electrical: According to state code, 150 amp service, toggle switches, one
   bath fan per bathroom, 5 TV jacks and 5 phone jacks, 6 kitchen can lights, 6
   porch can lights, 3 soffit outlets, 3 dimmers, A/C disconnect, 1 landscape
   circuit, 1 sprinkler outlet, 1 whirlpool tub, 2 fan/lights and 2 reading cans.
9. Specialty Wiring: Home theater pre-wire,3 rooms sound pre-wired.
10. Roofing: Roofing is to be Elk 30 year with standard vents, roof to wall
    flashing, painted vents, and #30 felt.
11. Fireplace: Fireplace is to be Superior 3530 direct vent with a wall switch.
12. Garage: 22'x22' - 2 car garage with 1 – 16'x8' series 311 insulated garage
    door with windows with 1 garage door opener and 2 remotes.

13. Insulation: House to be insulated with cellulose blown R-13 walls and R-38 ceilings, interior vapor barrier and anti-air infiltration system. R-19 Sound insulation in basement ceiling and R-11 at bathroom walls. Garage to be insulated with cellulose blown R-13 walls and R-19 ceilings.
14. Exterior Finishes: Masonite 1 x 6 siding, 12" soffit and 8" fascia. PVC lattice is to be used to skirt the front porch.
15. Drywall: ½" drywall on all, medium spray and knock-down on walls and ceilings with bullnose corners. Garage is to be fire taped as code requires. Window jambs are to be wrapped on 3 sides w/bullnose corners.
16. Painting: Exterior to be painted with one body color and one trim color. Interior walls and ceilings are to be primed and painted with one color throughout. Interior woodwork, doors, & mantle are to be painted with a second color. Stairway materials are to have a split finish. Contractor to give final approval on all colors.
17. Cabinetry: (See "Cabinetry Allowance" below) Canyon Creek Cabinetry to include: Alder Roman Arch Cabinets with 3" Crown molding, 36" uppers with 42" corners at kitchen, trash pull out, tilt outs in kitchen, grand height master vanities, bar cabinetry.
18. Interior Trim: Painted 3 ¼" case and 4 ¼" base, outside and inside corners, Carmelle doors with pine jambs, US10B hinges, US10B Hancock door locks, painted window sills, split finish stair railing in oak, and painted fireplace mantle. Bathroom towel bars and paper holders are to be polished chrome.
19. Specialty Iron: Window well ladder and 1 custom grate.
20. Floor Coverings: All labor & materials are to be supplied by Westpoint Interiors. Kitchen, Dining, and entry will have a Laminate wood floor. All Countertops are to be Formica. (See "Floor Coverings Allowance" below)
21. Appliances: Stainless Steel/Black Appliances, microwave is included (See "Appliance Allowance" below)
22. Light Fixtures: To be selected. (See "Light Fixture Allowance" below)
23. Glasswork: Mirrors & shower doors-1 shower door with panels, 2-standard mirrors and 1 oval mirror.
24. Closet Shelving: Wire shelving throughout. (See "Closet Allowance" below)
25. Rain Gutters & Exterior Piping: Factory painted seamless rain gutters and down spouts. (Purchaser to choose from chart.)
26. Final Cleaning, Final Grading
27. Trash Removal, Site Clean Up, Sanitation, Temporary Services and Misc.
28. Builders Risk Insurance
29. Radon Mitigation: None.
30. Home will be placed on lot with garage to be on west side and facing south.
Purchase price includes following allowances. Any overages will be paid by the Purchasers.

Cabinetry Allowance	$ 6000
Light Fixture Allowance	$ 800
Appliance Allowance	$ 900
Floor Coverings Allowance	$15 sq.yd.
Mirror and Shower Door Allowance	$ 600
Front Door Allowance	$ 400
Closet Allowance	$ 600
Total Purchase Price	$250,000
Total Paid.....................................$	
Total Due $	

Financing

Pre-approval

Before you fall in love with any builder, blueprint or model home, visit a mortgage banker or broker to be pre-approved for a loan amount. Typical items that you'll need to bring to this meeting are listed on page 12. You'll gain confidence that the amount you're planning to spend is reasonable and likely to be available to you when you need it. This makes model viewing real instead of just window shopping. This is a fun and exciting project and if you do it right, it will be very enjoyable.

The mortgage industry offers many choices to the new homebuyer. Be aware that lenders make their money by selling you a loan. Don't assume that the maximum amount they are willing to lend you is the right amount for you. Foreclosures are generally the result of buying more home than the owners could afford. While many loan packages look attractive, consider the size of payments over the entire life of the loan to be sure your loan is right-sized for you.

For custom buyers, construction and final loans that can be rolled into one have become a popular choice. See page 13 for information on choosing a good lender.

It's a good idea to know what your current credit score is, which is included as a total number on your credit report. See Website directory on page 234 for addresses of the three major credit bureaus.

Types of Mortgage Professionals

Mortgage *bankers* offer their bank's mortgage types and rates. Mortgage *brokers* shop around for other companies' mortgages and rates. Loans obtained through the Internet are typically administered by the lowest bidder, who comes to you without references.

Ask questions about types of mortgages and their advantages and disadvantages. Evaluate the lender's ability to communicate by how well you understand the answers to your questions. This is your money and you should have some level of confidence that you understand how the process works. Many people are intimidated by financial matters and professionals, which is not an enjoyable experience! A good lender will make you feel at ease.

Many homebuyers do well with a local bank that is in stiff competition with the big guys. Their competitive edge is their superb customer service. They want you as a customer for the long term and are therefore interested in giving you the best service they can.

It is important for homebuyers to know that having the money on the table on closing day is far from a guaranteed event. Having a lender that can step in to correct any problem along the way will be very much appreciated when all goes smoothly because of their personal attention to your needs.

Using "Old" Land

If you are building on land you have owned for some time, you may want to investigate using its equity as part of your construction financing.

Questions to Ask Lenders

Ask about the difference in charges, partial-month interest payments, the dollar difference to you between closings at the *beginning* of the month and closings at the *end* of the month. What is the difference between fixed-rate and variable-rate mortgages, and which is a better choice for your particular situation?

How early can you lock in an interest rate? How will making a larger or smaller down payment affect the interest rate? What are the advantages and disadvantages of taking out your own construction loan versus having the builder do so? What is a one-time close and how would that affect you? How can you avoid having to pay private mortgage insurance, which protects only the insurance company? Also be sure to ask for a Good Faith Estimate and Truth-in-Lending form before giving permission to have a credit report or application fee generated. These forms will disclose all charges, mandatory and additional.

Setting Your Budget

Questions of quantity and quality will influence your budget decisions. This can be square footage or number of bathrooms versus basic or best plumbing or lighting fixtures. See page 96 for a description of wants and needs and page 93 to read about some strategies for effective decision-making.

The coach and the scoreboard

A detailed budget will eliminate many surprise charges that you won't welcome after you've spent your money on something else. Make as thorough a list of categories as possible. You may want this budget to be on an erasable board so that you can be like the coach who changes his line-up and strategies as situations change.

"We think we want to spend an extra $550 on bathroom plumbing." Add the dollar amount in the Plumbing category and then decide if you want to deduct $550 from another category or take the money out of the upgrade or contingency budget. The important thing is for you to stay on top of the total budget. Be the "coach" of your own budget, and be in charge of it instead of letting it run you.

The Building Process

Builder's Role

A good builder earns his fee by owning the "bottom line" responsibility of delivering a house that meets all specifications and functions as designed in all of its many aspects. This is a complex task, parts of which are described below. After your home has been completed, you'll appreciate just how big this job was.

Obtain permits

The builder should file with the local authorities to obtain all required permits. If this process is your responsibility, contact these same local authorities for exact information on requirements and procedures for obtaining them.

Perform tests

The builder or you will pay fees for necessary tests including soils and percolation tests, tap fees for utilities and a survey. In some regions, the builder is required to provide the homebuyer with a copy of these reports.

Schedule trades

This is one of the builder's biggest challenges. Many factors can interfere with the construction schedule. This includes inclement weather, manufacturers' production or delivery delays, and labor delays caused by workers being unable to complete prior work on time. Too often, the builder's biggest problem is the homebuyer who can't make a decision, or who changes his mind after materials have been ordered and labor has been scheduled, or after work has been completed.

Builders know the craftsmen in each field and what they cost. If you've chosen a quality builder, he is keeping quality in mind when hiring subcontractors to work on your house. You don't want the apprentice crew practicing on your home, although new construction is where they often do practice. When you visit the site, watch for sloppy work and don't accept it. However, unless you have prior building experience, it will be difficult for you to distinguish between good and bad work. This is one reason why choosing a quality builder is so important.

Provide blueprints

See page 86 for a checklist of blueprints you should have. Also see page 123 for information on reading blueprints.

Builder site visits

It will be important for your peace of mind that the builder visits your building site frequently to ensure that the home is being built to specifications. Find out from prospective builders and their references how often these visits typically occur.

Maintain communication with buyer

As discussed in Contract Section, regularly scheduled meetings between builder and buyer are an excellent forum in which to have your questions and concerns addressed. Knowing that you will be having this meeting can diffuse fear and that awful feeling of being out of control of all that is happening.

Include builder's signature

A signature is a special feature or product that your builder likes to include with a particular home or with every home. Builders are professionals and can be creative if given the opportunity. If your builder takes pride in the product he's delivering, you will be the beneficiary.

Builder's insurance

Builders (or buyers) must carry liability insurance to cover builder errors and omissions and worker's compensation insurance to cover everyone who works on the house. These certificates should be on display or available upon request and their expiration date should be checked.

Obtain documentation that the house "works"

When the house is completed, all systems and appliances should be tested and results should be made available to you. Also see page 160 about performance testing. If anything does not meet requirements, it should be remedied as indicated in your contract.

Building Superintendent's Role

Many builders have a project manager or superintendent that handles building details. This is the field person in charge of daily construction. How much of the day will he or she be on site? He is responsible for having the blueprints followed correctly. It is his job to supervise those doing the work and see that the site is left reasonably clean.

This is an important job and requires knowledge of the whole building process. It is a very good idea to meet this person before signing your contract, because you will probably be dealing with him throughout construction.

A good question to ask prospective builders is how long their superintendents have been with them. Constant turnover on your building site means an increased opportunity for miscommunication and error.

The superintendent should be responsible for the care of systems, fixtures and all components of the house once they are installed. This includes covering all bathtubs, plumbing fixtures and appliances.

If the heating system is forced hot air, it should not be run because doing so would draw existing wallboard dust and debris into it. All vents should be covered to protect them. After carpeting and floors are installed, they should be covered with a plastic sheet to keep them clean until closing.

Buyer's Role

The buyer's job begins with determining what to build and how to finance it, choosing the right builder with care, signing a solid, thorough contract and making a commitment to get and stay organized.

Plan your shopping with deadlines in mind and make timely decisions. Be an effective advocate for all work being done correctly. Visit the site but without interfering with workers. Communicate any discrepancies from the blueprint to your builder or superintendent, in whatever manner has been agreed upon in advance.

Plan for scheduled payments and stay within your budget. Pay attention to the building schedule and, if there seems to be a delay, ask your builder if there is a problem. Accept the challenge to stay focused on success.

The Closing

Product Information

At the time of closing, the builder should provide you with product information about all products in your home. This can be in a notebook binder, with dividers by category, such as plumbing, fireplace, garage door openers, etc. Long after the builder is out of the picture, you will need to provide evidence of date of purchase, usually with your name, product detail and purchase price.

Certificate of Occupancy

The certificate of occupancy is a legal document issued by the local authority that contains a diagram of the land and buildings. The purpose of this certificate is to show that the house has been inspected by the local authorities and should therefore be of sound construction.

Lien Releases

You may want to request lien releases from all subcontractors who have worked on your home. Liens provides them with some protection in case they don't get paid. This protection is a legal infringement on your home. A conditional lien simply lets you know who will be doing the work. An unconditional lien release is the only document that completely relinquishes you from any claims by a subcontractor. Your attorney will know more about this in your particular jurisdiction.

Pre-closing Walkthrough Checklist

Your builder may have his own pre-closing form, or you can use checklists in this workbook on page 98 to assemble your own. As the house nears completion, use the form on page 245 to write down items that need attention. Look for quality of work. Notice anything that is missing. Small details can be added to your punchlist, which will be addressed after closing. Watch for anything that is so important that it must be addressed before closing.

Items That Must Be Corrected Before Closing

For significant issues, you may want to sit down with all necessary parties to determine how and when they will be resolved. Keep in mind that you will want to have your builder's cooperation for at least a year, as small (and occasionally big) problems surface. If you've been able to maintain a cordial and cooperative relationship, you should be able to come to agreement about any issues, and you'll be helping to make the upcoming year go smoothly.

Moving In

See checklist on page 99. It will be very helpful when moving into your new home to have all boxes clearly labeled, so that you will be able to tell movers exactly where boxes belong. This avoids unnecessary clutter in what is typically a confusing situation. Getting the kitchen organized as quickly as possible helps to reduce that feeling of being so unsettled.

Any boxes that need not be unpacked immediately can be placed in an out-of-the-way location, such as the garage or lower level. This allows you optimum space in which to organize the most important areas without feeling overwhelmed. Hiring a babysitter and eating out will make this big day more enjoyable.

Being on friendly terms with the purchasers of your old house can also be helpful. They may be willing to forward mail that the post office misses, and even send along an earring that was found under a carpet. You could leave a prepaid, pre-addressed envelope with them. It will also be a good deed to leave the old house as clean and empty as possible.

Protecting Walls and Floors

Moving day is a high-energy time. Protect your walls as best you can. Protecting the items entering the house accomplishes this most effectively. Use blankets or see that professional movers use their pads to avoid sharp edges coming near your new walls. Put protective coverings on every floor and carpet that will be the movers' traffic path.

Create a Punchlist

Your pre-closing/punchlist form on page 245 can be the beginning of your after-closing punchlist. You will probably discover other items after you've lived in your home for a little while. Rather than call the builder with every little thing you notice, he will probably prefer that you keep a list for an amount of time and then call in your whole list. The time limit varies, but usually builders fix and replace for at least one year from date of closing. In some areas, the punchlist may be subject to renewal if callbacks are required. Talk with your builder about this policy.

Sometimes big problems, such as a buckled or disintegrating driveway, won't become apparent until much later. If the builder sees that the problem is clearly due to faulty materials or workmanship and has a sense of pride in his work, he may take care of the problem after the warranty period has expired. Do not hesitate to speak up about defective items: a sink that chips or stains, a carpet whose loops are coming loose. You may need to contact the manufacturer of the particular item directly.

My sink story

After we had lived in our beautiful new home for about six months, I was forced to face the fact that our composite sink was staining and I could not make the stains go away. Ugly sink. But since it had been six months, I kept putting off contacting the company, anticipating resistance.

After another two more months went by, I summoned up the courage to contact the distributor of the sink. Within a few days, two men arrived at my door, looked at the sink, agreed that it was not acceptable, and ordered a different model (that I liked better) that they said would perform much better. It has.

Items that your builder purchased on your behalf should be free of defects or should be replaced by the builder or manufacturer during warranty time.

Remembering the very large number of parts that have gone into your new home can give you some perspective. We tend to jump on anything that goes wrong instead of having the attitude that *most* things have gone right! This attitude of gratitude makes it more enjoyable and easier to deal with the problems that do come up.

Long Term Protection Measures

Wood floors/tile

Wood floors that have been pre-finished or properly sealed should be protected for many years, depending on use. When areas of wood begin to look gray, the finish is no longer protecting the wood, and refinishing is necessary. Tile may or may not have a sealant applied. Your tile store or installer can advise you about recommended care of your particular tile.

Cabinets

Wood cabinets have probably been sealed but will show the effects of grease and fingerprints. Applying lemon oil or polish on a regular basis will keep them looking beautiful. Laminated cabinets should be easily and effectively cleaned with mild cleanser, polish or water.

Foam/caulking

If your builder used a high quality foam or caulk throughout the house, you shouldn't have to repair or replace it for a number of years. Keep an eye on areas where water is habitually present. If the caulk is cracked or missing, moisture can get behind the area and cause problems. You will eventually need to re-caulk on the exterior and interior.

Pay particular attention to the caulking around windows. If the caulk fails at the top but not the bottom, water can become trapped inside.

Grout

If you have wall tile, the grout will eventually need to be replaced. Some manufacturers recommend applying a sealant to help extend the grout's life. The grouting on floor tile should be very durable but may benefit from a professional cleaning.

Carpets

The best way to extend the life of your carpet is to vacuum it frequently. Locating cleaners that remove dirt and stains with natural enzymes instead of detergent may also give more satisfactory results, since it is difficult to remove detergent thoroughly.

Balancing ceiling fan paddles

If your ceiling fans shake when operating, they probably need balancing. On the top side of one or more paddles, you will find a small metal weight. Using trial and error, move these weights toward or away from the center of the fan until the paddles rotate smoothly.

Driveways/walkways

Applying sealant to your concrete areas will be an effective maintenance measure that will help to extend the life of your driveway.

Countertops and fixtures

Countertops and fixtures, including plumbing and tub/shower, can be treated with a protective coating. Various products, including silicone automobile polish are available, but never polish floors, as this would make them slippery. Treated surfaces repel dirt and soap scum for much longer than untreated ones.

Water heater(s)

Sediment collects at the bottom of water heaters at various rates, depending on the mineral content of your water supply.

$$$ Regular draining, by using the valve at the base of the water heater, will release these impurities, extending the life of the heater.

Furnace/duct system

Regular cleaning and tuning of your heating and cooling systems will help them to run more efficiently and last longer. Between initially clean ducts and a central vacuum system, your ducts should remain relatively clean. Especially if someone in the home is highly sensitive, having ducts cleaned can reduce dust and molds from reaching the air that you breathe. It is important to have both supply and return ducts cleaned thoroughly.

Follow Through with Your Punchlist

Keep your punchlist updated. Now is the time to speak up about anything that isn't right. Don't accept unsatisfactory work or products. Keep in mind that you paid for all of this. If items on your punchlist go unattended, call, call, call. Be polite, but persistent. Don't give up until all items are corrected or replaced.

Thank You Letter to Your Builder

Sometime between closing and the end of your first year, write your builder a letter, expressing gratitude for the excellent job accomplished and why you are pleased with your home. If the builder made beneficial suggestions, thank him for those specifically. You might also give your permission for him to post your letter for clients to read, and to serve as a referral for future homebuyers.

Celebrate

This isn't just a house you've moved into; this is your unique creation! Have a housewarming party to celebrate it with your family, your new neighbors and friends, and consider inviting your builder! If someone says they are thinking of building, suggest that they get a copy of this workbook. Hopefully, this copy has empowered you to be an educated consumer, has helped you to foster teamwork among all the participants in this project, and has provided information that encouraged you to be creative and to truly enjoy the building of your high performance home.

Glossary

air barrier Any product (e.g. wallboard, plastic sheeting) that is designed to stop air from penetrating it. Typically, some form of air barrier is placed on both sides of a wall with insulation (holding "dead" air) in between.

air exchanger This device, attached to the furnace, allows fresh air into the house through the return duct that is headed to the furnace. A filter can be placed over the fresh air opening so that the air is as free of pollutants and allergens as possible.

air infiltration This is the passing of air from one area to another. When it is hot or cold outside, air infiltration from a leaky thermal envelope can make the living space uncomfortable and energy-inefficient.

allowance The amount of money designated for purchases of a particular item.

arbitration clause Part of some contracts, this clause removes the buyer's right to litigate any disputes. A third party is paid to make a final decision.

backfill The process of replacing dirt all around the exterior foundation.

backsplash A special surface (e.g. tile or granite) on walls behind countertops to protect the walls from food debris and moisture.

blower door A device placed in the entire exterior door opening that gently pressurizes or de-pressurizes the closed house. Chalk dust from a special "gun" will be drawn into, or blown away from any leaks, showing areas that need to be foamed, caulked or otherwise insulated.

fresh air exchanger An electronic device that can be set to turn the furnace fan on intermittently throughout the day in order to circulate filtered fresh air throughout the house.

bullnose Rounded (like a bull's nose) instead of squared, this is a style of finishing wallboard corners. This is usually done with a rounded strip of metal that is then covered to match wallboard or plaster.

compaction The process of backfilling dirt against the foundation so that the dirt is solidly packed and won't "sink in" months or years later.

cantilevered An area of a home that is "bumped out," without any foundation beneath.

central flue The central ducting that is the main conduit for exhaust fumes to exit to the outside.

certificate of occupancy This certificate is issued by a municipal authority as a safeguard that all construction done has passed inspection. Most banks require a "C.O" that matches the structure before they will issue a mortgage.

cost-plus contract An open-ended contract that includes costs (materials, labor, other expenses) and the builder's profit.

covenants Covenants or CC&Rs (Codes, Covenants and Restrictions) are legally binding rules that are created and enforced by a local homeowners association or municipal authority.

curb appeal The term used to describe how attractive a house looks on the exterior from the front view.

dormers Areas of a home that protrude from the house with their own little roof. They can add living space and light to a room, or be decorative additions without function.

easements An easement is the right of someone else to use part of your property for a limited purpose, such as a right-of-way for underground utility lines.

elevation An architectural term for an exterior view of a home. Builders will often use this term to describe varying models of homes, e.g. Elevation A, Elevation B.

errors and omissions insurance This important insurance is for builders and architects for errors in design or construction.

e**scrow** An escrow account is set up, often by a financial institution, for the express purpose of paying for materials and labor as deemed appropriate by the escrow trustee.

expansive soils Soil that may shift with atmospheric conditions, often clay, provides an extra challenge to builders because, if the soil rises in places, the house is likely to suffer damage unless built to withstand this possibility.

fixed-price contract This contract itemizes all estimated costs for each phase's materials and labor plus additional fees and the builder's charge for a total project amount, which is the contracted rate.

flex room For "flexibility," this room is used for more than one purpose.

footlights The size of electrical outlets, these lights are placed on the wall very close to the stair (every few stairs) to light one's way at night.

hose bibbs A builder's term for exterior water spigots that are used for garden hoses.

housewrap An engineered permeable paper product that is installed all around the exterior walls before siding. It protects the house from wind and sheeting rain.

induced-draft This type of venting involves passive exhausting of gases from the appliance through the roof by way of a vent placed directly over the appliance.

impact fees These are municipal charges for future schools, parks, etc.

infrared photography A special camera that is used to take photographs of a house for the purpose of detecting heat loss. Dark, purplish colors on the photograph will indicate where heat is escaping, so that it may be properly sealed.

lien releases A lien is a legal infringment that can be claimed by a worker that has not been paid by the builder. Until an unconditional release has been issued, liens are possible and have the power to make the homeowner responsible for any monies owed the worker.

lot pins Lot pins are metal markers that are hammered into the ground by a surveyor. Their purpose is to mark your property lines.

low-E windows Low-E stands for low-emissivity, a coating placed on these windows. Its purpose is to repel heat in the summer and invite heat in during the winter.

mud room An entrance from the outside to a room that is most friendly to wet and muddy shoes and clothing. This is often a laundry room.

overhang An overhang is an extension of the edge of the roof. It serves to shelter the home from water and the heat of the sun, most effectively, southern.

power vent A power vent has an electric motor that actively sucks hot air out of an unconditioned attic in order to attempt to cool this space. A power vent can also be used to actively draw exhaust fumes from a water heater.

R-value Stands for resistance value of a particular thickness of insulation to resist air from passing through it. The greater the resistance, the higher the number. Typically, walls range from R-13 to R-19, attics can be R-38 or higher.

radon Radon is a noxious gas that can seep through the ground and find its way into the home. It is a by-product of uranium that is breaking down.

resilient channel This inexpensive metal strip is attached to wood joists before wallboard is installed. Its purpose is to block sound from being transmitted through the wall.

return registers Return registers suck "old air" into the return ducts, to be carried back to the furnace or air conditioner.

rough-in plumbing Rough-in plumbing is the underground laying and surface stub-out of pipes so that plumbing can be easily completed at a later time.

schematic A preliminary drawing, to ensure that room placement and other basic features are correct, before incurring the time and expense of detailed blueprints.

sealed-combustion This safe ventilation of water heater and furnace is done through two sealed, dedicated pipes: one bringing fresh air in, the other escorting poisonous exhaust fumes out. With this design, neither ever enters the home's breathing air.

setback The distance from the road to where the front of your house is placed, which is sometimes a regulated minimum or maximum.

SGHC Solar Heat Gain Coefficient, a rating assigned by the National Fenestration Rating Council, to determine how much solar heat is able to pass through the window.

soffits The underside of the roof rafters, often enclosed to protect the roof structure from moisture.

soils test This test, often required and always advisable, indicates any potential soil problems that should be considered before plans are finalized.

superintendent This term is often used for the person in charge of the construction site. He or she makes sure the blueprints are followed and that the work is done according to specificiations.

supply registers Supply registers blow conditioned air from the furnace or air conditioner into the room in which they are located.

surge protection (electrical) This electrical term means protecting a circuit from becoming overloaded by a device that demands more power than the circuit is designed to carry. When this situation occurs, the circuit breaker will shut off rather than supply power.

surge protection (plumbing) A device is placed in pipes that keeps the temperature of water sufficiently even so that if someone flushes the toilet, the one taking a shower won't be scalded.

tap fees These fees are charged to homebuyers to offset utility construction costs for water, sewer, natural gas, electric, etc.

thermal envelope This concept treats the entire house, including basement or crawlspace to attic floor or ceiling as one conditioned space with insulation and air sealing all around the exterior.

toe kick This is the area between cabinet base and floor that is at "toe" level when standing in front of cabinets.

Tyvek® Is Dupont's brand of housewrap.

vapor barrier A vapor barrier, usually of plastic or paper, is placed against the side of the wall where moisture may enter. Placement will vary depending on climate.

wet bar A sink usually located in an entertainment bar.

workers compensation insurance This is insurance for workers who suffer an injury on the job. It is a must to protect the builder and homebuyer who would otherwise be responsible for any on-site injuries.

Website Directory

Today's search engines (*Google, Yahoo, AOL*) are so good that you need only type in selected keywords to get the latest information on every subject of interest. Here are a few:

www.homebuildingcoach.com
   Home Building Coach's website, where workbooks and DVDs may be ordered

www.cfiinstallers.com - Directory of certified floor covering installers
www.eere.energy.gov
   A U.S. Dept. of Energy gateway to hundreds of websites and thousands of online documents on energy efficiency and renewable energy
www.efficientwindows.org -For window efficiency information
www.energyconservatory.com/index.html
   List of energy rating contractors using The Energy Conservatory line of blower doors and infrared cameras
www.equifax.com, www.experian.com, www.transunion.com
   Credit reporting agencies
www.energybuilder.com - Green building "primer"
www.energystar.gov
   Dept of Energy consumer and professional sources – ENERGY STAR
www.epa.gov/iaq - EPA website- indoor air quality
www.forms.org – Insulated concrete forms
www.greenbuildermagazine.com
   Green building practices and products for builders and consumers
http://hes.lbl.gov
   Utilizes homeowner zip code to provide energy costs for average and energy-efficient homes
hometips.com/help/tan1.html – Tank and tankless hot water and capacity
www.infiltec.com/inf-bdc.htm
   List of energy rating contractors using the INFILTEC line of blower doors
www.nahi.org - National Association of Home Inspectors
www.nahb.com
   National Association of Home Builders- Green Building Guidelines
www.namb.org - National Association of Mortgage Brokers
www.nkba.org - National Kitchen and Bath Association
www.nfrc.org
   National Fenestration Rating Council, window, door and skylights
www.nwfa.org
   National Wood Flooring Association
www.radiantpanelassociation.org
   Information of purchase and installation of radiant floor systems
www.realtor.org - National Association of REALTORS®
www.simplyinsulate.com - Available tax credits
www.sips.org – Structural insulated panels
www.solaraccess.com -Solar energy and home power generation information
www.timberframe.org-Source for information on log and timber frame homes

Alphabetical Index

Where to Shop

Name of store	Address/directions/email	Telephone	Contact name

Upgrade Worksheet

Builder's Name _____   Base price $_____

Phone._____   Total budget $_____

(See Creating Your Budget on page 12)   Upgrade budget $_____

	Item to add, subtract, or change	Date ordered	Add'l cost
1			
2			
3			
4			
5			
6			
7			
8			
9			
10			
11			
12			
13			
14			
15			
16			
17			

Upgrade Worksheet

Builder's Name _____ Base price $_____

Phone._____ Total budget $_____

(See Creating Your Budget on page 12) Upgrade budget $_____

	Item to add, subtract, or change	Date ordered	Add'l cost
18			
19			
20			
21			
22			
23			
24			
25			
26			
27			
28			
29			
30			
31			
32			
33			
34			

Change Orders Worksheet

Builder's Name _____ Contract price $_____

Phone _____ Total absolute maximum budget $_____

(See Creating Your Budget on page 12) Contingency budget $_____

	Item to add, subtract, or change	Date ordered	Add'l cost/ reduction
1			
2			
3			
4			
5			
6			
7			
8			
9			
10			
11			
12			
13			
14			
15			
16			

Funds Drawn by Builder

Date	Project Milestone	Amount	Running Total

	Pre-Closing Walkthrough/Punchlist Item to add, subtract, change	Date notified	Date completed
1			
2			
3			
4			
5			
6			
7			
8			
9			
10			
11			
12			
13			
14			
15			
16			
17			
18			
19			

Month _____

Sunday	Monday	Tuesday	Wednesday	Thursday	Friday	Saturday

Month _____

Sunday	Monday	Tuesday	Wednesday	Thursday	Friday	Saturday

Month _____

Sunday	Monday	Tuesday	Wednesday	Thursday	Friday	Saturday

Month _____

Sunday	Monday	Tuesday	Wednesday	Thursday	Friday	Saturday

Month _____

Sunday	Monday	Tuesday	Wednesday	Thursday	Friday	Saturday

Month _____

	Sunday	Monday	Tuesday	Wednesday	Thursday	Friday	Saturday

Month _____

Sunday	Monday	Tuesday	Wednesday	Thursday	Friday	Saturday

Month____

Sunday	Monday	Tuesday	Wednesday	Thursday	Friday	Saturday

Month _____

Sunday	Monday	Tuesday	Wednesday	Thursday	Friday	Saturday